Also by Marvin E. Gettleman

Vietnam: History, Documents and Opinions

Conflict in Indochina (with Susan Gettleman, Lawrence and Carol Kaplan)

The Failure of American Liberalism (with David Mermelstein)

THE DORR REBELLION

A Study in
American Radicalism:
1833-1849

THE DORR REBELLION

*A Study in
American Radicalism:
1833–1849*

Marvin E. Gettleman

Random House, New York

Library of Congress Cataloging in Publication Data

Gettleman, Marvin E
The Dorr Rebellion.
Includes bibliographical references.
1. Dorr Rebellion, 1842.   2. Dorr, Thomas Wilson, 1805–1854.   I. Title.
F83.4.G47   974.5'03   72-14312
ISBN 0-394-46470-2

Manufactured in the United States of America

First Edition

84160

for Susan

Preface

This study of a little-known but significant episode in the history of American radicalism originated as an academic project and in an earlier form was accepted as a Ph.D. thesis at The Johns Hopkins University.[1] The Dorr Rebellion was suggested to me as an inviting topic for investigation by Professor David Donald, who guided my work to its completion. Donald's own important contributions to nineteenth-century American history are widely known to a scholarly and general audience, and they need no additional mention from me. But his role as a teacher of graduate students and his supervision of apprentices, carried out with dedication, sympathy and insight, are known only to those of us who have been fortunate enough to study with him. Committed to different philosophical and political views than mine, and unable to share all my conclusions about American radicalism, Donald nevertheless helped me to develop and clarify my own ideas. He was my teacher in the most profound sense.

Susan Gettleman, to whom this book is lovingly dedicated, was a true comrade during the years it took to compose it. She helped in the archival research, criticized the early drafts, and encouraged the work in every way. While my initial urge is to specify and even exult in this encouragement and the relationship from which it sprang, I suppose I ought to recognize that some things are not appropriate for public acknowledgment.

Much useful advice, criticism and encouragement also came my way from friends and colleagues. Norman Dain of Rutgers University graciously shared extensive materials he had collected on the Dorr Rebellion. Eugene D. Genovese of the University of

---

[1] In this earlier form its title was "Reform, Radicalism and Party Development: A Study of the Dorr Rebellion and Rhode Island Politics, 1833–1849." The Ph.D. was awarded in the spring of 1972.

ix

Rochester extended a helping hand in a critical period of my graduate school apprenticeship and offered thoughtful criticism of an early draft. As this study was nearing completion, my old friend Dr. Bernard Horowitz tendered many helpful suggestions. Along with many other radical scholars, I owe a special debt of gratitude to the Louis M. Rabinowitz Foundation, which in my case provided financial support for a half-year free from teaching duties.

Early drafts of this work were also read and constructively criticized by Jean Baker of Goucher College; Patrick Conley of Providence College; Hugh Davis of Southern Connecticut State College; William Evitts of Hollins College; Frank O. Gatell of the University of California at Los Angeles; Jack P. Greene of The Johns Hopkins University; Lawrence Kaplan of The City College, New York; Michael Kraus, formerly of The City College, New York; Ann Lane of John Jay College; Jesse Lemisch of Roosevelt University; Staughton Lynd of Chicago, Illinois; William G. McLoughlin of Brown University; Sydney Nathans of Duke University; Michael Parenti of the University of Vermont; Murray Rothbard of the Polytechnic Institute of Brooklyn; William M. Wiecek of the University of Missouri; Irwin Yellowitz of The City College, New York; and Alfred Young of Northern Illinois University. The conventional listing here of these people's names should not obscure my special gratitude for the unique help that each of them provided.

The contributions of two additional persons were also much needed and are gratefully acknowledged. Claudia Reid, presented with a difficult manuscript, typed a final copy speedily and intelligently. Belying the cultural stereotype of a hostile mother-in-law, Eleanor Brown searchingly proofread and suggested useful changes in previous versions of some of the chapters and in the proofs.

And where would any of us historical researchers be without librarians? I would like explicitly to mention the staffs of the John Hay Library, Brown University; The Widener Library, Harvard University; and the New York Public Library. Janice Wolf of the Polytechnic Institute of Brooklyn Library, Phyllis Pelloquin of the Rhode Island State Archives in Providence, and Albert Klyberg, Marsha Peters, Noel P. Conlon and the wonderfully cooperative staff of the Rhode Island Historical Society Library were especially helpful to me.

Lists of acknowledgments usually close with a statement absolving all the previously mentioned people of responsibility for the final outcome of the work in question. I have always been opposed to this academic custom, on the grounds that it insufficiently recognizes the ideal of a community of responsible scholars which I as a radical hope will one day emerge from the chaos of contemporary academic life.

M. E. G.

June 1972

Contents

Tables

Illustrations

(following p. 136)

ABBREVIATIONS

Dorr MSS.   Sidney S. Rider Collection of Dorr War MSS., John Hay Library, Brown University

RIHSL   Rhode Island Historical Society Library

LC   Library of Congress

WLHU   Widener Library, Harvard University

Burke's Report   U.S. Congress, House, *Interference of the Executive in Affairs of Rhode Island,* Report No. 546, 28 Cong., I Sess., 1844.

[Further data on these sources and depositories may be found in the Bibliographical Essay, pp. 238-250.]

The manuscripts in the Sidney S. Rider Collection have been used by permission of the Brown University Library.

Material from the William L. Clements Library is used by permission of the University of Michigan.

The people are the sovereign power and agreable [*sic*] to our system they have a right to alter and amend their system of Government when a majority wills it, as a majority have a right to rule.

Andrew Jackson (on the Dorr Rebellion), to Francis P. Blair, May 23, 1842.

The great difficulty is that, in order to know them in our terms, it is first necessary to make the abnegation of learning them in their own terms.

Paul Goodman, "Politics Within Limits," *New York Review of Books,* XIX (August 10, 1972), 33.

Introduction

Rhode Island's political upheaval of the early 1840s, in which Thomas Wilson Dorr played a central role, is usually considered an oddity of the Jacksonian era. Treating the Dorr Rebellion as an instance of the nationwide suffrage reform impulse of the period, historians have frequently been puzzled or repelled by the radical actions of the Rhode Island agitators. The Rebellion's failure has often been cited to bolster an "American extension of the Whig interpretation of history" [1] by showing the superiority of determined, moderate protest to dangerous radicalism.

Although the Dorrite movement certainly embraced reformist aims, it evolved a radical thrust during the course of the struggle. Opposing powerful conservative forces in Rhode Island, the rebels gradually and reluctantly came to strive for a measure of popular control over the political process far beyond any yet (or since) achieved in America. They developed a radical ideology [2] that at key points challenged the dominant values of

---

[1] The phrase is J. R. Pole's from "The American Past: Is It Still Usable?" *Journal of American Studies,* I (April 1967), 64. Pole does not mention interpretations of the Dorr Rebellion in his historiographical essay. For my evaluation of the literature, see the bibliographical essay.

[2] The development of the concept "radicalism" is suggestive of the way in which it is used in this study. Originating in mathematics as the root of a number, the most basic and fundamental way it can be expressed, "radical" took on political meaning and by the late eighteenth century had come to be descriptive of political beliefs and movements that aimed at fundamental change in the direction of greater democracy. The term retained some of its original connotations in that radicals usually claim to strip social reality of its mystifications and lay bare the roots of social problems to facilitate popular action to remedy them. See "radical" in Samuel Johnson, *Dictionary of the English Language* (London, 1755), no pagination. *Oxford English Dictionary,* 12 vols. (Oxford: The Clar-

antebellum society and implied that vast political and social changes might be necessary. In the pursuit of these radical objectives Dorr and some of his followers resorted to violent measures that showed how far the movement had gone beyond its originally reformist goals.

This study of the Dorr Rebellion is offered as a contribution to the history of radical movements in the United States. I attempt to show how the nation's revolutionary beginnings transmitted an undercurrent of genuine radicalism which lay close to the surface of antebellum American political life. But the Rebellion also reveals the limited nature of that radicalism—its unwillingness to delve deeply into social and economic issues, its racism, its commitment to the sanctity of private property, its respect for constitutional forms, and its historical nostalgia. These factors, which led to the defeat of Dorrite radicalism, were to a great extent products of America's eighteenth-century revolutionary experience, and they suggest the constraints under which radicals usually find themselves in the United States.

My aim is to show how these cross-pressures affected particular groups of politically aroused people in Rhode Island during the early nineteenth century. I have made a special effort to distinguish various groups and classes involved in the Rebellion. When viewed in this way, the data shows a coalition of diverse forces making up the radical movement. Middle-class professionals served as leaders and ideological spokesmen. But plebeian elements, also attracted to the radical cause, occasionally expressed more extreme convictions than the leading "gentlemen" were willing to endorse. These differences within the rebel movement were vividly revealed by changes in its social composition as it approached and passed its dramatic confrontation with the conservative opposition.

*   *   *

---

endon Press, 1933), VIII, 99–100; Peter Gay, *The Enlightenment: An Interpretation. The Rise of Modern Paganism* (New York: Vintage Books, 1966), p. 280. While some would reserve the label "radical" only for Marxist movements that totally negate the existing society, or for earlier anticipations of such ur-radicalism, I believe that gradations among radical movements ought to be recognized. Along any spectrum, Dorrism would be a weak, compromised and ambiguous radical movement, but a radical movement nonetheless.

Although this study is intended to be a contribution to local history—a genre recently wrested from the exclusive domain of antiquarians and provincial panegyrists[3]—it is also intended as a case study in what may be called the natural history of radicalism. Particular emphasis has been placed on the development of a radical ideology and on the interrelations between ideology and political tactics. There is little mention in the pages that follow of fashionable concepts such as "internal war" and "collective violence." I have carefully searched the burgeoning literature generated by anguished public responses to ghetto uprisings and campus revolts,[4] and I not only find this material irrelevant to an understanding of the Dorr Rebellion but also have doubts as to whether such concepts adequately illuminate the contemporary events they were intended to deal with.[5] Radicalism, it seems to me, still retains usefulness as an exploratory concept.

Instructive as the Dorr Rebellion can be as an episode in antebellum radicalism, it can hardly serve as an exemplary model for

---

[3] See, for examples, Sumner Chilton Powell's Pulitzer Prize-winning study of colonial Sudbury, Massachusetts, *Puritan Village: The Formation of a New England Town* (Garden City, N.Y.: Doubleday Anchor Books, 1965); and John Demos, *A Little Commonwealth: Family Life in Plymouth Colony* (New York: Oxford University Press, 1970).

[4] I began with Hugh Davis Graham and Ted Robert Gurr, eds., *Violence in America: Historical and Comparative Perspectives* (New York: Signet Books, 1969) and other publications of the National Commission on the Causes and Prevention of Violence. While in the National Archives, Washington, D.C., I looked at many of the unpublished studies of this Commission as well. Insofar as I sought enlightenment for my inquiry into the Dorr Rebellion, it was a fruitless search.

[5] This is obviously no place for systematic criticism of a large body of scholarship, but one main shortcoming of the literature on "internal war" and "collective violence" is particularly glaring. Almost all of this material has a deep bias against the movements under study, and seems mostly concerned with prevention and suppression. Ted Robert Gurr, in his influential *Why Men Rebel* (Princeton, N.J.: Princeton University Press, 1970), p. x, suggests that his work is as useful to rebels as to rulers, but this claim to impartiality is not borne out by the rest of the volume. Gurr, however, is almost the only one to raise this issue. Other writers simply assume that the task of scholarship is to show how rebels can be defeated. Without the benefit of sophisticated terminology, much of the scholarship on the Door Rebellion (as I show in the bibliographical essay, pp. 246–250) is similarly biased in an antiradical direction.

the present. In my opinion, historians—radicals especially—are not obliged to constitute themselves into a cheering section for the presumed Heroes of Our Radical Past, not even to redress the hostile interpretations of conservative and liberal writers.[6] The most sympathetic apologist could hardly disguise the fact that most Dorrites were racists who rejected black suffrage and sought political equality exclusively for whites. Nor is it easy to overlook the painful naïveté of the rebels, who believed in some sort of automatic triumph for their principles. In addition, many of them demonstrated a marked unwillingness in the showdown of spring and summer 1842 to fight for their announced beliefs. Heaven help any subsequent radical movement that emulated the Dorrites of Rhode Island!

---

[6] For discussion of these hostile interpretations, see the bibliographical essay. On the tasks of radical historiography, I find myself in almost complete agreement with Aileen S. Kraditor, whose paper "American Radical Historians on their Heritage," *Past & Present,* No. 56 (August, 1972), 136–153, is insightful and provocative.

THE DORR
REBELLION

*A Study in
American Radicalism:
1833-1849*

1

Class, Party and Reform
1833 to 1837

If any American political developments in the early nineteenth century could be called inevitable, they were the growth of white manhood suffrage and popular political parties in the United States. So natural were these innovations to an expanding and wealthy new nation that democratic institutions seem to have appeared effortlessly as by-products of larger social changes. Limitations of political rights to whites also seem to have developed naturally in a society that tolerated slavery in over half of its territory. Slavery was swept away in the great mid-century conflagration. But conflict did mark some of the other political transformations of the period as conservatives fought a series of rear-guard actions to stem the democratic tide. The most dramatic and bitter battle of the antebellum period took place in Rhode Island, where the movement for political reform took a radical and even revolutionary character.

The greatest formal barrier to democratic political change was the venerable Charter of 1663, issued to the "Collonie of Rhode Island and Providence Plantations, in New England, in America" when Roger Williams was still the community's leading spirit. This charter remained in force until 1843. Its guarantees of "a full libertie in religious concernments" are justly celebrated, but the Charter also included noteworthy provisions for self-government in the colony. Effective political power was in the hands of the General Assembly chosen by the freemen. Neither the governor of the colony nor the local courts enjoyed any independent authority. One enthusiastic supporter of this legislative dominance was reported to have stated in 1818 that the powers of a General Assembly were "unlimited." Legislators, he said, "have as much right to govern the affairs of this state and its citizens as the supreme ruler of the Universe has to manage his affairs." [1] Another important feature of the Charter was an apportionment fixed in 1663, whereby Newport (the most populous town in the seventeenth century) had six representatives, Portsmouth, Warwick and Providence each had four, and each new town was to have two.[2]

Rhode Island's charter, along with that of Connecticut, escaped abrogation by royal authority before the American Revolution. Neither state carried through a constitutional change during the Revolution, although a Rhode Island legislative committee was empowered to take action on the subject in 1777.[3] So extensive were the provisions for self-government in these old charters and so complete was the support for independence among the ruling groups that there was no crisis of local authority at the time of independence. Since governmental functions continued as before, there was no urgent need for constitutional revision.[4] Eventually Connecticut replaced its charter with a

---

[1] Remarks of Elisha R. Potter, Sr., quoted in Thomas Wilson Dorr, Newspaper & Other Extracts, n.d., Dorr MSS.

[2] The Charter of 1663 may be found in John Russell Bartlett, ed., *Records of the Colony of Rhode Island and Providence Plantations in New England,* 10 vols. (Providence: A. C. Greene, 1856–1865), II, 3–21; and in Arthur May Mowry, *The Dorr War: Or, The Constitutional Struggle in Rhode Island* (Providence: Preston & Rounds, 1901), Appendix A. Mowry's study is the major published work on the Rhode Island upheaval. See my discussion of it in the bibliographical essay, pp. 242 n, 247–248.)

[3] The committee's failure to report may have had as much to do with wartime conditions as with resistance to constitutional change. See Mowry, *Dorr War,* p. 27.

[4] In some other states there was a period of veritable anarchy, with almost all governmental functions suspended between independence and the drafting of a new constitution. See Allan Nevins, *The American*

modern constitution.[5] In other states, too, greater democratization resulted from constitutional and political reform movements in the antebellum period.[6] Rhode Island, with its seventeenth-century charter still in force, remained something of a political anachronism.

States During and After the Revolution, 1775–1789 (New York: Augustus M. Kelley, Publishers, 1969), Chaps. 2, 3; Fletcher M. Green, *Constitutional Development in the South Atlantic States, 1776–1860: A Study in the Evolution of Democracy* (New York: Norton Library, 1966), Chap. 2.

[5] The circumstances which brought about constitutional reform in neighboring Connecticut did not exist in Rhode Island. In Connecticut there was another potent issue in addition to the issues of restricted suffrage and unequal apportionment—namely, an established church. Most of the leading divines were Federalists, and after the Hartford Convention the Federalist Party was discredited. A reforming party could thus use established political techniques and appeal to already franchised voters in Connecticut in a campaign against an entrenched conservative government. This is essentially what happened in 1816, when the Federalists were voted out of office and a Republican administration pledged to reform took power. A constitutional convention followed, the delegates to which were chosen by the landholding voters. The constitution for Connecticut which went into force in 1818 not only disestablished the Congregational church and reapportioned legislative seats, but also swept away property qualifications for voting. This development is ably narrated in Richard J. Purcell, *Connecticut in Transition, 1775–1818* (Washington, D.C.: American Historical Association, 1918), especially Chap. 8. Some of these conditions that allowed constitutional reform to take place in Connecticut were missing in Rhode Island.

[6] For political reform movements in this period, in comparison to which Rhode Island's situation is largely atypical, see John Bach McMaster, *The Acquisition of Political, Social and Industrial Rights of Man in America* (Cleveland: Imperial Press, 1903); Louis Hartz, *The Liberal Tradition in America: An Interpretation of American Political Thought Since the Revolution* (New York: Harcourt, Brace & World 1955), Chap. 3; Carl N. Degler, *Out of Our Past: The Forces that Shaped Modern America* (New York: Harper & Bros., 1959), pp. 137–144; Seymour Martin Lipset, *The First New Nation: The United States in Historical and Comparative Perspective* (Garden City, N.Y.: Doubleday Anchor Books, 1967), Chap. 2; Gilman Ostrander, *The Rights of Man in America, 1606–1861* (Columbia, Mo.: University of Missouri Press, 1960), Chap. 8; but especially Chilton Williamson, *American Suffrage: From Property to Democracy, 1760–1860* (Princeton, N.J.: Princeton University Press, 1960), which also includes an extended account (Chap. 13) of the Dorr Rebellion based on primary sources.

Ironically, although independence brought no formal political change in Rhode Island, it did add an element of rigidity to the state's constitutional system. The Charter of 1663, like all colonial charters, had no explicit amendment procedure. If change was to be accomplished, it would have to be done by petitioning the imperial authorities in London.[7] After 1776 such appeal to England had no meaning. Thus, unless the established authorities in Rhode Island were willing to grant reforms, there seemed no regular way to effect constitutional change.

Dissatisfaction with the Charter centered on three major points. First, during the early nineteenth century the fixed system of apportionment became increasingly unfair to citizens in the growing population centers in northern Rhode Island. Second, legislative domination did not accord with notions of a precise separation of powers, and particularly of judicial independence. The third basis for dissatisfaction was the limited suffrage. Although the Charter of 1663 did not explicitly restrict the electorate, it did imply that determination of community affairs in Rhode Island would be the province of the freemen. Subsequent acts of the General Assembly defined the term "freeman" in terms of landed property; by the opening of the nineteenth century $134 of real estate, or rental of such property for $7 a year, entitled a citizen of Rhode Island, along with his oldest son, to apply at his local town meeting for the status of freeman. When formally "admitted" as a freeman, a Rhode Islander could then vote and assume the role of active citizen of the state.[8]

Before the Revolution almost every resident was a landholder, and few citizens were disfranchised by these landholding qualifications. David Lovejoy estimates that as many as 75 percent of

---

[7] As Thomas Dorr put in 1834: "[S]ince the Declaration of Independence, no appeal can be had, as formerly [against the Charter authorities], by an aggrieved party, to a tribunal of the mother country." Ironically, then, the American Revolution rendered Rhode Island in some sense less free. Dorr, and others, Address to the People of Rhode Island, 1834, *Burke's Report,* p. 158. For the circumstances under which Dorr and a group of reformers composed this Address, see below, pp. 22–24.

[8] For evolution of the landed requirement, see Mowry, *Dorr War,* pp. 19–21; Edwin Maxey, "Suffrage Extension in Rhode Island Down to 1842," *American Law Review,* XLII (July–August 1908), 545–566; Irwin H. Polishook, *Rhode Island and the Union, 1774–1795* (Evanston, Ill.: Northwestern University Press, 1969), pp. 22–26.

the adult males in Rhode Island could meet these qualifications in the eighteenth century.[9] The proportion decreased with the emergence of manufacturing centers in the Blackstone River valley and with the growth of immigration, so that by the 1830s considerably less than half the adult white male population could vote.[10] With the passage of time the proportion of non-landholders grew, the number of disfranchised persons mounted, and with it the potential pressure for suffrage reform.

The growth of industrialism, which underlay much of the reform agitation, was little short of spectacular in early nineteenth-century Rhode Island. As Peter J. Coleman has shown, entrepreneurs in the tiny state eagerly grasped at economic opportunity, transforming Rhode Island's traditional mercantile economy into a booming industrial one by the 1830s.[11] Not every region of the state shared in the upsurge of manufactures. Agricultural districts in the south and west remained economically backward bastions of political conservatism. But in the manufacturing regions, the growth of a working class unable to exercise political rights contributed to the reformist ferment that eventually brought Rhode Island to a revolutionary crisis.

Rhode Island politicians helped to bring on the crisis by refusing to take any stand on the issues of constitutional reform, preferring to play the traditional game of politics in the state. Even before the Revolution Rhode Island politics was characterized by vigorous factional disputes and embryonic party struc-

---

[9] David S. Lovejoy, *Rhode Island Politics and the American Revolution, 1760–1776* (Providence: Brown University Press, 1958), pp. 13–18. Cf. similar estimates in Williamson, *American Suffrage*, p. 243; Patrick T. Conley, "Rhode Island Constitutional Development, 1636–1775: A Survey," *Rhode Island History*, XXVII (June 1968), 92.

[10] Advocates of free suffrage probably accurately estimated in 1833 that only 5,000 of a potential electorate of 12,000 (if a taxpayer suffrage were instituted) could actually vote in Rhode Island. William I. Tillinghast, report to suffrage meeting, May 10, 1833, Dorr MSS. A decade later, at the time of the Dorr Rebellion, both the number of freemen and the total of citizens disfranchised increased, the latter group far more rapidly. See Williamson, *American Suffrage*, pp. 244–245; Appendix B.

[11] Peter J. Coleman, *The Transformation of Rhode Island, 1790–1860* (Providence: Brown University Press, 1963), Chaps. 2–5. This book, while not clarifying all the problems of antebellum Rhode Island, is the indispensable basis for all further study. I have relied heavily upon it.

tures that coalesced around leading men who represented the major sectional and class issues. By the second quarter of the nineteenth century the party divisions were openly acknowledged: manufacturing and farming interests—identified with the Whig and Democratic parties, respectively—fought fierce battles for the freemen's votes and regularly succeeded each other in the spoils of office. Outsiders were aghast at the shameless licentiousness of Rhode Island politics, and even local citizens sometimes expressed disgust at the more sordid maneuvers.[12] But by the third decade of the century this political system was functioning smoothly, with a tacit agreement among leading politicians to sidestep the issues of constitutional reform in the state and thus avoid exciting "the prejudices of the people" and creating "hostility between town & country." [13]

Sustaining the resistance of Rhode Island politicians to any tampering with the Charter or with the political system that developed under its provisions were fears of change among the franchised landholders. The state's farmers enjoyed relative immunity from taxation. Only three times since the Revolution had temporary land taxes been levied, the last in 1822.[14] If the suf-

[12] See John Brown Francis to Elisha R. Potter [Sr.?], August 28, [1825?], Potter Collection, RIHSL. Cf. Nevins, *American States,* pp. 225–233; Lovejoy, *Rhode Island Politics and the American Revolution,* pp. 29–30, 194 and *passim.* As early as 1767 a Massachusetts observer complained that Rhode Islanders were "divided into furious parties; they bribe, they quarrell, they hardly keep from blows. The parties are so nearly equal that they change governors and magistrates almost every year." Rev. Andrew Eliot, quoted in Bernard Bailyn, *The Origins of American Politics* (New York: Alfred A. Knopf, 1968), p. 158.

[13] For an unusually candid invocation of this agreement, see the important exchange of letters between two rising Rhode Island politicians in 1830, from which the quotations are taken: James Fowler Simmons to John Brown Francis, December 18, 1830 (draft?); Francis to Simmons, December 30, 1830, Simmons Papers, LC. Francis was soon to become governor of the state, and both men served in the U.S. Senate in the 1840s.

[14] Thomas Dorr, undated notes for a speech [1842?], Dorr MSS.; Williamson, *American Suffrage,* p. 246. Political campaigns in Rhode Island often were occasions for one party to charge that the other was in favor of land taxation. See, for example, *Address to the Landholders and Farmers of Newport County, Delivered by Hon. Tristam Burges at a Meeting of the Friends of Messrs.* [Duttee J.] *Pearce and Burges . . .* (Providence: Office of the *Daily Advertiser,* 1829), p. 20.

frage were enlarged to include nonlandholders, or if legislative apportionment took power from the rural regions of the state, this immunity from taxation of real property might end. Some suspicious conservatives dreaded sharing power with the lower orders of society who, because they lacked property, were presumed to lack "a common interest with the rest of the community . . . in the wise administration of justice" and were deemed "unfit to be invested with any control over the property or rights of others." [15] Even before the arrival of large numbers of Irish Catholics,[16] these conservative sentiments took on a nativist tone. One staunch upholder of tradition in Rhode Island denounced the newcomers in 1829 as being in "as degraded a condition as men can be brought by abject servitude, poverty, ignorance and vice." [17] In addition, opposition on the part of some conservatives to sharing power found expression in vague fears that the lower orders would use such power to plunder the state treasury, decree a general division of property and degrade the landholders to servile status.[18]

This concerted opposition by politicians and their constituencies ensured hostile responses to reform appeals. Humble petitions sent to the General Assembly from town meetings and

---

[15] Report of Benjamin Hazard to the Rhode Island General Assembly, against extension of suffrage, 1829, in *Burke's Report*, pp. 384–386. On Benjamin Hazard, Rhode Island's archconservative and Thomas Dorr's political opponent in the struggles over reform in the 1830s, see below, pp. 17, 26–27.

[16] Coleman, *The Transformation of Rhode Island,* pp. 219, 229–230, 241–242, dates the great surge of foreign immigration from the late 1840s. But as Ray Allen Billington has shown (*The Protestant Crusade, 1800–1860: A Study of the Origins of American Nativism* [Chicago: Quadrangle Books, 1964], Chap. 2), anti-immigrant and anti-Catholic sentiment could flourish without many immigrants or Catholics. Professor Patrick T. Conley of Providence College has suggested to me that this "premature" nativism of the Rhode Island conservatives was a "first Negro on the block" reaction.

[17] Benjamin Hazard, in *Burke's Report*, p. 386.

[18] *Ibid.;* [John Pitman], *A Reply to the Letter of the Hon. Marcus Morton, Late Governor of Massachusetts on the Rhode Island Question, by One of the Rhode Island People* (Providence: Knowles and Vose, 1842), pp. 30–31; *Address of John Whipple, to the People of Rhode Island on the Approaching Election* (Providence: Knowles and Vose, 1843), pp. 14–16; W. C. Gibbs to James Fenner, March 26, 184[2], RIHSL.

conventions of "friends of reform" received little serious consideration from the Rhode Island authorities. Such proposals
were either ignored, rejected, or submitted to the freemen and
voted down. For decades a majority of franchised landholders
and their representatives made clear their opposition to tampering with the Charter.[19] They also indicated that ordinary attempts to accomplish change would be easily turned aside. One
working-class orator summed up this situation in 1833 by lament-
ing that reformers "might as well petition Engine Company No.
2" as the Rhode Island General Assembly. "Both would throw
a vast quantity of cold water and in a very short time; the Engine Company to extinguish fire, and the General Assembly to
extinguish the flame of liberty." [20]

A muted tradition of political radicalism, stemming from
America's eighteenth-century revolutionary experience, seemed
to offer some fuel for the torch of liberty in Rhode Island. The
successful struggle for independence had shown the people
precisely how to "alter or to abolish" a hated system of political
domination and "institute new Government, laying its foundation
on such principles and organizing its powers in such form, as to
them shall seem most likely to effect their Safety and Happiness." These revolutionary doctrines of 1776, as Gordon Wood
has recently shown, underwent reinterpretation in the subsequent
decade that deprived them of much of their radical content.[21] But a residue of radicalism remained in the American
political atmosphere, and even before 1842 some people in
Rhode Island had thought of carrying out political reform by
applying the principles of the Declaration of Independence.

---

[19] For these early, sporadic reform efforts, see Jacob Frieze, *Concise
History of the Efforts to Obtain an Extension of Suffrage in Rhode Island
From the Year 1811 to 1842* (Providence: B. Moore, 1842), Chap. 2;
various petitions to the General Assembly, Dorr MSS., Vol. 3; Mowry,
Dorr War, Chap. 3; Maxey, "Suffrage Extension," pp. 545–566; Cole-
man, *Transformation of Rhode Island,* pp. 262–270.

[20] William I. Tillinghast, report to suffrage meeting, May 10, 1833, Dorr
MSS. Cf. Pauline Maier, *From Resistance to Revolution: Colonial Radicals . . . 1765–1776* (New York: Alfred A. Knopf, 1972).

[21] Gordon Wood, *The Creation of the American Republic, 1776–1787*
(Chapel Hill, N.C.: University of North Carolina Press, 1969) brilliantly
describes the transformation of early American political ideology.

One of these Rhode Islanders was a Federalist stalwart named George R. Burrill. As a leading Providence lawyer, Burrill delivered a memorable Fourth of July oration in 1797 urging that the Charter be replaced by a new constitution more favorable to equal rights. To accomplish this, Burrill believed, the people themselves would have to act, without the help of the established governmental authorities. Appeal to the General Assembly was both wrong and futile. No legislature could "create a constitution; since the legislature itself is a creature of the . . . constitution . . . , posterior and subordinate to it." Moreover, the Rhode Island legislature, representing the landholding interest, would never accede to the request that it surrender political power. It "is not in human nature to grant" such a requisition, Burrill observed.[22] Rhode Islanders remembered his admonition that fundamental reform in their state would have to be sought outside regular political channels.

A decade later an anonymous Rhode Island pamphleteer renewed the suggestion that the people, the ultimate repository of political power, establish a constitution independent of legislative authorization. The author spelled out the steps more explicitly than Burrill had. The people would first meet in town conventions throughout the state to choose delegates to a constitutional convention. The framework of government that emerged would be submitted to all the people for approval. "[T]hen let there be a time appointed on which the new system shall go into operation. All this could be done without the least danger to the public welfare, and without putting to hazard individual rights." [23]

Neither Burrill nor the pamphleteer of 1807 discussed the likelihood that the Charter Government might not agree to fade away at the appointed time. In the early 1840s radicals under

---

[22] Burrill's oration, reported in the *Providence Gazette,* July 8, 1797, was reprinted in the reform organ *New Age,* December 20, 1841, and was incorporated into *Burke's Report,* pp. 271–274. On Burrill, see Providence *Evening Bulletin,* January 7, 1874; Mowry, *Dorr War,* p. 27. In some of his later political writing Dorr used the pseudonym "Burrill." See Dorr MSS. For the earlier development of doctrines of legitimate political action by "the People Out-of-Doors," see Wood, *Creation of the American Republic,* pp. 319–343, 516 and *passim.*

[23] *A Few Observations on the Government of the State of Rhode Island & c. by A Citizen* (Providence: John Carter, 1807), copy in RIHSL.

the leadership of Thomas Wilson Dorr, acting on the previous suggestions, also failed to foresee determined opposition to reform from the government they intended to replace.

II

Dorr was an unlikely revolutionary. He was born in Providence on November 5, 1805, the oldest son of Sullivan and Lydia Allen Dorr. His father had amassed a fortune in China trade. Returning to the United States from Canton in 1800, Sullivan Dorr settled in Providence and took a wife from one of the most distinguished families of Rhode Island. A self-made man of imposing demeanor, he invested in various manufacturing and commercial enterprises in the state, headed a leading insurance company, became a trustee of Brown University, took a place of prominence in the Whig Party, and erected a magnificent house in Providence.[24] Sullivan Dorr's achievements must have constituted for his sons a positive challenge to accomplish something noteworthy in life. In 1832, at age twenty-seven, Thomas Dorr confessed that he had not "yet lived to a purpose," but was hop-

---

[24] Sullivan Dorr's early business career may be traced in the Dorr Family Papers, Massachusetts Historical Society, some of which have been edited by Howard Corning and printed in *Proceedings of the Massachusetts Historical Society,* LXVII (1941–1944), 178–364. See also Corning, "Sullivan Dorr, China Trader," *Rhode Island History,* III (July 1944), 75–90; Jane Louise Cayford, "The Sullivan Dorr House in Providence, Rhode Island" (M.A. Thesis, University of Delaware, 1961); which contains much biographical and genealogical data; and see Anne Mary Newton, "Rebellion in Rhode Island, The Story of the Dorr War" (M.A. Thesis, Columbia University, 1947), pp. 42–43. For Sullivan Dorr's political affiliation, see the Whig electoral broadside, July 20, 1837, Broadside Collection, RIHSL. There is a photograph of the Dorr House in Mowry, *Dorr War,* facing p. 264. In the Dorr House is a striking portrait of Sullivan Dorr. Existing data permit little more than speculation about the psychological dynamics of the Dorr household. There may be significance in the fact that none of Sullivan Dorr's four sons ever married, whereas his three daughters married well and raised families. Did Sullivan Dorr set so high a standard of manhood that none of his sons felt capable of equaling him, except perhaps the eldest, Thomas, who defied his father to become a leader of the rebel movement in Rhode Island? For Sullivan and Lydia Dorr's attitude toward their son's political efforts in the 1840s, see p. 86.

ing to embark soon on some useful life's work.[25] There was no indication in his family background that this work might include a stint as insurrectionist.

Thomas' family not only contributed to his conviction that he must live "to a purpose"; they also provided him with every advantage of wealth, social position and education for the realization of honorable ambition. According to a childhood neighbor, the boy was studious and retiring. Small of stature and pudgy like his mother, young Thomas "kept himself from the pranks and extravagances which boys are prone to." [26] He attended the Latin Grammar School in Providence and Phillips Exeter Academy in New Hampshire, and he entered Harvard College in 1819 at the age of fourteen.

It was hardly necessary to urge the young college student, as one of his uncles did, to avoid pranks and frivolity at Cambridge and dedicate himself to civic and religious responsibility.[27] Thomas Dorr was the very model of a docile, well-behaved undergraduate, despite the general tumultuousness at Harvard. Campus unrest had been simmering for some time. The issues were student roistering and the consequent punishments administered by the faculty. In early November 1820 a series of campus battles brought disciplinary action against two students, whereupon most of the other members of the class temporarily left Cambridge in protest. A small group supported the college authorities and were entered on a "Black List" by their dissident classmates.[28] Dorr was prominent enough among the "Blacks"

---

[25] Dorr to William B. Adams (copy?), May 28, 1832, Dorr MSS.

[26] Catherine R. Williams, "Recollections of the Life and Conversation of Thomas W. Dorr, First Governor of Rhode Island Under the People's Constitution" (unpublished draft, n.d.), Dorr MSS. There is a graceful portrait of Lydia Allen Dorr in the Dorr House, Providence.

[27] James A. Dorr (writing from Canton) to Thomas Dorr, March 17, 1820, Dorr MSS.

[28] Pickering Dodge, "Brief Account of the Class of 1819–23," in Samuel Eliot Morison, "The Great Rebellion in Harvard College and the Resignation of Pres. Kirkland," *Transactions of the Colonial Society of Massachusetts, 1927–8* (Boston: the Society, 1929), pp. 64–95; Morison, *Three Centuries of Harvard, 1636–1936* (Cambridge, Mass.: Harvard University Press, 1936), pp. 230–231.

to merit a stanza in verses that were published by the rebel students:

> Then the mathematician [Dorr] of true gothic size,
> Whose cheeks are so huge, you can scarce see his eyes;
> That mighty young mammoth so highly renown'd
> For *gift of the gab*, though 'tis all empty sound.[29]

Students on the Black List were "very much irritated at the neglect and coldness they receive[d] from the class, and to avenge themselves" became *"spies* and *informers."* [30] It is not known whether Dorr actually spied or informed, but rebels did celebrate the second anniversary of the Black List in the spring of 1823 by taking his shower bath from his fourth-story quarters in Stoughton Hall and burning it in the college yard. This event was duly celebrated as "the splendid conflagration of Dorr" in verses revised for the occasion.[31] When disorders continued into May, the authorities expelled forty-three students out of a class of seventy.[32] Dorr still refused to associate himself with student rebels. One of a handful who took his degree in course, he submitted a senior thesis in mathematics and delivered an English oration at commencement.[33]

---

[29] "The Convention," March 10, 1821, broadside, Harvard College Library. (I wish to acknowledge the assistance of my nephew, S. Andrew Jacobs, a sophomore in Harvard College when he gathered data for me on the class of 1823).

[30] Dodge, "Brief Account . . . ," in *Transactions of the Colonial Society of Massachusetts, 1927–8,* p. 72.

[31] "Black List Convention," 2nd ed., August 27, 1823, Harvard College Library.

[32] *Transactions of the Colonial Society of Massachusetts, 1927–8,* pp. 79–88. The issues, not directly relevant here, included apparently trumped-up charges of dissipation against John Paul Robinson, which students suspected were spread by one of the "Blacks." In the wake of this rebellion President John Kirkland resigned and a general reform at Harvard was begun.

[33] Harvard Faculty Record, X (July 14, 1823), 46. Dorr's thesis was on "Calculation and Projection of a Lunar Eclipse of 1825," dedicated to the sorely pressed Harvard president, John Kirkland (in Harvard College Library). Dorr's Harvard diploma is in the Dorr MSS. Another later rebel, or at least nonconformist, who as a Harvard senior upheld the college authorities in 1823 against his rebellious fellow students, was

Soon after graduation, at the age of twenty, Thomas Dorr went to New York City to pursue a legal career. He studied with Chancellor James Kent, who had just retired from the State's Court of Chancery and was delivering the lectures that would eventually appear as the magisterial *Commentaries on American Law* (four volumes, 1826–1830).[34] Dorr attended these lectures for two winter terms, also getting some instruction from Kent's former associate, Vice Chancellor William T. McCoun.[35] Later Dorr occasionally spiced his reform orations with a reference to Kent's *Commentaries,*[36] but there seems to have been little direct influence on the young man from the conservative jurists who trained him.[37] However, a certain obsessive legalism that he carried with him, even into the Rebellion of 1842, may betray the impact of his early study of the law.

Dorr continued his legal studies in Providence with some of

George Ripley, the founder of Brook Farm. Years later Dorr was charged with being a fervent rebel at Harvard in 1823, backing down only when the faculty showed force and then attempting to curry favor with the authorities. See the Washington *National Intelligencer,* November 23, 1844; New York *Journal of Commerce,* November 20, 1844; *Providence Journal,* November 27, 1844. Dorr's father vehemently denied these charges (*Providence Journal,* December 10, 1844), and George Ripley privately substantiated this denial. Ripley to Francis O. Dorr, December 24, 1844, Dorr MSS. For Dorr's own recollections of the rebellion, see Dorr to [Walter S. Burges], December 12, 1844, Dorr MSS.

[34] William Kent to Moss Kent, November 9, 1824, Kent Papers, LC; Perry Miller, ed., *The Legal Mind in America: From Independence to the Civil War* (Garden City, N.Y.: Doubleday Anchor Books, 1962), p. 93.

[35] [Frances H. (Whipple) McDougall], *Might and Right by a Rhode Islander,* 2nd ed. (Providence: A. H. Stillwell, 1844), p. 327; Dan King, *The Life and Times of Thomas Wilson Dorr, with Outlines of the Political History of Rhode Island* (Boston: published by the author, 1859), p. 285; William T. McCoun to Dorr, November 3, 1827, Dorr MSS.

[36] See [Dorr and others], Address to the People of Rhode Island, 1834, in *Burke's Report,* p. 154, where Kent was invoked as an authority on the desirability of the separation of judicial and legislative power.

[37] In fact, codification of the law that Kent abhorred (see Perry Miller, *The Life of the Mind in America: From the Revolution to the Civil War* [New York: Harcourt, Brace and World, 1965], pp. 246–264) was Dorr's "favourite plan." Henry C. Dorr to T. W. Dorr, May 28, 1841, Dorr MSS.

Rhode Island's leading lawyers.[38] He was admitted to the state bar in 1827. After a trip through the South and West, he returned to Providence and legal practice.[39] He specialized in maritime and commercial cases, earning the respect of fellow attorneys in his own city and elsewhere.[40] Detractors were later to charge that he enjoyed no professional advancement in the law and that he embraced radicalism to gain fame and attention.[41] The available evidence [42] suggests, however, that he took advantage of family connections and achieved considerable success in his chosen calling.[43]

----

[38] [McDougall], *Might and Right,* p. 327. One of them was John Whipple, who in 1842–1843 was one of the leaders of the anti-Dorr movement and in 1848 served as anti-Dorr counsel in the Supreme Court case of *Luther v. Borden,* 7 Howard 1 (1849). See Chap. VII below.

[39] Certificates of admission to the bar and to the U.S. Circuit Court, Rhode Island District, Dorr MSS.; [McDougall], *Might and Right,* p. 327.

[40] Thomas P. Tappan to David B. Ogden, February 20, September 21, October 17, 1827; William T. McCoun to Dorr, November 3, 1827; draft autobiographical note by Dorr stating his qualifications for admission to the New York State Supreme Court, May 16, 1831; Dorr to John Whipple and Henry Rogers (copy), May 27, 1831, all in Dorr MSS.

[41] [George Ticknor Curtis], *Merits of Thomas W. Dorr and George Bancroft as they are Politically Connected, by a Citizen of Massachusetts* (Boston: John H. Eastburn, [1844]), pp. 5, 28; Broadside, *"To the Freemen of Providence,"* August 29, 1837, by "Franklin," Broadside Collection, RIHSL.

[42] Rhode Island court records for the 1830s and early 1840s do not list the attorneys arguing particular cases. I have examined the dockets in Dorr MSS., Vol. 2, and the Supreme Judicial Court Minute Books, MSS., in State Records Center, Providence. The first printed *Docket of the Court of Common Pleas for the County of Providence, December Term, A.D. 1841* (Providence: B. Cranston, 1841) lists Dorr among the other lawyers practicing in the county but provides no data on the extent of this practice.

[43] I concur with the conclusions reached by Chilton Williamson on this point; see his "Disenchantment of Thomas W. Dorr," *Rhode Island History,* XVII (October 1958), 97; and his *American Suffrage,* p. 274. Newton ("Rebellion in Rhode Island," p. 42) uncritically accepts the conservative canard that Dorr's reform involvement was the result of professional failure. It is not necessary to credit Dorr with absolute, selfless purity of motive either, as his partisans did. See [McDougall], *Might and Right,* p. 69; King, *Life and Times of Dorr,* pp. 286–287. A combination of motives brought Dorr to reform and radical commitments. A "spirit of philanthropy" (King, *Life and Times,* p. 286) was certainly

Dorr's early prominence in Rhode Island civic and political life was a measure of his professional success. Before the age of thirty he became a member of the General Assembly, representing Providence's fourth ward. The portly young lawyer actively championed expanded public education, abolition of imprisonment for debt, and banking reform. The legislature appointed him bank commissioner to investigate alleged abuses, and it passed an important banking statute in 1836 that he helped draft.[44] Outside the General Assembly, Dorr was a prominent defender of religious liberty [45] and an abolitionist. He endorsed immediate Congressional action to abolish slavery in the District of Columbia and expressed confidence that the abolitionist campaign for public enlightenment would soon bring

---

present, along with political and psychological factors. On the interpretation of the growth of radical commitment, I have benefited from Silvan S. Tomkins, "The Psychology of Commitment: The Constructive Role of Violence and Suffering for the Individual and for His Society," in Martin B. Duberman, ed., *The Antislavery Vanguard: New Essays on the Abolitionists* (Princeton, N.J.: Princeton University Press, 1965), pp. 270–298; and Charles Hampden-Turner, *Radical Man: The Process of Psycho-Social Development* (Cambridge, Mass.: Schenkman Publishing Co., 1970), Chaps. 3, 4.

[44] See Edward Field, *State of Rhode Island and Providence Plantations at the End of the* [Nineteenth] *Century: A History,* 3 vols. (Boston and Syracuse: Mason Publishing Co., 1902), I, 329; Charles Carroll, *Rhode Island: Three Centuries of Democracy,* 4 vols, (New York: Lewis Historical Publishing Co., 1932), I, 433; Coleman, *Transformation of Rhode Island,* p. 198; Dorr MSS., Vols. 22, 23 (banking affairs), 25 (imprisonment for debt), 28 (education). See also Dorr's bitter debate on imprisonment for debt with Rhode Island archconservative Benjamin Hazard in Providence *Manufacturers and Farmers Journal,* January 5, 1837.

[45] Dorr protested the blasphemy conviction of Massachusetts deist Abner Kneeland in 1839. See draft petition in Newspaper Articles and Notes, 1837–1840, Dorr MSS. For the Kneeland case, see Henry Steele Commager, *The Era of Reform, 1830–1860* (Princeton, N.J.: D. Van Nostrand Co., 1960), pp. 159–161; Leonard W. Levy, *The Law of the Commonwealth and Chief Justice Shaw: The Evolution of American Law, 1830–1860* (New York: Harper Torchbooks, 1967), Chap. 4. Dorr also fought in the General Assembly against legislation to restrain use of property by religious sects, and again found Benjamin Hazard in opposition. See Providence *Manufacturers and Farmers Journal,* January 19, 1835.

about the demise of the peculiar and evil institution of slavery.[46] But as a public-spirited young reformer, Dorr fought his most memorable political battles in the 1830s over the issues of constitutional revision and suffrage extension.

III

He entered the political arena in a new era of intense agitation for reform. Efforts to achieve constitutional change in Rhode Island before the 1830s had been limited to sporadic exhortations by individuals and uncoordinated requests from some of the northern industrial towns. But after the Presidential election of 1832, nonlandholders began vociferously demanding the vote. In the spring of 1833 Providence barbers, shoemakers, blacksmiths, stonecutters and other "mechanics" took the initiative in reform organization. Within the next year they would be joined by lawyers, physicians, and newspaper editors, who would moderate somewhat the radical tone of the movement. But in the early phase, when the workingmen were the most active, a militant tone predominated.

Workingmen delivered impassioned orations on their grievances and voiced the elements of a radical political philosophy. Even their enemies admitted that these speeches

> . . . exhibited considerable talent; and though often spiced with satire and sarcasm, afforded evidence that those who delivered them had felt much and thought much, if they had not learned much. It was fashionable . . . to give the landholders the appellation of aristocrats and ruffled shirt gentry; and the speakers and their associates prided themselves in occupying an opposite standing. Hence they frequently appeared . . . arrayed in green baize jackets to address the audience. . . .[47]

---

[46] On Dorr's antislavery views and connections, see William Chace to Dorr, July 18; Dorr to Chace, July 25, 1837 (copy); Dorr to James G. Birney (copy), December 26. 1837, all in Dorr MSS. For my discussion of the role of the Negro question in the Dorr Rebellion, see below, pp. 45–47, 49, 142, 145, 148, 157.

[47] Frieze, *Concise History,* pp. 22–23.

The most noteworthy and forceful of the radical speeches of 1833 was Seth Luther's *Address on the Right of Free Suffrage,* which expressed a point of view that remained alive for a decade in Rhode Island. Luther was a carpenter and a labor spokesman, a self-educated seeker whose influence was felt even beyond his native Providence.[48] He spoke against class prejudice and in behalf of a concept of community that included respect for the rights of all Rhode Islanders. He ridiculed the pretensions of "the *mushroom lordlings, sprigs of nobility*" and *"small potato aristocrats"* of his state, who monopolized political power. These landholders, he said, "fly from the green baize jacket on the back of a mechanic, as from the infection of the Asiatic Spasmodic Cholera." Workingmen continually heard that politics were beyond their ken and were only of concern to "good society." A just political community involved an "implied contract" between citizens, in which the working-class members received due recognition for their contributions to the community —displaying craftsmanly skills, fighting fires, performing militia duty and paying taxes. Quoting Jefferson as an authority on the principle of political equality, Luther went further than the Monticello sage in championing the social rights of "the unlearned rabble and unpolished mob." His protests were not against divisions in society as such, but rather against the exaggeration of those divisions by pretentious ladies and gentlemen who acted as if they were "a different 'class,' if you please." Luther's philosophy was a radical Jeffersonian communitarianism, which accepted economic inequalities in society but insisted upon political equality, social civility and mutual respect.[49]

---

[48] Louis Hartz, "Seth Luther: Working Class Rebel," *New England Quarterly,* XIII (September 1940), 401–418; Edward Pessen, *Most Uncommon Jacksonians: The Radical Leaders of the Early Labor Movement* ([Albany]: State University of New York Press, 1967), pp. 87–90. Luther was planning a compilation of economic statistics in 1840, and he asked the aged Jeffersonian financier Albert Gallatin to supply him with information. See Luther to Gallatin, July 23, 1840, Gallatin MSS., LC.

[49] Seth Luther, *An Address on the Right of Free Suffrage, Delivered by the Request of Freeholders and Others of the City of Providence, Rhode Island, in the Old Town House* . . . (Providence: S. R. Weeden, 1833), pp. 3–6, 21–23 ("All Men Are Created Equal" on the title page). Some of Luther's ideas about community are developed at greater length

Luther's *Address* led to conclusions about independent political action similar to those reached by George Burrill and the anonymous pamphleteer of 1807.[50] The radical carpenter urged disfranchised Rhode Islanders to protest their political status by refusing to cooperate with the Charter Government, refusing to pay taxes and refusing to serve in the militia or fire brigades. But in addition to this protest, Luther called upon "the whole people" of Rhode Island to frame their own new republican constitution for the state, regardless of the existing government.

> [The people] . . . have a right to assemble in primary meetings, and appoint delegates to a Convention. That convention have [*sic*] a right to form a Constitution, and submit it to the people. If they adopt it, it is the law of the land.

He said that the General Assembly, established under the Charter of 1663 and representing only the landholders of the

---

in *An Address to the Workingmen of New-England. On the State of Education and On the Condition of the Producing Classes in Europe and America* . . . (Boston: published by the author, 1832). The conjunction of equal-rights radicalism with communitarian ideas in Seth Luther suggests a possible revision of the now fashionable idea that antebellum radicals were uniformly anti-institutional in outlook. See Stanley M. Elkins, *Slavery: A Problem in American Institutional and Intellectual Life* (New York: Grosset's Universal Library, 1963), pp. 27–37, 140–157; John L. Thomas, "Romantic Reform in America, 1815–1865," *American Quarterly, XVII* (Winter 1965), 656–681; and George M. Fredrickson, *The Inner Civil War: Northern Intellectuals and the Crisis of the Union* (New York: Harper Torchbooks, 1965), Chap. 1. David J. Rothman, in his provocative *The Discovery of the Asylum: Social Order and Disorder in the New Republic* (Boston: Little, Brown & Co., 1971) shows how institutional innovation *was* a central concern of antebellum reformers. It also seems to me that another difficulty with the prevailing view is that it does not discriminate sufficiently between the class origins of different reform spokesmen. There is no doubt that many middle-class reformers of the period were anti-institutionalists (although even this point is certainly overemphasized in some recent literature), but the generalization might not hold for the working class. Of course, the latter group leaves fewer records, so that its aims and goals are more difficult to discover, but that does not mean that they are negligible. For some of the issues of writing history "from the bottom up," see Jesse Lemisch, "Toward a Democratic History," *Radical America,* I (1966), 43–53.

[50] See pp. 10–11.

state, had no right to interfere with such proceedings.[51] Just let the five thousand landed "aristocrats" of Rhode Island try to suppress the twelve thousand unfranchised citizens of the state, warned a Providence barber associated with Luther: they would taste the power of the majority.[52]

In 1833, however, workingmen were far more radical in utterance than in action. They organized a few mass meetings in Providence, but little that was decisive resulted. Attending these meetings were a number of opponents of free suffrage who, "not having the effrontery" to admit their true reasons for opposing reform, referred instead to the allegedly dire consequences of the taxpayer suffrage in neighboring Massachusetts.[53] On the defensive and unsure of how to proceed, the workingmen agreed to correspond with Massachusetts leaders and with local men to gauge public opinion on suffrage extension. The out-of-state and local replies were more favorable than the opinions of Rhode Island politicians,[54] but the data gathered was small recompense for months of waiting. Workingmen radicals suspected that they had been maneuvered into conducting the correspondence so as to blunt their determination to change Rhode Island's political system.[55] The result, whether intended or not, was that reform initiative passed out of the hands of radical workingmen to another, more respectable middle-class group between 1833 and 1834. However, the belief in radical action independent of the established authorities lingered on as a latent

---

[51] Luther, *Address on the Right of Free Suffrage,* p. 24.

[52] William I. Tillinghast in *ibid.,* Appendix, p. x.

[53] Tillinghast and others to Martin Van Buren, May 31, 1833, in Marvin E. Gettleman and Noel P. Conlon, eds., "Responses to the Rhode Island Workingmen's Reform Agitation of 1833," *Rhode Island History,* XXVIII (August 1969), 81–82. This collection of correspondence provides data on the occupational status of the suffrage radicals of 1833, clearly showing that workingmen were the most intensively involved at that point in the agitation for constitutional change.

[54] For the responses of Rhode Island political figures, see *ibid.,* pp. 84–87, 92–93.

[55] See the letter from Tillinghast and others to Martin Van Buren, May 31, 1833, *ibid.,* pp. 81–82.

possibility, to be revived in the 1840s when once again working-men became politically active in the state.[56]

IV

The new group that absorbed and supplanted the working-men's reform efforts of 1833 was the Rhode Island Constitu-tional Party, organized in the spring of 1834. Leaders of this party, mostly business and professional men from the northern industrial towns in the state,[57] exerted a moderating influence on the workingmen-radicals. While generally endorsing the idea of independent political action, these gentlemen believed that the issue of unequal legislative representation of the northern towns was as important as the question of suffrage extension.[58] They urged workingmen-radicals to rally behind respectable leaders who would best represent the common interest in reform.[59] And they ignored the inflammatory talk about direct action and passive resistance by proceeding to organize in more conven-tional ways.

Early in the year these moderate reformers from the northern towns, having previously corresponded with each other and with the radical Providence workingmen, issued an invitation to a general meeting "to promote the establishment of a State Con-stitution." [60] Delegates from Newport and ten of the northeastern

---

[56] I do not mean that the strategy of popular constitutional action was a working-class doctrine. As has been previously noted, even a Federalist lawyer in 1797 could advocate it, and Thomas Dorr became its most fervent advocate in the early 1840s. What I do mean is that before such a strategy could actually be put into force in Rhode Island, a working-class movement had to appear. For the formation of this new coalition of suffragist radicals in the 1840s, see pp. 34 ff.

[57] See Table I, p. 23.

[58] Metcalf Marsh to William I. Tillinghast, November 11, 1833, Dorr MSS.

[59] Dan King to Tillinghast, February 20, March 4, 1834; Marsh to Til-linghast, December 26, 1833; Christopher Robinson to [Tillinghast], Oc-tober 14, 1833; all in Dorr MSS. [McDougall], *Might and Right,* pp. 68–69; Frieze, *Concise History,* p. 23.

[60] [Dorr and others], Address to the People of Rhode Island, February-March 1834, in *Burke's Report,* p. 151; Mowry, *Dorr War,* p. 37.

towns, those most adversely affected by the archaic apportionment of seats in the legislature, gathered in February at the

TABLE I   MEMBERS OF THE CONSTITUTIONAL
PARTY, 1834–1837 *

Metcalf Marsh	Manufacturer, Smithfield
Charles N. Tilley	Hotel manager, Newport
George Knowles	Lawyer, Newport
William Peckham	Commission merchant, Newport
Thomas W. Dorr	Lawyer, Providence
Dan King	Physician, Charlestown
Charles B. Peckham	Proprietor of Vapor Baths, Newport
Joseph K. Angell	Lawyer, Providence
Christopher Robinson	Lawyer, Woonsocket
Charles Randall	Newspaper editor, Warren

* Sources: Providence and Newport Directories; Abraham Payne, *Reminiscences of the Rhode Island Bar* (Providence: Tibbitts & Preston, 1885); Dorr MSS., correspondence of the 1830s. I have been unable to find occupational data for any other members of this party, but this list includes the men whom Dorr, Constitutionalist State Secretary, corresponded with most regularly. While I have no full roster of Constitutional Party membership, my impression is that it enjoyed no mass following, and consisted of no more than a few dozen men of similar status as those listed here.

State House in Providence to "devise the best means to effect the adoption of a Constitution for this state, embracing an equalization of representation, an extension of Suffrage, limitation of the powers of the legislature, an improvement of the Judiciary, and other important objects." [61] The marked sectional pattern of responses to this call indicated deep political divisions in Rhode Island. The agricultural regions in the southern part of the state, along with the smaller Narragansett Bay towns, already enjoying disproportionate political power through the landholding suffrage requirement and rural overrepresentation, showed little interest in constitutional reform.[62] In future years

[61] *Rhode-Island Constitutionalist* (Providence), March 12, 1834.

[62] The most thorough treatment of Rhode Island sectional patterns in this period is Coleman, *Transformation of Rhode Island,* pp. 255–256, 264–270.

these regions would continue to function as centers of opposition to political change.[63]

The reform proposals that emerged from the meetings and deliberations of the Constitutional Party were distinctly less radical than the demands of workingmen agitators the year before. The moderate Constitutionalists disclaimed "the slightest disrespect" toward the "noble forefathers" who established the Rhode Island colony in the seventeenth century. They also disavowed any intention to engage in "narrow party affair[s]" or pursue "secondary or sinister ends." The party was sincerely dedicated, they said, to the achievement of equal representation, suffrage extension, a reformed judiciary and a bill of rights defining the limits of legislative power.[64] On the question of how to bring about these reforms, the Constitutionalists were significantly ambivalent. Their elaborate Address of 1834, of which Thomas Wilson Dorr was principal author, promoted the doctrine of Popular Constituent Sovereignty—the doctrine that the people possessed ample wisdom and authority to form a new constitution without prior government action.[65] Despite this invocation of popular radicalism, the Constitutional Party merely requested that the General Assembly call a convention to draft "a liberal and permanent constitution." In order to facilitate "the exercise by the people of the great original right of sovereignty in the formation of a constitution," the reformers also asked the legislature not to require that delegates to this convention be chosen by the restricted electorate of landholders. Allowing "the people at large" to vote would be the American way.[66]

Before the General Assembly could act on the request for a convention, the Constitutional Party prepared to participate in

---

[63] See pp. 55, 79, 87–88, 249–250, and Appendix B.

[64] [Dorr and others], Address to the People of Rhode Island, February–March 1834, in *Burke's Report,* pp. 152–154; *Rhode-Island Constitutionalist,* March 12, 1834.

[65] [Dorr and others], Address to the People of Rhode Island, February–March 1834, in *Burke's Report,* p. 185. For a full discussion of Popular Constituent Sovereignty, which would soon become the central tenet of the radical ideology of the Dorrite movement of 1841–1842, see below, pp. 63–73.

[66] [Dorr and others], Address to the People of Rhode Island, February–March 1834, in *Burke's Report,* p. 185.

the annual state election. Apparently such open electoral activity was not included in the category of "narrow" partisanship that the reformers disavowed, but certain political realities of this canvass must have been clear to the Constitutionalists. The Democrats were the dominant party in Rhode Island, drawing their electoral strength from the agricultural regions where the proportion of franchised freemen was relatively high. Of the major parties in the mid-1830s only the Whigs stood to gain by constitutional reform that would assign more political weight to the manufacturing and commercial centers in the northern party of the state. Most members of the Constitutional Party were Whigs, including Dorr, who was soon to stand for election as representative from Providence to the General Assembly. Hence the slate of candidates chosen by the Constitutionalists was essentially the same as the Whig ticket that year.[67] Heading that ticket as nominee of both Whig and Constitutional parties for Governor was Nehemiah R. Knight, who had been serving as United States Senator from Rhode Island for most of the previous decade.[68] The choice of Knight by the Constitutionalists was an act of political opportunism, for he had expressed distinctly lukewarm views on reform in his response to the workingmen's agitation the previous year.[69] In the spring elections Knight was

---

[67] *Rhode-Island Constitutionalist,* March 12, April 7, 1834; *Northern Star* (Warren), April 5, 1834; and two broadsides: *Constitution to the People of Rhode Island* (n.p., [April 12, 1834]); *Union Convention* [i.e., Whig] *Ticket* (n.p., [1834]), both in Broadside Collection, John Hay Library, Brown University.

[68] Knight, who led the Republican Party to victory over the Federalists in 1817, was elected to the United States Senate in 1823. See Samuel H. Allen, "The Federal Ascendency of 1812," *Narragansett Historical Register,* VII (October 1889), 394; Carroll, *Rhode Island: Three Centuries of Democracy,* I, 564. In the Senate, Knight opposed the banking policies of the Jackson Administration, and so drifted into the Whig camp. See Knight to James Fowler Simmons, December 9, 1831, Simmons Papers, LC.; Knight, *Address to the Farmers of Rhode Island* (Providence: Cranston & Hammond, 1832). Cf. *Biographical Directory of the American Congress,* 1774–1949, Document No. 607, 81 Cong., 2 Sess., 1950, p. 1176, where Knight's Whig affiliation is not acknowledged.

[69] See Knight to [William I. Tillinghast and others], September 2, 1833, in Gettleman and Conlon, eds., "Responses to Reform Agitation," pp. 85–87. (The account of workingmen's reactions to Knight's candidacy,

defeated by Democratic, anti-Masonic incumbent John Brown Francis,[70] a defeat which inauspiciously closed the Constitutionalists' first electoral effort.

No less fraught with difficulties was the Constitutional Party's subsequent attempt to achieve reform through a constitutional convention. The 1834 General Assembly debates on the bill to call the convention pitted young Dorr against Benjamin Hazard of Newport, a venerable conservative who five years earlier had issued a scathing attack on schemes for constitutional change in Rhode Island.[71] His views unchanged in 1834, Hazard led off with a personal attack on "the young gentleman from Providence," whose Constitutional Party Address, he said, had included lengthy abuse of Rhode Island's "institutions and our ancestors" coupled with excessive amounts of visionary social theory. Supposing that it must be "mortifying for the relations of these young gentlemen" to know that their offspring were politically associated with stonecutters, barbers, carpenters and other low types, Hazard denounced the dangerous "spirit of levelling" abroad in the state.[72] Dorr, an aggressive debater,[73] made a

---

ibid., note 20, is mistaken.) On the complementary opportunism of Knight and the Constitutionalists, see also Dorr to Knight, April 3, 1834, Dorr MSS.; Knight to James F. Simmons, February 22, 1836, Simmons Papers, LC.

[70] Francis won by only 150 votes. See Field, *State of Rhode Island and Providence Plantations,* I, 326–327; Philip A. Grant, Jr., "Party Chaos Embroils Rhode Island [II]," *Rhode Island History,* XXVII (January 1968), 24–25.

[71] In 1829 the General Assembly referred appeals for suffrage extension and constitutional reform to a select committee chaired by Hazard. The committee's report, drafted by the chairman, was an impassioned defense of Rhode Island's traditional political system. Hazard's report is reprinted in *Burke's Report,* pp. 384–386. Cf. above, pp. 9, 17 n. For Hazard's long political career, including his participation as a Federalist in 1815 in the Hartford Convention, see Caroline E. Robinson, *The Hazard Family of Rhode Island, 1635–1894* (Boston: printed for the author, 1895), pp. 83–85; David H. Fischer, *The Revolution of American Conservatism: The Federalist Party in the Era of Jeffersonian Democracy* (New York: Harper & Row, 1965), pp. 282–283.

[72] Debates in the General Assembly, June 1834, reported in *Manufacturers and Farmers Journal* (Providence), September 1, 1834.

[73] On Dorr's forensic abilities, see [McDougall], *Might and Right,* p. 230.

spirited reply, accusing "the gentleman from Newport" of voicing the "old fashioned prejudices" of Rhode Island's farmers. The young reformer defended his party's search for reasonable remedies of "palpable" abuses such as unfair apportionment, which gave the inhabitants of one town fifteen times the political power of those of another, and disfranchisement of sober, industrious nonlandholders. Dorr dismissed Hazard's attack as the sort of thing that might be expected of "a common Barroom politician."

> He impeaches the motives of the most active members of the Constitutional Party; and in the course of his vituperations, after charging upon them the crime of being young men, he tells you that they are acting against the opinions of their relatives, not perceiving that if this were true he was contradicting himself by an acknowledgement of their integrity in postponing private interests to what they deemed the welfare of the state.

Dorr did not exactly endear himself to that "certain class of politician[s]" whose power was based on the prevailing political injustices in Rhode Island when he stated that the very idealistic reformers they scorned would bring about their downfall.[74] Yet the reform issue was raised so insistently that the conservatives who dominated the General Assembly agreed to call a constitutional convention that fall.[75] Such an agreement, however, fell far short of full commitment to the reform program.

Rhode Island conservatives expressed their cautious intentions both in the balloting for delegates and in the convention sessions. Since the General Assembly had rejected Dorr's motion for a temporary relaxation of voting requirements in advance of the convention,[76] only the traditional restricted electorate of freemen was eligible to choose delegates. The voting took place at

---

[74] General Assembly debates reported in *Manufacturers and Farmers Journal* (Providence), September 1, 3, 8, 1834.

[75] Act of the General Assembly, June 1834, in *Burke's Report*, pp. 643–644.

[76] For Dorr's modest proposal to allow all those native residents of Rhode Island paying taxes on $134 of real *or* personal property to choose delegates, see *Manufacturers and Farmers Journal*, September 11, 1834; Frieze, *Concise History*, pp. 24–26; Mowry, *Dorr War*, p. 41; Maxey, "Suffrage Extension," p. 572.

the regular town meetings in August, and the group chosen was merely a miniature version of the legislature. Benjamin Hazard was one of the delegates, as was Dorr.[77] The relative strength of reform and conservative contingents at the convention was revealed when Dorr proposed that a taxpayer suffrage be instituted; the proposal won only seven votes.[78] The convention not only refused to extend suffrage, it also failed to recommend broad legislative reapportionment or any change in legislative and executive powers. Only minor changes in apportionment of legislative seats and in judicial tenure won the support of a majority of delegates.[79] But even these minor changes were blocked when the conservatives stayed away altogether, preventing a quorum and bringing the convention to a humiliating halt. At the last session in June 1835, only Dorr and fellow Constitutionalist Metcalf Marsh of Smithfield were present; [80] Rhode Island conservatives had won still another battle in their struggle against political change.

Outmaneuvered and defeated in the contest over a constitutional convention, the Constitutional Party nevertheless continued its campaigns for basic political change. At first Constitutionalist leaders tried to enter into coalitions with the Whigs, who were anxious to win votes in the industrial towns to counterbalance Democratic strength in the rural areas.[81] But the re-

---

[77] Frieze, *Concise History,* pp. 24–26.

[78] *Manufacturers and Farmers Journal,* September 11, 1834. This sympathetic Whig semiweekly contains the only extant account of the 1834 convention, but it provides no roster of delegates or roll call votes. Dorr's convention proposal provided for an expanded electorate consisting of white male citizens (native *or* naturalized) who paid taxes on at least $200 of personal property. See his notes in folder of draft convention proposals, John Hay Library, Brown University.

[79] *Manufacturers and Farmers Journal,* September 15, 1834.

[80] Mowry, *Dorr War,* p. 41; Newton, "Rebellion in Rhode Island," pp. 16–17. The cynical intentions of Rhode Island conservatives may easily be inferred from their actions in 1834–1835, but there is also contemporary corroborative evidence in Frieze's *Concise History,* pp. 26–27, where the author, an anti-Dorrite, brands official sponsorship of the constitutional convention a "sham . . . designed to amuse that portion of the citizens of the state who were loudest in their demands for a constitution and an extention of suffrage."

[81] The Dorr MSS. are rich in materials on Constitutional Party affairs of the 1830s. See especially Metcalf Marsh to Dorr, February 22, 1835;

formers, lacking political strength, found it "next to impossible" to hold endorsed candidates to the Constitutionalist cause. "I am apt to think if we had a few *good fat offices* to dispose of," wrote one reformer, "we should not be troubled for candidates." [82] Unable to advance their cause through electoral coalitions, the Constitutionalists ran their own ticket in the spring elections of 1837 and won enough votes to believe they had made a good showing.[83] Emboldened by the results of this canvass, Constitutionalist leaders decided to run their own men for Congress later in the year, including Thomas Dorr as candidate for an at-large seat in the United States House of Representatives.[84]

The decision to compete against the major parties in an electoral contest with national implications opened wide fissures in the reform party. Many Whig Constitutionalists vehemently opposed Dorr's candidacy for Congress as tending to weaken opposition to the hated policies of the Van Buren Administration in Washington.[85] When forced to choose between national political commitments and the local reform cause, many Rhode Islanders chose the former. After Dorr and Dan King, who ran for Rhode Island's other Congressional seat, won a ludicrously small total of votes in 1837, Dorr vowed to exert himself no longer in the cause of electoral reform until nonlandholders themselves took the initiative.[86] He did not have to wait long.

Charles Randall to Dorr, November 11, 1835, for discussions of party strategy. For the Whigs' willingness to work with the Constitutionalists, see Nehemiah R. Knight to James F. Simmons, February 22, 1836, Simmons Papers, LC.

[82] Charles Randall to Dorr, July 12, March 16, 1837, Dorr MSS. (emphasis in original).

[83] *Providence Journal,* April 20, 21, 1837.

[84] See Constitutionalist ticket, shown in Plate 3, Dan King to Dorr, July 24, 1837, Dorr MSS.

[85] Charles N. Tilley to Dorr, July 15, 1837; Charles Randall to Dorr, August 10, 1837, Dorr MSS.

[86] Dorr won only a few score votes out of the more than seven thousand cast. See Mowry, *Dorr War,* pp. 42–43. Dorr complained that disfranchised Rhode Islanders "seemed quite willing to have [Tyranny's] foot set upon their necks. Such being the case, they deserve their fate. We owe it to self-respect to make no more vain calls to ears dead to all questions relating to political liberty and equal rights." Dorr's remarks on reverse of Philip B. Stinness to Dorr, November 18, 1837, Dorr MSS.

2

Fresh Efforts
1838 to 1841

I

After the collapse of the Constitutional Party in 1837, Rhode Island's party system lapsed into its traditional pattern of intense partisanship, fierce struggle for patronage, wholesale corruption and erratic shifts of allegiance among the factions that formed around the state's leading politicians.[1] As in the past, neither Democrats nor Whigs took a clear stand on constitutional reform. The Democrats, whose "country party" was strong in the southern part of the state, were unwilling to risk the displeasure of farmers who enjoyed a near monopoly of political power under the Charter. And any tendency among the Whigs, who more clearly represented the industrial regions of north-

---

[1] Richard P. McCormick, *The Second American Party System: Party Formation in the Jacksonian Era* (Chapel Hill, N. C.: University of North Carolina Press, 1966), pp. 76–86. On the personal nature of political groupings in Rhode Island, see Thomas Dorr's denunciation of "man worship," in the Address of the Constitutional Party, 1834, in *Burke's Report*, p. 153: "There has been too much strife in this state about *men;* too much *man worship.* Party after party has come into power . . . , [b]ut we have the mortification of perceiving that very little has been done for the improvement of our political condition from the fear of endangering this or that man's office—from the fear of offending, or from a desire to conciliate, this or that prominent politician. . . ."

eastern Rhode Island,[2] to advocate reapportionment and extended suffrage was inhibited by the fact that in order to win an election they had to draw enough farmers' votes to offset the usual Democratic majorities. As the 1830s drew to a close, Rhode Island politics had the same unchanging character it had exhibited for decades.

The Presidential canvass of 1840 acted as a catalyst, generating sufficient excitement to revive the issues of suffrage extension and constitutional reform. Early in the year an anonymous campaign pamphlet appeared, urging the voteless majority in Rhode Island to band together and choose delegates to a constitutional convention. Under a newly drafted constitution, a government would be elected, and its Congressional delegation would place its claims alongside those of the Charter Government. Thus Rhode Island's political dilemma would be solved peacefully by the Federal Government in Washington.[3] Suggestions for unau-

---

[2] The sectional basis of Rhode Island's parties may be seen in the hard-fought gubernatorial canvass of 1840, in which the Whig electoral strength in the expanding northern industrial towns of Providence and Kent counties offset Democratic majorities in the predominately agricultural districts. See voting returns in *Providence Herald,* November 4, 1840, and in Appendix B. The 1840 balloting was the largest voter turnout in the state's history, with 4,798 ballots in favor of the Whig candidate, Samuel Ward King, and 3,417 for his Democratic opponent, Thomas F. Carpenter. King, a former physician, and later a bank official in the Providence County town of Johnston, had been elected state Senator in 1839. Because of feuds among the Whigs, no governor was elected that year, and King became acting governor until he was elected in his own right in 1840. See *Representative Men and Old Families of Rhode Island,* 3 vols. (Chicago: Beers, 1908), I, 345; Edward Field, *State of Rhode Island and Providence Plantations at the End of the* [Nineteenth] *Century: A History,* 3 vols. (Boston and Syracuse: Mason Publishing Co., 1902), I, 331; Charles Carroll, *Rhode Island: Three Centuries of Democracy,* 4 vols. (New York: Lewis Historical Publishing Co., 1932), I, 571. Reelected in 1841 and 1842, King was officially Governor of Rhode Island during the critical phase of the Dorr Rebellion. For a frank and irreverent portrait of him at that time, see S[amuel] Blatchford to William H. Seward, June 30, 1842, Seward Papers, Rush Rhees Library, University of Rochester.

[3] *Address to the Citizens of Rhode Island, Who are Denied the Right of Suffrage* [Periodical No. 3, "Social Reform Society of New York"] (n.p., 1840), copy in RIHSL. I have not been able to identify the organization whose name appears on this pamphlet. It does not seem to have been the

thorized constitutional initiatives by the people had been made earlier, although without any plans for appeal to the central authorities.[4]

As before, reformist ideas elicited no party support. Whigs were sure that the Van Burenites of New York were behind these proposals and angrily denounced them at their state convention in 1840.[5] But local Democrats were no more hospitable to suggestions of action outside the established political framework. The state's leading Democratic newspaper, the *Republican Herald,* vehemently denied the party's responsibility for the pamphlet. The *Herald* defended Rhode Island's traditional landholding requirement and charged that the obnoxious suggestions had originated in New York, denouncing them as "indecent and unwarrantable" interference in Rhode Island's internal affairs.[6]

Soon leading Democrats became more sympathetic to reform measures. As the Whigs swept the state elections in 1840 and were about to win Rhode Island for "Tippecanoe and Tyler too," Democrats wondered if their party had been mistaken in opposing suffrage extension. Thomas Dorr, who had severed his ties to the Whigs by 1838 [7] and had become state chairman of

---

New York Society of Land Reformers, which took an active interest in Rhode Island affairs, in 1844 (see Chapter 6). It is most likely that the pamphlet originated in Rhode Island. George Marshel Dennison's account ("The Constitutional Issues of the Dorr War: A Study in the Evolution of American Constitutionalism, 1776–1849" [Ph.D. Thesis, University of Washington, 1967], pp. 169–70, 72) is confused. He seems at first to accept the notion that New York agitators stimulated the reform revival in Rhode Island and then, a few pages later, to doubt his own conclusion. Even the often uncritical Mowry is skeptical of the putative New York origins of this pamphlet. See Arthur May Mowry, *The Dorr War: Or, The Constitutional Struggle in Rhode Island* (Providence: Preston and Rounds, 1901), p. 48.

[4] See pp. 10–11, 18–22.

[5] Field, *State of Rhode Island and Providence Plantations,* I, 332.

[6] Providence *Republican Herald,* February 1, 1840, quoted in Mowry, *Dorr War,* p. 49.

[7] Dorr's reasons for switching to the Democrats probably stemmed from the factional quarrels within the Whig Party that seemed to have intensified his distaste for "man worship" (see note 1, p. 30). The particular dispute with which Dorr was most closely connected was the intraparty struggle for succession to the Senate seat held since 1823 by

the Democratic Party, was only slightly ahead of his fellow Rhode Island Democrats. He declared in September that the state's archaic suffrage requirements constituted a major obstacle to the party's electoral success:

> 16,000 of the 24,000 white males over 21 years in this State are deprived of the right of suffrage by the operation of our landed system, which has been sustained to this time equally by the democratic and whig farmers. Our friends in the country are now reaping the fruit of disfranchising their natural allies, the mechanics and workingmen. . . .[8]

His implication was that disfranchised plebeians in Rhode Island would have resisted the "log cabin and hard cider" blandishments of the Whigs in 1840 to find common interest with farmers in the Democratic Party. Even if wrong,[9] Dorr expressed

---

Nehemiah R. Knight, who had promised to retire in favor of some other deserving Whig. Dorr favored the heir apparent, Tristam Burges, who had served as Whig member of the U.S. House of Representatives from 1825–1835. When Knight and a group of other Whigs decided to dump Burges, Dorr struck back with an anonymous pamphlet, *Political Frauds Exposed: or a Narrative of the Proceedings of the "Junto in Providence" Concerning the Senatorial Question From 1833–1838, by Aristedes* ([Providence, 1838]), and a broadside, *Explanation of an Old Affair by Aristedes* (n.p., [1838]), in Broadside Collection, RIHSL (misfiled, 1835). But Dorr's gallant efforts had little effect; Burges never held public office again. For an account of this episode from the point of view of the winning faction, see N[ehemiah] R. Knight to J[ames] F. Simmons, December 23, 1838, Simmons Papers, LC. As late as 1845 Dorr was still fulminating against the Whig politicians who denied Burges advancement. See Dorr to [Catherine] W[illiams], April 10, [1845], Dorr MSS. There is no adequate study of Rhode Island politics in the 1830s. Philip A. Grant, Jr., "Party Chaos Embroils Rhode Island," *Rhode Island History,* XXVI (October 1967), 113–125; XXVII (January 1968), 24–33, is almost exclusively concerned with local reactions to national political questions.

[8] Dorr to Amos Kendall, September 24, 1840 (copy), in Dorr MSS. Kendall was national Democratic Party leader, one of the earliest of a new breed of American politicians, as Lynn T. Marshall shows in "The Strange Stillbirth of the Whig Party," *American Historical Review,* LXXII (January 1967), 445–468.

[9] It is probable that he was wrong, for recent scholarship has tended to show that new voters in this period were not especially likely to gravitate to either major party, but rather tended to divide roughly equally between

the willingness of Democratic politicians in Rhode Island to identify their party's fortunes with local constitutional reform, a tendency that would soon become more marked.

II

Providence mechanics and workingmen, still excluded from the electorate and unable to hold office, founded a new, militant free suffrage organization in the spring of 1840. They gave it a dignified name: the Rhode Island Suffrage Association. The immediate impetus seems to have been an act of the General Assembly in January fixing criminal penalties for avoiding militia duties, which politically disadvantaged groups saw aimed at them.[10] But the general increase in political excitement that election year also underscored the plight of voteless Rhode Islanders. Only two survivors of the workingmen's agitation of 1833 participated in the Association's activities—carpenter Seth Luther and stonecutter Franklin Cooley.

In a forceful public statement the Association blasted the pretentions of the landholding minority, who denied even the name

---

Whigs and Democrats. See Richard P. McCormick, "Suffrage Classes and Party Alignments," *Mississippi Valley Historical Review,* XLVI (December 1969), 397–401; Edward Pessen, *Jacksonian America: Society, Personality and Politics* (Homewood, Ill.: Dorsey Press, 1969), Chap. 7.

[10] Act in Amendment to an Act to Regulate the Militia (January Session, 1840), Acts and Resolves of the General Assembly, Vol. 42, p. 127, Rhode Island State Archives, Providence. On the origins of the Rhode Island Suffrage Association, see [Frances H. (Whipple) McDougall], *Might and Right by a Rhode Islander,* 2nd ed. (Providence: A. H. Stillwell, 1844), pp. 70–72; Jacob Frieze, *Concise History of the Efforts to Obtain an Extension of Suffrage in Rhode Island From the Year 1811 to 1842* (Providence: B. Moore, 1842), pp. 28–29; [Anon.], *Facts Involved in the Rhode Island Controversy, With Some Views Upon the Rights of Both Parties* (Boston: B. B. Mussey, 1842), p. 15. Dorr's Address to the People of Rhode Island, 1843, *Burke's Report,* p. 733; [George Ticknor Curtis], *Merits of Thomas W. Dorr and George Bancroft As They Are Politically Connected by a Citizen of Massachusetts* (Boston: John H. Eastburn, [1844]), p. 5. The secondary sources that date the origin of this organization from the fall of 1840 (Mowry, *Dorr War,* p. 50; John Bell Rae, "The Issues of the Dorr War," *Rhode Island History,* I [April 1942], 37–38) are in error.

"freeman" to citizens who lacked "a few square feet of land." The anonymous authors of the Association's constitution invoked in a fiery preamble the doctrine of equal natural rights, refuting the belief that only those who demonstrated a stake in society by owning land ought to participate in politics. The social compact was made for all members of society, they argued, and consequently "the acquisition of property, however necessary and laudable, neither increases nor multiplies the natural rights of its possessors, nor diminishes the natural rights of those who possess it not." [11] "The whole people of Rhode Island" demanded extended suffrage and were determined to attain their goal through action of "the people in their primary capacity." [12]

The Rhode Island Suffrage Association had in mind a long campaign for political rights. Economic and social grievances certainly underlay this new movement,[13] but disfranchised mechanics had good reason to believe that winning political rights was a necessary preliminary to solving all other problems.[14]

---

[11] *Preamble and Constitution of the Rhode Island Suffrage Association . . . March 27, 1840* (Providence: B. T. Albro, 1840), p. 3. For some reason Dennison ("Constitutional Issues of the Dorr War," p. 233) credits Jacob Frieze with the authorship of this document. Frieze, author of the anti-Dorr *Concise History of Efforts to Obtain an Extension of Suffrage,* never made the claim himself. Dennison offers no firm evidence for his attribution of authorship.

[12] *Preamble and Constitution,* pp. 6, 9. Just how far the proposed expansion of suffrage could go was left vague in the early spring of 1840. During the year and a half that followed, a more precise position including the issue of suffrage for blacks was hammered out within the councils of the Rhode Island Suffrage Association. See pp. 46–47. The doctrine that people can act politically in a "primary capacity" was one of the main ideological issues in the Dorr Rebellion; for earlier Rhode Island precedents, see pp. 10–11, 20–21.

[13] Seth Luther, the Providence housewright, who was active in the Rhode Island Suffrage Association, had indicated what these social and economic demands were. See the discussion of Luther's ideas on pp. 19–21.

[14] Some writers have attempted to establish a direct link between economic grievances and the rise of a radical political movement in Rhode Island. See Beryl Lee Crowe, "The Dorr Rebellion: A Study of Revolutionary Behavior" (M.A. Thesis, University of California [Berkeley], 1961), Chap. 4, esp. pp. 45–51, and James C. Davies, "Toward a Theory of Revolution," *American Sociological Review,* XXVII (February 1962), 8-10. Crowe erects an elaborate theoretical superstructure on a ludi-

Moreover, Rhode Island's archaic political system was becoming increasingly objectionable to many of the state's citizens, and the founders of the Association could be reasonably certain of eventual widespread support. Exclusive focus on common political grievances would best attract such support. Also, the Presidential contest of 1840, which brought out enormous numbers of new voters almost everywhere but Rhode Island,[15] underscored the need for political reforms. The tasks of broadening political participation were formidable enough without raising the potentially divisive issue of what ideologies and programs the enlarged electorate would endorse.

In accordance with these prudent considerations, the Association moved cautiously at first. Local branches were set up in towns throughout the state, most notably in the northern districts of Providence County.[16] In December 1840 the Association acquired a weekly newspaper, *The New Age and Constitu-*

---

crously inadequate empirical foundation, whereas Davies relies on Crowe's work for his even more speculative theory of a "J-Curve of Rising and Declining Satisfactions." The Crowe-Davies theory hinges on Rhode Island's textile workers having played a key role in the Dorr Rebellion, for which they present not a shred of evidence. In his later work (e.g., "The J-Curve . . . ," in Hugh Davis Graham and Ted Robert Gurr, eds., *Violence in America: Historical and Comparative Perspectives* [New York: Signet Books, 1969], Chap. 19) Davies drops the Dorr Rebellion. See below, pp. 120, 133, for an occupational breakdown of those Rhode Island working-class rebels for whom data is available.

[15] Richard P. McCormick, "New Perspectives on Jacksonian Politics," *American Historical Review,* LXV (January 1960), 288–301. In fact, the elections of 1840 brought more Rhode Island landholders to the polls than had ever voted before—8,579 in all.

[16] [McDougall], *Might and Right,* pp. 70–75; Frieze, *Concise History,* pp. 30–31; Mowry, *Dorr War,* p. 50. Cf. Peter J. Coleman, *The Transformation of Rhode Island, 1790–1860* (Providence: Brown University Press, 1960), p. 273, where the Association is charged with "extremism" at this early stage, an attitude that is compared unfavorably with Dorr's moderation. Aside from the gratuitous value judgments, Coleman is wrong on two grounds: the Association's tactics in 1840 and well into 1841 were quite moderate, and Dorr was not associated with the organization until late 1841. See also Robert L. Ciaburri, "The Dorr Rebellion in Rhode Island: The Moderate Phase," *Rhode Island History,* XXVI (July 1967), 79–80, which captures the early moderation of the movement but, like Coleman's account, erroneously assumes that Dorr participated in the founding of the Association.

tional Advocate, which carried appeals for constitutional reform, suffrage extension and popular rights.[17] The same month the Association made its final appeal to the General Assembly, respectfully requesting

> the abrogation of the Charter granted to this state by King Charles the Second of England, and . . . the establishment of a constitution which should more efficiently define the authority of the Executive and Legislative branches, and more strongly recognize the rights of the citizens.

Casually dismissing the question of black suffrage, which soon would agitate Association meetings, the reformers argued that an extension of the suffrage to a greater portion of "the white male residents of the State, would be more in accordance with the spirit of our institutions, than the present system. . . ." [18]

The legislature's response gave the reformers scant satisfaction. The General Assembly tabled the Association's petition when it was introduced in February 1841. But at the same time, the legislature responded to a similar memorial from the northern town of Smithfield, which requested relief from the "extreme inequality of the present representation [i.e., apportionment]," by authorizing a constitutional convention the following November. Reformers felt they could place little confidence in the General Assembly's action, in which no explicit mention was made of suffrage extension. Moreover, the official call for a convention made no provision for reapportionment in assigning seats of delegates or for relaxation of landholding qualifications in the

---

[17] This paper had been founded in November by "Dr." John A. Brown, a "botanical physician" and manufacturer of root beer in Providence. He hired a young graduate of Brown University, Charles Congdon, to edit the newspaper. In December the Association agreed to support the *New Age* by collecting subscriptions and appointing members to act as agents. In return, the *New Age* tailored its editorial policy to the wishes of the Association. See [McDougall], *Might and Right,* p. 77; Charles T. Congdon, *Reminiscences of a Journalist* (Boston: James R. Osgood, 1880), pp. 106–107; Mowry, *Dorr War,* pp. 54–55. Dennison ("Constitutional Issues of the Dorr War," *passim*) assumes that Congdon continued to edit the organ through 1841 and 1842, which was not the case.

[18] *New Age,* December 18, 1840; *Burke's Report,* pp. 402–403. For a discussion of the Association's handling of the black suffrage issue, see below, pp. 46–47.

choice of these delegates. Thus the forthcoming convention would represent mainly those who had a stake in the existing political inequities, and the Association believed no good would come of it.[19]

Its own petition ignored, the Association continued its political agitation in ways that were relatively new to Rhode Island. Until 1840, when the Whigs introduced the practices of modern party campaigns in the state, public political spectacles were rare because of the limited suffrage and the state's consequent political immaturity.[20] The Association's campaign for reform

---

[19] Mowry, *Dorr War,* pp. 58–59. The official convention, which met in November 1841, was known as the Landholders' Convention. Reformers feared that it would be a repetition of the distressing constitutional convention of 1834–1835, for which, see pp. 27–28.

[20] Until after the Dorr Rebellion, Rhode Island's parties were more like the "connexions" of traditional English politics than like parties in the modern sense. See Lewis B. Namier, *The Structure of Politics at the Accession of George III,* 2nd ed. (London: St. Martin's Press, 1965) on this older pattern. Recent scholarship has begun to reveal the dynamic forces that led to the development of the modern party in America with a stable mass base and an efficient organizational structure. One study in particular that has indirectly influenced my thinking about Rhode Island's party system is Lynn T. Marshall, "The Strange Stillbirth of the Whig Party," *American Historical Review,* LXXII (January 1967), 445–468. Marshall shows how the archaic pattern of "leadership oriented" political groupings, in which groups of friends coalesce around leading men, persisted on the national level into the period of the second party system in the 1830s. Marshall's dynamic typology also enables us to understand party development on the local level, such as in Rhode Island, where the limited suffrage "froze" the political system at an archaic level and hindered the operation of national political forces that elsewhere led to the emergence, or reemergence after 1828, of modern parties. (Cf. Richard P. McCormick, "Political Development and the Second Party System," in William Nisbet Chambers and Walter Dean Burnham, eds., *The American Party Systems: Stages of Party Development* [New York: Oxford University Press, 1966], pp. 90–116; McCormick, *The Second American Party System,* esp. pp. 346–356; Michael Wallace, "Changing Concepts of Party in the United States: New York, 1815–1828," *American Historical Review,* LXXIV [December 1968], 453–491: Richard Hofstadter, *The Idea of a Party System: The Rise of Legitimate Opposition in the United States, 1780–1840* [Berkeley: University of California Press, 1969].) The Dorr Rebellion, from this point of view, shook Rhode Island's party system out of its archaic form and facilitated the creation of modern parties in the state. See Chapter 6.

through the spring and summer of 1841 was appropriate to the aims of a group that wished to open and widen the political process. Parades, spectacles, processions and collations were organized to stimulate nonlandholders to assert their political rights and to persuade freemen that other classes in the population had as good a right as they to vote.

The Association's parade and celebration in Providence on April 17, 1841, was the first such event, and it was a resounding success. As many as three thousand Rhode Islanders may have participated in the procession, which was headed by Providence butchers in white aprons. Paraders carried banners with slogans such as "Worth makes the man, but sand and gravel make the voter"; Virtue, Patriotism and Intelligence versus $134 worth of dirt"; and the more ominous "Peaceably if we can, forcibly if we must." The barbecue culminating the celebration included a roast ox, a loaf of bread ten feet long, and several barrels of beer.[21] Conservatives muttered about these disreputable political agitations,[22] but some respectable Rhode Island politicians were beginning to give active support to the Association. Two local Democrats, Duttee J. Pearce of Newport and Samuel Y. Atwell of Glocester, addressed the Providence gathering on the need to extend the franchise and to replace Rhode Island's archaic charter with a modern constitution.[23]

Thomas Dorr was not yet active in this new reform movement. The corresponding secretary of the Association asked him to

---

[21] Field, *State of Rhode Island and Providence Plantations,* I, 337–338; Mowry, *Dorr War,* p. 63; Anne Mary Newton, "Rebellion in Rhode Island: The Story of the Dorr War" (M.A. Thesis, Columbia University, 1947), pp. 49–50. Dorr seems to have taken no part in this event.

[22] See [John Pitman], *To the Members of the General Assembly of Rhode-Island* (Providence: Knowles & Vose, [January] 1842), p. 22, where one of the most vehement opponents of the reform cause fulminated against roasting of oxen, processions for political ends and, worst of all, inflammatory "speeches from the orators of the human race." The author of this anonymous pamphlet was federal district judge for Rhode Island, who later presided over the leading case to come out of the Dorr Rebellion, *Luther v. Borden,* 7 Howard 1 (1849). See below, pp. 57–58, and Chapter 7.

[23] Field, *State of Rhode Island and Providence Plantations,* I 337–338.

address a rally scheduled for Newport in May 1841,[24] but he was not ready to become involved in another crusade for popular rights. The memory of his unsuccessful efforts in 1840 were still fresh, and he could not forget that nonlandholders had failed to support the Constitutional Party in the 1830s,[25] so he coolly acknowledged the invitation. "Should I be in Newport that day," he wrote, "it would give me great pleasure to take part in the mass meeting." But his continued enthusiasm for the cause of political reform could not be disguised. He confessed "no ordinary gratification" in witnessing the determination of Rhode Island's nonlandholders "to vindicate to themselves a just and equal participation in political power, and to become the *citizens* rather than the *subjects* of a state, now only nominally republican." [26] Despite his reluctance to engage in the Association's organizational work in 1840 and early 1841, his sympathetic attitude presaged eventual involvement.

Although the Newport "mass convention" in May was not so well attended; [27] it represented a fateful step in the Association's campaign for political change in Rhode Island. The opening procession was impressive, and some of the participants marched with guns and swords.[28] Resolutions adopted by the assemblage denounced the Charter of 1663 as an "insufficient and obsolete"

---

[24] Jesse Calder to Dorr, May 3, 1841, Dorr MSS. For the widespread, erroneous belief that Dorr had been involved with the Association from the outset, see note 16, p. 36, and Chilton Williamson, *American Suffrage: From Property to Democracy, 1760–1860* (Princeton, N.J.: Princeton University Press, 1960), p. 251, which is also mistaken on this point.

[25] See p. 29.

[26] Dorr to Jesse Calder (draft), May 4, 1841, Dorr MSS.

[27] Although the Providence meeting of the previous month had attracted about three thousand people, the Newport gathering had only about half that number (Mowry, *Dorr War,* p. 65). Mowry accounts for the falling off in part by observing that "Newport headed the opposition to any change in the form of government." But a majority of the landholding voters of Newport later supported the People's Constitution in March 1842, which contradicts Mowry's assertion. A more plausible explanation may be found in the simple fact that Newport's population was just a third of Providence's. See the population table in Coleman, *Transformation of Rhode Island,* p. 220; Appendix B.

[28] Mowry, *Dorr War,* p. 65.

document that "should be laid aside in the archives of the State, and no longer be permitted to subsist as a barrier against the rights and liberties of the people." The Association called for replacement of the Charter by a new constitution that would extend the franchise to "the mechanics, the merchants, the workingmen, and others—who own no land" as well as bring about "a new assignment of representatives among the towns, according to population." Dismissing the General Assembly's own call for a constitutional convention as a sham, the Newport gathering nevertheless "respectfully" called upon the very authorities who had so often scorned change to take fresh action on reform demands. As if perceiving the futility of their appeal to the government they sought to supplant, they also empowered a commitee to initiate plans for a People's Convention that would work outside regular authorized channels to draft a constitution.[29]

The ambiguous and contradictory purposes of the Association were implicit in the Newport meeting. Its cautious—even humble—attitude toward the state authorities contrasted with the firm belief that Rhode Island's political institutions, with the exception of "the immortal declaration and guarantee of religious freedom," [30] were fundamentally unjust. The reform group was beginning to consider itself the embodiment of popular will in the state, or at least the agency by which that will, long pent up by established authority, would find expression. In May the Association initiated a radical invocation of popular power against the existing government. Such action could be called revolutionary, and the appearance in Newport of armed suffragists flaunting militant slogans looked threatening. Yet these men, naïvely believing that the American Revolution legitimized their plans for unauthorized measures, seemed unable to conceive that anyone could seriously view their activities as illegal. It was to be their fatal flaw.

The Charter Government was both unwilling and unable to take any action that would satisfy the Association. At its regular spring legislative session the General Assembly tried rather in-

---

[29] Resolutions of the Newport "mass convention," May 5, 1841, in *Burke's Report,* pp. 256–259, 404–407; Mowry, *Dorr War,* pp. 64–66.

[30] Resolutions of the Newport "mass convention," May 5, 1841, in *Burke's Report,* pp. 256, 404.

effectually to conciliate the rising tide of radicalism. It decided to reapportion representation for the Charter Government's official constitutional convention coming in November. But the apportionment was not as extensive as reformers wished.[31] The *New Age* scorned this proposal as "a feint to draw the attention of the friends of equal rights from the [greater] object that they have in view." [32] At the June legislative Assembly the state authorities were given ample opportunity to take the sort of action the Association favored. Samuel Y. Atwell, representative from the northern town of Glocester, proposed to admit all taxpayers to vote along with the freemen in the choice of convention delegates. After a long debate, Atwell's measure was overwhelmingly defeated.[33] The Association took this action as a final demonstration that the authorities would reject any reasonable proposal for democratic political change.

The spring of 1841 was a turning point for the reformers; they began seriously planning radical action. Behind this transformation was a vivid conviction of having exhausted all regular political channels. "[I]t is quite apparent," stated the Association's July Address, that the people of Rhode Island "can find no redress through the ballot box, from which, by law, they are excluded."

> Nor is it much more likely that they will derive it from legislative aid; the members of the legislature being exclusively the representatives of the minority, who wield the power. . . . The laws of the State are against them; the legislative authority is against them; the custom of more than a half a century is against them; and, no doubt, the opinions, interests, political aspirations, and the prejudices and prepossessions of a majority of the landed interest are against them.

In face of these formidable antagonists "the friends of reform," the Address concluded, would have to "depend on their own active energies." They would have to resume the "exercise of their original and natural rights and powers" to draft a constitution independent of the usurping officials who then governed

---

[31] See Appendix C.

[32] *New Age,* May 14, 1841.

[33] Mowry, *Dorr War,* pp. 68–69.

the state. This was not thought to be a very difficult task; the obstacles to political change would turn out to be "shadowy and unsubstantial, and a single act of the majority of the whole people of Rhode Island will be found sufficient to sweep them all away."

> The people—the "numerical force"—have but to proclaim their will, to resume their original powers, and assert their original rights. It is but for the people to arouse themselves to action, to array themselves in the majesty of their strength, and to speak with united voice. "WE THE PEOPLE," *decree it,* is a legitimate sanction to the warrant that consigns an unequal government to the grave.[34]

This heady belief in the majesty of popular power signaled a subtle but important shift in the Association's aims, as the conviction of the people's right to act independently of constituted authority began to overshadow the advocacy of specific reforms.

III

The next logical step in the Association's program of constitutional change outside official channels was a convention to draft a new framework of government for Rhode Island. The call for such a convention was issued by the Association's State Central Committee in late July. Delegates would be chosen by universal male suffrage and under an apportionment that gave due weight to the population centers in the northern part of the state.[35] Dorr, invited to stand for election to the People's Constitutional Convention,[36] responded eagerly and positively.[37]

---

[34] Address of the State Suffrage Committee, July 1841, in *Burke's Report,* pp. 261–268. This Address was prepared by a committee of eleven men, including Charles Collins and Duttee J. Pearce of Newport and Samuel Wales and Benjamin Arnold of Providence.

[35] Address of the State Suffrage Committee, July 24, 1841, *ibid.,* pp. 269–271. Male adult citizens (naturalized or native) residing one year in the state could vote. The Association did not specifically exclude blacks. This Address was different from the Address cited in note 34. Elected chairmen and secretaries at each of the balloting places (presumably local Association members) were directed to certify these elections. For the apportionment see Appendix C.

[36] See Parley M. Mathewson and D. Brainard Blake to Dorr, August 11, 1841, Dorr MSS. Dorr's correspondents, a grocer and a watchmaker

The balloting in late August was disappointingly light. Although virtually anyone could vote, only 7,512 bothered to endorse the uncontested slate of convention delegates put forward by the Association. Probably fewer than half the voters were landholding freemen. Three towns in the southern agricultural region of the state failed to elect any delegates at all.[38] Clearly the Association had not yet proven that it spoke and acted in the name of any popular majority in Rhode Island.

Only three days after these unofficial elections, the landholders gathered at the regular town meetings to choose delegates to the November constitutional convention authorized by the legislature.[39] In Providence there was some overlap in the delegations to the two conventions; Dorr and four other Suffragists were elected to both.[40] Samuel Atwell, another reformer, represented the freemen of Glocester in the Landholders' Convention.[41] These reformers were a minority in a convention chosen by freeholders reluctant to share power and suspicious of reform measures.

By contrast, the delegates to the People's Convention in October were enthusiastic reformers who drafted a constitution with

---

respectively (see *Providence Directory, 1838* [Providence, 1838], pp. 22, 80), were representative of the men who dominated the Association at this point.

[37] Dorr to Parley M. Mathewson (draft), August 12, 1841, Dorr MSS. There is no reason to conclude (as does Williamson, *American Suffrage,* p. 251) that Dorr's political beliefs were any less radical than those of the working-class organizers of the Association. In fact, his younger brother urged Dorr not to take "so leading a part" in the reform movement lest he "alarm the freeholders . . . with the extreme liberality" of his views. Henry C. Dorr to Thomas W. Dorr, October 25, 1841, Dorr MSS.

[38] Mowry, *Dorr War,* p. 95.

[39] It is possible that the suffrage vote was diminished by the close conjunction of the election dates, underscoring the unauthorized nature of the election. When the People's Constitution was ratified later that year (see pp. 51–54), there was no competition from any other proximate ratifying vote. This may help to explain the considerable popular vote for that Constitution.

[40] Mowry, *Dorr War,* p. 95.

[41] See the account of the Convention proceedings in *Providence Journal,* November 2–15, 1841. For the results of this Convention, see pp. 49–50.

zeal and dispatch.[42] Sweeping aside Rhode Island's traditional landholding requirements, they opened the suffrage to adult male citizens of a year's residence (the same electorate that three months earlier had chosen them).[43] They also equalized apportionment of legislative seats among the towns, greatly increasing the power of the expanding commercial and industrial towns in Providence, Kent and Bristol counties.[44] Except for the question of black suffrage, delegates disagreed only on minor points —tenure of judges, punishment of legislators who took fees for cases coming before the General Assembly, and other criminal penalties.[45] A few questions, including the issue of jury trials for "persons in this State, who are claimed to be held to labor or service under the laws of any other State," remained undecided.[46] The convention decided to hold a final session one

---

[42] The People's Constitution first appeared in draft form, *Articles of a Constitution Adopted by the People's Convention, Held October 4, 1841, and Postponed to November 16, for Final Consideration* (Providence: Office of the *New Age,* [October] 1841), and was widely circulated throughout the state. For textual differences between this *October Draft* and the final People's Constitution, which was revised in November, see Appendix A.

[43] See People's Constitution, Article II, in Appendix A.

[44] People's Constitution, Article V, Sections 2, 3, in Appendix A. For details on the apportionment changes, see Appendix C, especially the explanatory note.

[45] *Providence Journal,* October 8, 9, 1841. No proceedings of this convention were published, and the hostile *Journal's* is the fullest extant account, which mercilessly exposed the disagreements and disputes among suffragists. In columns adjoining the news reports on the People's Convention, the *Journal* published articles by "Town Born" (a pseudonym for William G. Goddard, Professor of Moral Philosophy at Brown University) ridiculing the reformers. For the resolution of the disputed issues, see People's Constitution, Article XI, Section 3, in which Dorr's desire for life tenure for judges (*Providence Journal,* October 7, 1841) gained inclusion in terms that somewhat obscured their implication, and Article IV, Section 5, which dealt with the issue of legal fees, in Appendix A.

[46] See Article I, Section 14, in Appendix A, for this expression of the antislavery sentiments that prompted many of the Personal Liberty laws in the antebellum period. The Association offended proslavery sentiment with this clause. See *Trouble in the Spartan Ranks, Old Durham in the Field* ([1843]), Broadside Collection, RIHSL, reproduced in Mowry, *Dorr War,* facing p. 207, where Dorr is pictured with the cloven hoof of

month hence to clear up all outstanding questions and put the People's Constitution in final form.

The Convention fashioned a constitution that was intended not only to attract as many votes as possible at the ratifying election in late December,[47] but also to serve soon after as the fundamental law of Rhode Island. Since the unauthorized mode of framing this constitution was radical enough in the eyes of many, the Association's leaders did not wish to jeopardize the possibility of success by advocating "advanced" or outlandish reforms. They proposed, therefore, "no Greek temple of ideal democracy, but rather a solid homely City Hall structure," [48] filled with the ordinary details of state politics—fishing and clamming rights, tax provisions, governmental agencies and procedures—as well as those of citizens' rights.

Haunting the People's Convention and earlier Association gatherings was the issue of extending the franchise to blacks. The question had arisen at September 1841 meetings of the Providence Suffrage Association, when a black barber of the city, Alfred Niger,[49] was proposed as treasurer of the local group. Nominating him was an outspoken opponent of black suffrage who had acted, he explained, to discover "how many 'wolves in sheep's clothing' [i.e., abolitionists] there were among them." Niger's nomination was defeated, and hotly contested resolutions were introduced urging the convention to restrict the vote to whites in the new constitution.[50] When the People's Convention met in October, the issue so agitated delegates that they adjourned convention sessions early in the afternoon in order to have time to caucus. Both in caucus and on the floor of the con-

---

abolitionism because of this clause. Ironically, advocates of free suffrage actually lost the favor of abolitionists and blacks by their failure to endorse black suffrage in the People's Constitution.

[47] For the ratification arrangements, see Article XIV in Appendix A.

[48] Newton, "Rebellion in Rhode Island," pp. 54–55.

[49] A follower of William Lloyd Garrison, Niger was an active abolitionist. See *Providence Directory, 1841* (Providence, 1841), p. 185; J. Stanley Lemons and Michael A. McKenna, "Re-enfranchisement of Rhode Island Negroes," *Rhode Island History,* XXX (February 1971), 6.

[50] *Ibid.,* pp. 7–8; *Providence Journal,* September 27, 1841; Irving H. Bartlett, "The Inconsistency of Thomas Dorr," *New England Social Studies Bulletin,* XI (May 1954), 3–4.

vention the leading proponents of black suffrage were Benjamin Arnold, a Providence grocer, and Dorr. On behalf of the black community, Dorr and Arnold introduced an eloquent resolution which argued that the Association's claim to defend popular rights would be undermined if blacks were excluded from the electorate created by the new constitution.[51] But there was much opposition. One delegate from Smithfield opposed granting the vote to blacks because, he explained to the presiding officer of the convention, if they could vote they could also be "elected to office; and a nigger might occupy the chair where your honor sits. A pretty look that would be." [52] Other influential men, such as Atwell and Duttee J. Pearce, opposed black suffrage on the grounds that a constitution with such a provision would never be ratified in Rhode Island.[53] When the issue came to a final count (on a motion to strike the word "white" from the specifications of the electorate) only eighteen delegates upheld the rights of blacks; forty-six voted no.[54] Their hopes for political rights destroyed by the People's Convention, Rhode Island blacks had little choice but to oppose the new constitution and subsequent measures of the Association.

Despite its conservatism on the race question, the People's Convention, assembled "without the least pretense of authority," was to many Rhode Islanders an "illegal and revolutionary"

---

[51] *Providence Journal,* October 7, 1841. This petition, forcefully arguing that the Association's commitment to the Declaration of Independence and to political equality would be compromised unless blacks were permitted to vote, is reprinted in *Burke's Report,* pp. 111–113. The group that prepared the petition included James Hazard (clothier), Ransom Parker (teacher), Ichabod Northrup and Samuel Rodman (laborers), and George J. Smith (coachman) as representatives of the black community in Rhode Island. Black minister Alexander Crummell conveyed the petition to the convention. See Lemons and McKenna, "Re-enfranchisement of Negroes," pp. 6, 8; *Burke's Report,* p. 113; W. E. B. DuBois, "Of Alexander Crummell," in *The Souls of Black Folk* (Greenwich, Conn.: Fawcett Publications, 1961), Chap. 12. For an occupational profile of the black community in Providence, see Table II, p. 48.

[52] Smithfield delegate Nathaniel Mowry, quoted in *Providence Journal,* October 9, 1841.

[53] *Ibid.,* October 8, 9, 1841.

[54] *Ibid.,* October 11, 1841; Barlett, "Inconsistency of Dorr," pp. 4–5. No roll call was recorded on this vote.

TABLE II OCCUPATIONAL PROFILE OF PROVIDENCE NEGRO POPULATION, 1841 *

Laborers	85	Whitewasher-	
Pilot-mariners	27	painters	2
Barbers	14	Gardeners	2
Carters and		Engineers	1
draymen	10	Liverymen	1
Small business	9	Carpenters	1
Waiters	8	Teachers	1
Clergy	3	Bakers	1
Cooks	3	Coachmen	1
Shoemakers	3		

Total for whom occupational data is available: 172

* Sources: Julian Rammelkamp, "The Providence Negro Community, 1820–1842," *Rhode Island History,* VII (January 1948), 20–33; J. Stanley Lemons and Michael A. McKenna, "Re-enfranchisement of Rhode Island Negroes," *ibid.,* XXX (February 1971), 3–13; but especially *Providence Directory, 1841* (Providence, 1841), pp. 181–187, listing the town's "coloured" population.

gathering.[55] The *Providence Journal* ran scathing attacks on the Convention and denounced its leaders, "whose true object" was said to be not "civil freedom or regulated liberty in any form, but *agitation* and *revolution.*" [56] But the conservatives were unable to take action against the radicals, since the latter had committed no crime and had made no actual threat to the established government. Sorely misunderstanding their opponents, some conservatives believed that "a few leading men" could "blow the whole affair to the winds" merely by declaring suffrage measures to be absurd.[57] The radicals were contesting the very domination

[55] Elisha R. Potter, Jr., to Duttee J. Pearce (copy), December 20, 1841, Potter Collection, RIHSL.

[56] *Providence Journal,* August 21, 1841.

[57] Elisha R. Potter, Jr., to John Brown Francis, October 21, 1841, Francis Collection, RIHSL. Democratic Party leader in southern Rhode Island, Potter lamented his own inability to speak out against the Suffrage radicals. As he explained to former Governor John Brown Francis, local political embarrassments in Washington County prevented him from raising his voice. Both Potter and Francis would in 1842 become leading

of "leading men," and their efforts would not easily be swept aside. The established authorities would have to develop a more successful political program of their own to oppose the radicals' bold assertion of popular power.

IV

The Landholders' Constitutional Convention was the place to develop such a program, but the conservatives who dominated the convention refused to be rushed into embracing reform. As the main proponent of suffrage extension at the Landholders' Convention, Dorr tried to get the delegates to adopt the People's Constitution or at least its major reform provisions.[58] But conservative leaders such as Richard K. Randolph of Newport opposed him. Skillfully exploiting the Association's divisions over the question of black suffrage, Randolph explained that the landholders would reject an enlarged suffrage for the same reason that the People's Constitution rejected extension of the vote to blacks—such a constitution would never be ratified by the freeholders of Rhode Island.[59] In vain did Dorr and a handful of reformers in the Landholders' Convention urge that if an enlarged electorate, and not just landholders, were permitted to vote on ratification, the passage of a revised constitution would be assured. The delegates were in no mood to relax their defense of the landholders' voting privilege. Dorr's motion to expand the

---

members of the antiradical Law and Order coalition. See Chapters 3 and 4.

[58] The only accounts of the Landholders' Convention I have been able to find are in the *Providence Journal,* November 2–13, 1841, and in the Dorr MSS., Vol. 32. Neither contains roll call votes.

[59] *Providence Journal,* November 13, 1841. When, as a last minute maneuver on the closing day of the convention, a delegate moved to strike out "white" from the draft constitution (a move that would have allowed blacks to vote), his suggestion was voted down 16–51. *Ibid.,* November 15, 1841. The Rhode Island Antislavery Society's executive committee found the Landholders' Constitution and the People's Constitution "equally objectionable" in their disfranchisement of blacks. The society's resolutions urged abolitionists to oppose both constitutions. See *New Age,* March 18, 1842.

suffrage lost by a vote of 61 to 8.[60] Atwell also appealed to the convention to allow some extension of suffrage, lest the people of Rhode Island be forced to choose between "blind submission or open rebellion." [61] The appeal went unheeded, and the Landholders' Convention adjourned until February 1842 without producing anything like a full draft constitution.[62] This lack of action, combined with the conservatives' hostile attitude toward the radicals accelerated the tendency within the Association to favor "open rebellion."

---

[60] *Providence Journal,* November 13, 1842.

[61] *Ibid.*

[62] The *Draft of Constitution of the State of Rhode-Island and Providence Plantations . . . , November, 1841* (Providence: Knowles & Vose, 1841), copy in John Hay Library, Brown University, appeared with key sections, including those on suffrage and apportionment, missing. It was not certain that the full and complete Landholders' Convention would actually reconvene in February. Mowry's account is grossly inaccurate and biased on the side of the conservatives, especially where he implied (*Dorr War,* pp. 99–100) that the Landholders' Constitution was produced by the November convention.

3

The Specter of Conflict
1841 to 1842

I

Although the Rhode Island Suffrage Association had seized the initiative by drafting a constitution proclaiming itself champion of the people, it had not yet called forth great popular support. Reformers realized that their efforts to democratize the state demanded some magnificent "single act of the majority of the whole people" in support of their program.[1] It was crucial for any party that claimed to speak for the people to mobilize the twenty thousand potential voters of the state, a figure that included the eight thousand registered freemen with some twelve thousand disfranchised citizens.[2] The legitimacy of the new

---

[1] Address of the State Suffrage Committee, June 1841, in *Burke's Report*, p. 267.

[2] The radicals calculated that of the approximately 108,000 people the 1840 census found in Rhode Island, 25,000 could vote under the People's Constitution, though it was unlikely that all of them would come to the polls. They arrived at their figure of 12,000 disfranchised citizens by assuming that only about 20,000 of the 25,000 were potentially active citizens, a figure that included the more than 8,000 landholding freemen who had voted in the hard-fought electoral struggle of 1840. The difference, then, was 12,000. For these calculations, see *New Age*, November 20, 1840; Dorr's message as Governor on May 4, 1842; *Ibid.*, May 7, 1842; Dan King, *The Life and Times of Thomas Wilson Dorr, With*

government hinged largely on the magnitude of the vote to ratify the People's Constitution in late December. Just before the election Dorr was hoping that enough nonfreemen would cast ballots to produce a total of twelve thousand votes. A thousand more, he calculated, would be enough "to place the result beyond all doubt or cavil," and fourteen thousand could be called a "triumphal majority." [3]

To ensure a vast outpouring of votes, the Association not only permitted nonfreemen to cast ballots,[4] but also conducted an extensive campaign of exhortation and mobilization. Party orators visited all parts of the state, calling upon the citizens to act for equal rights.[5] Broadsides and newspaper articles amplified the appeal and elaborated the argument that in America the people could legitimately act without authorization other than their own to create new governments.[6]

There was little effective opposition to suffrage measures in the late fall and winter of 1841. Those conservatives who favored continuation of the Charter of 1663 or looked upon the People's Constitution as an illegitimate and unauthorized in-

---

Outlines of the Political History of Rhode Island (Boston: published by the author, 1959), p. 49; Edward Field, *State of Rhode Island and Providence Plantations at the End of the* [Nineteenth] *Century,* 3 vols. (Boston and Syracuse: Mason Publishing Company, 1902), I, 339; Arthur May Mowry, *The Dorr War: or, The Constitutional Struggle in Rhode Island* (Providence: Preston and Rounds, 1901), p. 113. Cf. Appendix B.

[3] Dorr to Duttee J. Pearce, December 13, 1841, Dorr MSS.

[4] That is, adult white males permanently resident in Rhode Island were permitted to vote. The only exceptions were lunatics, persons under guardianship, and those convicted of "bribery, forgery, theft, or other infamous crime, [who] . . . shall not be restored except by an act of the General Assembly." The People's Constitution, (Article II, Sections 2 and 4) also specified that only citizens who paid taxes on $150 of "ratable property" could vote in town or ward meetings on "any question of taxation." But this restriction did not apply to the vote on ratification. See Articles II and XIV in Appendix A.

[5] Dorr and David Parmenter, a shoemaker, were among the most successful orators for the suffrage cause. See Dorr to Samuel Allen, December 13, 1841 (draft); Dorr to Duttee J. Pearce, December 31, 1841, both in Dorr MSS.

[6] See broadsides: *Dear Sir. To Act in Concert* (n.p., December 1841), *Vote. A Proposed Form* (n.p., n.d.), both in Dorr MSS. See also *New Age,* December, 1841, *passim.*

strument carried out no counter-efforts; they simply ignored the radicals and stayed away from the polls. Many moderates who repudiated the doctrine of Popular Constituent Sovereignty nevertheless supported the People's Constitution and voted in December as a symbolic gesture, indicating the desirability of political liberalization in Rhode Island.[7] The only organized opposition came from abolitionists who protested the disfranchisement of blacks in the People's Constitution. While Garrison's *Liberator* denounced the Suffrage Association for its inconsistency in championing democratic rights and then arbitrarily excluding a portion of the population,[8] some of the most energetic New England abolitionists—including Stephen Foster, Abby Kelley and Frederick Douglass—came to Rhode Island late in the fall of 1841 to agitate against the People's Constitution.[9] But these efforts could not prevent the ratifying election.

The procedure for casting and registering votes was nearly as orderly and regular as it would have been had it been carried out by an authorized government. At public meetings in every

---

[7] Jacob Frieze, an anti-Dorr pamphleteer, admitted that he voted for the People's Constitution in December 1841, "as an expression of opinion," without any belief that the document had "binding force." *Concise History of the Efforts to Obtain an Extension of Suffrage in Rhode Island From the Year 1811 to 1842* (Providence: B. Moore, 1842), p. 124. Cf. voting lists for Providence, *Burke's Report,* p. 486. A few other Rhode Island conservatives, including industrialist William Sprague (soon to become United States Senator) also cast ballots for the People's Constitution, though they were unsympathetic to the Constitutional Party and soon became its most "violent persecutors" (*ibid.,* pp. 354–355).

[8] See *The Liberator,* November 19, 1841, p. 187; December 24, 1841, pp. 205–206. While Garrison was away from Boston in the summer of 1842, *The Liberator* carried a series of pro-Dorr articles by abolitionist Elias Smith (July 8, p. 107; July 22, p. 115; August 5, p. 123), but on Garrison's return the abolitionist weekly returned to condemnation of both the Charterites and the Dorrites (*ibid.,* August 19, p. 131; October 14, 1842, p. 163).

[9] See *Burke's Report,* pp. 110–116; cf. the lengthy account by Abby Kelley, reprinted from the *National Anti-Slavery Standard* in *The Liberator,* January 21, 1842, p. 3. Kelley described antislavery meetings in Newport which were broken up by raucous mobs and the proslavery harangues of such prominent reformers as Duttee J. Pearce. The abolitionists got little better treatment in Providence, where Kelley and the others were pelted by "snowballs and other missiles."

town of the state and in the six wards of Providence, citizens chose moderators and clerks to receive the signed ballots of voters.[10] Proxy votes were accepted from those who because of "sickness or other causes" were "unable to attend and vote in the town or ward meetings. . . ."[11] One observer, watching Rhode Island seemingly set aside its old government and publicly institute a new one "without opposition from the existing authorities," saw in the process "a pretty good proof [of] . . . the sovereignty of the people."[12]

The election returns fulfilled Dorr's most optimistic predictions. On January 12, 1842, a committee appointed by the People's Convention inspected the ballots and reported that 13,947 Rhode Island citizens had endorsed the People's Constitution.[13] Only 52 votes were cast in opposition, most of them from the static and declining agricultural towns in the southern part of the state. The committee joyfully added that 13,947 was not only a clear majority of the enlarged electorate created by the People's Constitution but also, because it included 4,925 voters qualified under the landholding requirement, a putative majority of Rhode Island's approximately 8,000 freemen.[14]

---

[10] See People's Constitution, Article XIV, Sections 3 and 4, in Appendix A.

[11] People's Constitution, Article XIV, Section 2. In an uncautious moment, Newport reformer Duttee J. Pearce suggested that the ratifying vote be swelled by permitting aliens to cast ballots in violation of the provision in the People's Constitution (Article XIV, Section 1) allowing only citizens (native or naturalized) to vote. Dorr firmly rejected this suggestion, but when Dorr's opponents captured his correspondence later in 1842, they gleefully reprinted Pearce's letter (but not Dorr's reply) to prove how dishonest and fraudulent was the vote for the People's Constitution. See Duttee J. Pearce to Dorr, [November] 21; Dorr to Pearce, December 13, 1841, Dorr MSS.; Newport *Herald of the Times,* December 22, 1842.

[12] A[lexander?] H[ill?] Everett to an unidentified correspondent, November 8, 1841, Dorr MSS. This letter was apparently forwarded to Dorr by some Massachusetts well-wisher.

[13] There are annoying minor errors in the reporting and tabulation of the ratification vote. The radicals reported both 13,944 and 13,955 (cf. *Burke's Report,* pp. 119, 353). My own calculation, based upon town reports, is that 13,947 Rhode Islanders voted for the People's Constitution. See Appendix B.

[14] See the voting frequencies in Appendix B.

In the flush of victory it was easy for the reformers to minimize several disquieting results of the apparent ratification of the People's Constitution. For one thing, there was a marked sectional pattern to the voting, which both presaged struggle in the near future and echoed earlier divisions on reform questions.[15] Support for the People's Constitution was strongest in the industrial and commercial centers of the Blackstone-Pawtuxet river valley in the northern part of the state, where 64 percent of those eligible to vote did so. In the predominately agricultural districts of southern and western Rhode Island only 42 percent cast ballots, considerably below the state's average turnout of 55 percent.[16] In both areas the nonfreemen were relatively apathetic, as shown in Table III. The large total vote obscured the extent to which disfranchised Rhode Islanders were willing to endure the injustices that the Association was striving to eradicate.

TABLE III   PROPORTIONS OF FREEMEN AND NONFREEMEN VOTING ON RATIFICATION OF THE PEOPLE'S CONSTITUTION *

	Freemen	*Nonfreemen*	*All voters*
Industrial towns (Senate districts 1–6)	65%	51%	64%
Agricultural towns (Senate districts 7–12)	64%	38%	42%

* Source: calculated from the voting frequencies shown in Appendix B.

Reform leaders did perceive something like class cleavage in the December balloting. In a speech celebrating the ratification of the People's Constitution, Dorr sadly noted how few men of

---

[15] In an earlier constitutional referendum in 1824 the voting varied sharply from town to town. "With few exceptions, northern industrial and commercial towns supported reform while southern and western [agricultural] communities opposed it." Peter J. Coleman, *The Transformation of Rhode Island, 1790–1860* (Providence: Brown University Press, 1963), p. 266.

[16] See Table III, and Appendix B.

professional distinction or learning had come out publicly to champion popular rights.[17] The reformers did not yet anticipate that the indifference of Rhode Island's elite would soon turn into active hostility, or that they might have to assay riskier and more dangerous measures. No one imagined that the sheer magnitude of the vote in December would force the Association, now trustee of the solemnly expressed people's will, to embrace a desperate radicalism in order to uphold the constitution that had been so overwhelmingly ratified.

II

Rhode Island conservatives reacted slowly and hesitantly to the ratification. Believing the proceedings of the Association "absurd," they were amazed that the community accepted them so readily.[18] Almost no one publicly spoke out against what had been done. It was not until months later that the cry of electoral fraud was raised to discredit the People's Constitution.[19]

---

[17] See Dorr's notes for a speech at a Providence suffrage celebration, January 7, 1842, Dorr MSS. For an insightful analysis of the response of Rhode Island's intellectual elite to the upheaval in 1842, see Wilson Smith, "Francis Wayland and the Dorr War," *Professors and Public Ethics: Studies of Northern Moral Philosophers Before the Civil War* (Ithaca, N.Y.: Cornell University Press, 1956), Chap. VII. See also, William M. Wiecek, "Popular Sovereignty in the Dorr Rebellion: The Conservative Counterblast," (unpublished MSS., to be submitted to *Rhode Island History,* which I have consulted by courtesy of Professor Wiecek).

[18] See William Rhodes to James F. Simmons, January 3, 1842, Simmons Papers, LC.

[19] Conservatives raised this cry only after their own constitution (a discussion of which follows) had been defeated in March 1842, and it was subsequently taken up by almost every anti-Dorr pamphleteer. See, among the many examples, Elisha R. Potter [Jr.], *Considerations on the Question of a Constitution and Extension of Suffrage in Rhode Island* (Boston: Thomas H. Webb, 1842), appendix; [John Pitman], *A Reply to the Letter of the Hon. Marcus Morton, Late Governor of Massachusetts, On the Rhode Island Question. By One of the Rhode-Island People* (Providence: Knowles and Vose, 1842), p. 8; *Address of John Whipple to the People of Rhode-Island, On the Approaching Election* (Providence: Knowles and Vose, 1843), p. 11; [George Ticknor Curtis], *Merits*

An exception to this lethargy was a federal judge, John Pitman of Providence, who decades earlier had been a champion of suffrage extension.[20] In January 1842 Pitman rushed into print a twenty-four-page anonymous pamphlet addressed to members of the General Assembly. Believing the Rhode Island Suffrage Association to be a "revolutionary movement" gotten up by outside agitator "Augustus [sic] O. Brownson," Pitman urged the state government to suppress it immediately. He feared that the revolutionaries would proceed in their schemes to take over Rhode Island with such a great show of legality that the lethargic legislature would refrain from using the necessary force. To Pitman the essential question was not suffrage extension or any other specific reform proposal, but the manner in which political change and constitutional revision should take place. The measures of the Association, taken without authorization, were in his view dangerously criminal.[21] Supporters of the People's Con-

---

of *Thomas W. Dorr and George Bancroft as they Are Politically Connected, by a Citizen of Massachusetts* (Boston: John H. Eastburn, [1844]), pp. 16, 19. At first Mowry ("The Constitutional Controversy in Rhode Island in 1841," *Annual Report of the American Historical Association for the Year 1894* [Washington: U.S. Government Printing Office, 1895], pp. 366–367) concluded that the vote had been "fairly free from fraud or error, at least for one cast under such unusual circumstances." But in his later work (*Dorr War,* pp. 133-188) he uncritically accepted biased opinion and suspect testimony to reach the conclusion that a majority in Rhode Island may not have ratified the People's Constitution. Even Dorr and his closest associates admitted, both privately and publicly, that some fraudulent votes were probably cast. There is, however, no firm evidence to contest the overwhelming impression of contemporaries that the Association had indeed mobilized a majority of the electorate created under the People's Constitution. See Dorr's Address to the People of Rhode Island, August 1843, in *Burke's Report,* p. 736; Aaron White to Dorr, September 5, 1842, Dorr MSS.

[20] See draft of an act to extend suffrage, introduced in the General Assembly by John Pitman in 1811, *Burke's Report,* pp. 206–208. Pitman's opposition to reform measures in 1842 prompted reformers to search for his earlier statements. On this search, see Dorr to [Duttee J. Pearce], January 17, 1842, Pearce Papers, Newport Historical Society.

[21] [John Pitman], *To the Members of the General Assembly of Rhode-Island* (Providence: Knowles and Vose, [January] 1842); Pitman to Joseph Story, January 24, 1842, Pitman-Story Correspondence, William L. Clements Library, University of Michigan. Although Orestes Brownson, the Massachusetts reformer, was a correspondent of Dorr and a

stitution could dismiss Pitman's arguments as "a tissue of learned, farfetched and captious sayings," [22] but the arguments apparently impressed many members of the General Assembly and helped set the tone of the ideological debate over rival constitutions that soon raged in the state.

In January the General Assembly had its first opportunity to pronounce judgment on the People's Constitution. The Association had communicated to the legislature the news that a new constitution had been drafted and would soon become the supreme law in Rhode Island.[23] At about the same time, Samuel Y. Atwell, suffragist representative from Glocester, introduced a trio of reform bills in the lower house. First he proposed that the legislature voluntarily disband itself on the day before the People's Constitution was scheduled to go into force. When this idea was rejected, Atwell proposed a formal inquiry by the General Assembly to see if the People's Constitution had been legally ratified. In no mood to confer even the small measure of legitimacy that such an inquiry implied, the legislators rejected this suggestion as well.[24] Nor was there much support for Atwell's third proposal, which was to resubmit the People's Constitution to the voters through an act of the General Assembly itself.[25]

Unwilling to endorse in any way schemes of electoral reform originating with the Association, the General Assembly did en-

---

sometime supporter of the Rhode Island Suffrage Association, the main reason Pitman singled him out as the chief instigator of the radical agitation in the state seems to have been psychological and domestic. One of Pitman's sons was showing symptoms of transcendentalism, refusing to see the profession of law as an honest calling, and the father may have been venting his rage at Brownson, a convenient target. See Pitman to Joseph Story, September 13, 1842, *ibid.*

[22] Providence *Republican Herald,* January 19, 1842. Authorship of this pamphlet quickly became known in Rhode Island and elsewhere.

[23] Resolution of the General Assembly, January 1842, in *Burke's Report,* p. 167.

[24] [Francis H. (Whipple) McDougall], *Might and Right by a Rhode Islander,* 2nd. ed. (Providence: A. H. Stillwell, 1844), p. 157; Dorr's notes on General Assembly debates, Dorr MSS.; Mowry, *Dorr War,* pp. 121–122. For Atwell's equally unsuccessful sponsorship of reform measures in 1841, see above, pp. 42, 50.

[25] See records of the General Assembly, January session, 1842, in *Burke's Report,* p. 443; Mowry, *Dorr War,* pp. 121–122.

tertain proposals from its more conservative members who wished by means of timely concessions to head off conflict. After the defeat of Atwell's measures, Charles Jackson, a young Whig representative from Providence, proposed an expansion of the electorate to include most taxpayers. This proposal caused consternation in the legislature. Mindful of John Pitman's warning against being stampeded into hasty action by the radicals, the conservative majority voted it down.[26] But the General Assembly's members, who weeks earlier would have been as likely to agree on "a bill to establish Mohamedanism" as to endorse suffrage extension, began to see the wisdom of limited concessions.[27] They therefore passed a law directing the Landholders' Convention, adjourned since November, to relax the qualifications for voting on the new constitution that it was soon to present to the citizens of Rhode Island.[28]

Along with this mild and ambiguous concession [29] the General Assembly passed a strongly worded resolution denouncing the attempt by "a portion of the people of this State, without the forms of law" to frame a constitution as being a "violation of the rights of the existing government, and of the rights of the people at large." The resolution continued:

---

[26] On Charles Jackson's proposal, see J. H. Richmond to James F. Simmons, January 27, 29, 1842; C[harles] Jackson to Simmons, January 28, 1842, Simmons Papers, LC.; Dorr's notes on General Assembly debates, Dorr MSS.

[27] Henry B. Anthony to James F. Simmons, February 2, 1842, Simmons Papers, LC.

[28] Act of the General Assembly, January 1842, in *Burke's Report,* p. 646.

[29] The General Assembly's request that the Landholders' Convention relax suffrage restrictions had questionable constitutional sanction. Dorrites later claimed that this was an insubstantial gesture, especially since no complete constitution had yet been reported out of the Landholders' Convention, whereas the People's Constitution had been drafted and ratified. The General Assembly's Act of January 1842, unconvincing to reformers, also contained a provision—the enlargement of the suffrage so that all citizens who would be franchised by the Landholders' Constitution could vote on its ratification—that was potentially dangerous to the conservatives. It permitted many voters who had cast ballots in favor of the People's Constitution in December to vote against the officially authorized constitution in March. Cf. below, pp. 78–79.

[T]he convention called and organized in pursuance of an
act of this General Assembly . . . is the only body which we
can recognize as authorized to form such a constitution; and
to this constitution the whole people have a right to look, and
we are assured they will not look in vain.

Even as it contemplated its own orderly demise in favor of the
new regime to be set up by the Landholders' Convention, the
Charter Government warned that it would "maintain its own
proper authority." [30] This determination raised the specter of
conflict in Rhode Island, for some of the radical reformers were
just as determined to uphold the legitimacy of the People's Constitution.

Prodded into reconvening,[31] the Landholders' Convention
turned in February with greater earnestness than before to the
task of drafting a constitution to replace the Charter of 1663.
The task was complicated by the appearance of a formidable
rival constitution. In November the delegates to the first session
had been able to afford leisurely debate on whether suffrage
extension was needed or desirable. Now, three months later,
they were busily calculating the minimum amount of reform that
would calm the discontents and still leave political power in the
hands of those manufacturing and landed interests who tradi-
tionally ruled the state. If the convention did its work well, wrote
Senator James F. Simmons from Washington, "a conservative
majority on all [important] . . . questions" would be assured.[32]

---

[30] Resolution of the General Assembly, January 1842, in *Burke's Report,*
p. 167.

[31] Delegates to this convention were understandably hostile to reform, as
they were chosen by the restricted electorate that would have to share
power by any extension of suffrage or more equitable reapportionment.
After its inconclusive deliberations in November 1841, the Landholders'
Convention might not have reconvened. The events of 1834–1835 (see
pp. 27–28) provided ample precedent for the petering out of a constitutional convention due to the cynicism and apathy of its members. But
the People's Constitution, in spurring the General Assembly into action,
stimulated the work of the Landholders' Convention as well.

[32] James F. Simmons to an unidentified correspondent (draft), February
11, 1842, Simmons Papers, LC. This lengthy letter contained detailed
suggestions on how to draft a constitution that would ensure conservative
hegemony. That Senator Simmons, a powerful Whig politician, only

By mid-February the Landholders' Convention had produced
a constitution which, although it included some suffrage extension and reapportionment, was less broadly equalitarian than
the People's Constitution. The conservatives granted the vote
to all native, white, adult citizens, and heeding the legislature's
suggestion, permitted this enlarged electorate to vote on ratification the following month.[33] Both constitutions stipulated property qualifications for voting on questions dealing with the ap-
propriation of funds and taxation.[34] The apportionment provisions of the Landholders' Constitution were so favorable to the
thinly populated agricultural districts in the southern part of the
state that the Association denounced them as an unfair "gerry-
mander" designed to perpetuate the "rotten borough system"
of Rhode Island.[35] Even conservative Whigs believed the apportionment discriminatory to the northern industrial areas.[36]

On a number of minor but symbolic points the Landholders'
Constitution also suffered by comparison with its rival. Although
it promised remedies, under the law, for all legitimate grievances,
it did not explicitly guarantee to the people the "unalienable and
indefeasible right . . . to ordain and institute government, and
. . . to alter, reform or totally change the same, whenever their
safety or happiness requires" that was guaranteed in the People's
Constitution. The latter Constitution also contained a "Declaration of Principles and Rights," specifying that Rhode Island was
a "democracy" in which the "laws should be made not for the

---

drafted his suggestions in February supports the hypothesis that no serious proposals came out of the November meetings and that if the radicals had not put forward their constitution and ratified it so overwhelmingly, the conservatives might have done nothing in the way of
constitutional reform.

[33] Article II, both constitutions, in Appendix A; Mowry, *Dorr War,* pp.
326, 350.

[34] *Ibid.* In the People's Constitution those owning $150 of taxable prop-
erty could vote on financial questions presented to the towns in referenda,
whereas in the Landholders' Constitution $134 of real estate (the previ-
ous qualification for all voters) was required before a citizen could vote
on such questions. See Article II, in Appendix A.

[35] *New Age,* March 4, 1842.

[36] S[amuel F.] Man to James F. Simmons, February 21, 1842, Simmons
Papers, LC. For the apportionment in the Landholders' Constitution, see
Appendix C.

good of the few, but of the many" and requiring that no "favor or disfavor be shown toward any man, or party, or society or religious denomination." [37] Critics of the Landholders' Constitution attacked its indistinct separation of powers, according to which the General Assembly would exercise many judicial functions and the Governor would be unable to veto legislation or pardon criminals.[38] The People's Constitution, which sharply divided legislative from executive authority, stipulated that "in all criminal cases the jury shall judge both of the law and the facts," a clause abhorrent to the conservative framers of the Landholders' Constitution.[39] On economic matters the People's Constitution gave the General Assembly wide powers to control corporations chartered in Rhode Island, a feature not found in the rival instrument.[40] Finally, partisans of the People's Constitution objected to the Landholders' Constitution on the grounds that the latter contained "no offering of gratitude to the Governor of the universe, for his good Providence toward our [fore]fathers and their successors in the State." [41] Minor differences between the two Constitutions, however, were less important than the suffragists' belief that their Constitution had already been ratified by procedures that had perhaps been unconventional but had nevertheless been, by the canons of American democracy, thoroughly legitimate.

Conservatives leaped to the defense of the Landholders' Constitution with arguments against the legality of the Association's

---

[37] Article I (both constitutions), in Appendix A; Mowry, *Dorr War,* pp. [322]–326, [347]–350.

[38] The People's Constitution, Article III and Article IV, Section 12, in Appendix A; Landholders' Constitution, Articles III, IV, VIII, in Mowry, *Dorr War,* pp. 327–330, 352–354, 357–358; *New Age,* March 4, 1842. (This issue of the *New Age,* containing the Association's most extensive critique of the Landholders' Constitution, was printed as a broadside for wide public notice. I have consulted the copy in the WLHU.)

[39] The People's Constitution, Artcle I, Section 13, in Appendix A. For the importance of this issue of the relative power of judges and juries, see my discussion of the treason trials of Dorrites and of Dorr himself in Chapter 6. The People's Constitution also provided for jury trials in fugitive slave cases (Article I, Section 14, Appendix A).

[40] The People's Constitution, Article IX, in Appendix A.

[41] *New Age,* March 4, 1842. The People's Constitution did refer to the Deity in the Preamble and in Article I. See Appendix A.

measures and with threats to the supporters of the People's Constitution. Early in March the widely publicized *ex cathedra* opinion of the three judges of Rhode Island's Supreme Court appeared in response to a request from some citizens of Providence who wished to know whether or not the People's Constitution was a legal instrument.[42] Without hesitation the judges replied that it was not. Votes in favor of it, they said, had been mere expressions of public opinion, which had no "binding force." To support the People's Constitution further by attempting to carry it into effect would be, the judges warned, "treason against this State, if not against the United States." [43] Many Rhode Islanders who had previously supported the Association's reform efforts now paused to consider whether they were prepared to risk treasonable acts.

III

Upholders of the People's Constitution soon responded to such attacks and threats, contributing to a polemical "war of the constitutions" [44] in the spring of 1842. This ideological dispute, which would eventually erupt in armed struggle, was no longer over details of suffrage extension or sectional issues of legislative

---

[42] Charles Dyer and others to the Hon. Job Durfee, Levi Haile and William R. Staples, Judges of the Supreme Judicial Court [March 1, 1842], in *Citizens of Rhode Island! Read! Mark! Learn!* (n.p. [March 1842]), Broadside Collection, WLHU. At least two of the inquirers, Joseph Veazie and Thomas Fletcher, were landholding freemen of Providence who had voted for the People's Constitution. See voting lists for Providence in *Burke's Report*, p. 476. By March, however, they were declaring their intention to support the Landholders' Constitution.

[43] Durfee, Haile and Staples to Dyer and others, March 2, 1842, in *Citizens of Rhode Island! Read! Mark! Learn!*

[44] Thomas A. Jenckes to his daughter, Jeanie, March [13], 1842, Jenckes MSS., John Hay Library, Brown University. Jenckes was a leading Rhode Island lawyer, an active opponent of the Dorrites, who served in the United States House of Representatives from 1863 to 1871, part of that time as a moderate Republican. See *Biographical Directory of American Congress, 1774–1949*, House Document No. 607, 81 Cong., 2 Sess., 1950, p. 1118; David Donald, *The Politics of Reconstruction, 1863–1867* (Baton Rouge: Louisiana State University Press, 1965), p. 103. The Jenckes MSS., LC, do not contain material on the early 1840s.

apportionment. Such minor questions receded as larger ones loomed ominously: Where is the locus of ultimate sovereignty in the community? Can the people act on their own to revise and alter fundamental law? Is prior authorization from the outgoing regime necessary before a new government can come into being? What constitutes an authentic expression of popular will? Contributing greatly to the reformers' persistence in pursuing these questions to their radical conclusions was the prior ratification of the People's Constitution, which many of them believed represented a majestic and irrevocable act of Popular Constituent Sovereignty to be defended at all costs.

Association spokesmen, building on Enlightenment ideas of popular rights and natural law and extending the theories of earlier Rhode Island advocates of constitutional reform,[45] threw this fresh set of explosive questions before the public. Themselves not entirely free from confusion and mystification, these spokesmen attempted to lay bare the political process to show how the people by their own efforts could achieve political rights. A group of nine lawyers, anxious to refute attacks on the People's Constitution such as the State Supreme Court's *ex cathedra* opinion, fashioned the Association's definitive manifesto.[46] Though it did not quite express every strain of opinion in the Association, the *Nine Lawyers' Opinion* was the major radical weapon in the ideological battles of 1842.

Historical interpretations of the American Revolution (in the society created by that Revolution) were at the center of the ideological dispute in Rhode Island.[47] Although Association

---

[45] See above, pp. 10–11.

[46] The lawyers included Samuel Y. Atwell, Dorr, Duttee J. Pearce and others. Their pamphlet was entitled: "Right of the People to Form a Constitution: Statement of Reasons," March 14, 1842, ed., Sidney S. Rider, *Rhode Island Historical Tracts,* no. 11 (Providence: S. S. Rider, 1880). It shall be cited here as the *Nine Lawyers' Opinion.* For a complete citation of all nine co-authors (Dorr seems to have been the principal author), see the bibliographical essay, p. 242.

[47] I am not arguing here that suffrage ideology constituted some set of suprahistorical ideals passed on to the Rhode Island rebels by the heroes of 1776. The connection between the two movements is more complicated. Rhode Island radicals of the 1840s explicitly acknowledged that the Declaration of Independence had taken on a different meaning, as will be discussed. On the general problem of understanding the ideology of

spokesmen had frequently delivered their views on that struggle,[48] the *Nine Lawyers' Opinion* went most thoroughly into the matter.

> At the American Revolution, the sovereign power of this State passed from the king and Parliament of England to the People of the State; not to a portion of them, but to the *whole* People, who succeeded as tenants in common to this power.

The freemen of Rhode Island did not become the sovereigns of the state after 1776, the lawyers argued, for that would have rendered the nonlandholding majority less free, mere subjects of the landholders, unable any longer to appeal to English authorities for relief from local grievances. Advocates of free suffrage would never concede that the freedom of Americans had diminished as a result of the Revolution.[49]

The recorded actions of the Rhode Island authorities during the American Revolution committed the state, in the view of the Association, to a broad conception of popular power. In July 1776 the General Assembly had formally ratified the Declaration of Independence with its guarantees of citizens' rights "to institute new government, laying its foundation on such principles, and organizing its powers in such form as to them shall seem most likely to effect their safety and happiness." [50] The state

---

radical movements, Aileen S. Kraditor's "American Radical Historians on their Heritage," *Past & Present,* No. 56 (August, 1972), 136–153, expresses a viewpoint that has informed this study.

[48] See [Dorr and others], Address to the People of Rhode Island, February–March 1834; Address of the State Suffrage Association Committee, June 1841; Dorr's speech to the People's Convention, November 1841, in *Burke's Report,* pp. 155, 262–263, 850.

[49] *Nine Lawyers' Opinion,* pp. 68–69, 71.

[50] Declaration of Independence, quoted *ibid.,* p. 71. Cf. David S. Lovejoy, *Rhode Island Politics and American Revolution, 1760–1776* (Providence: Brown University Press, 1958), p. 193. Recently a historian of early American radicalism has aptly described the later impact of the famous manifesto of 1776: "For all its ambiguies . . . , the Declaration of Independence is the single most concentrated expression of the revolutionary intellectual tradition. Without significant exception, sub-variants of American radicalism have taken [it] as their point of departure and claimed to be the true heirs of the spirit of '76." Staughton Lynd, *Intellectual Origins of American Radicalism* (New York: Pantheon Books,

ratifying convention in 1790 that had brought Rhode Island into
the new union had specifically resolved: "[since] all power is
naturally vested in, and consequently derived from, the people,
. . . [such power] may be reassumed by the people, whenever
it shall become necessary to their happiness." [51] Dorr and the
Nine Lawyers stated that it was up to the people to determine
when the moment had come to exercise such power. Failure to
act in 1776 or at any later time could not bind subsequent generations.[52] "The necessity for a total reformation [of Rhode
Island's government] has been increasing during the last forty
years; and, in the judgment of the people, has now become absolute." [53]

The Nine Lawyers drew on earlier American radical thought,
including previous Rhode Island formulations, for their con-

1968), p. 4. This is true as far as it goes. But see the critique of Lynd's
often ahistorical approach in Kraditor, "Radical Historians"; and
Eugene D. Genovese, *In Red and Black: Marxian Explorations in Southern and Afro-American History* (New York: Pantheon Books, 1971),
Chap. 16. Neither Lynd nor the other students of Jefferson's influence
deal with the impact of Jeffersonian ideas on the Rhode Island rebels of
1842. See Charles Maurice Wiltse, *The Jeffersonian Tradition in American Democracy* (New York: Hill and Wang, 1960); and Merrill D.
Peterson, *The Jefferson Image in the American Mind* (New York: Oxford
University Press, 1962), which only casually mentions (on p. 82) the
Dorr Rebellion. Supporting these rebel claims in 1842 was ailing ex-
President Andrew Jackson, who wrote from the Hermitage in support
of the Rhode Island rebels. "The people are the sovereign power and
agreable [*sic*] to our system they have the right to alter and amend their
system of Government when a majority wills it, as a majority have a right
to rule." Jackson to Francis P. Blair, May 23, 1842, in John Spencer
Bassett, ed., *Correspondence of Andrew Jackson*, 7 vols. (Washington,
D.C.: Carnegie Institution, 1926–1935), VI, 153. Blair apparently kept
this communication private, for there is no evidence that the radicals
knew of Old Hickory's expression of sympathy. If they had known, they
certainly would have widely publicized the news.

[51] Resolutions of the Rhode Island ratifying convention, May 29, 1790,
quoted in *Nine Lawyers' Opinion*, pp. 79–80. The most recent study of
how Rhode Island was almost coerced into the union in 1790 is Irwin
Polishook, *Rhode Island and the Union, 1774–1795* (Evanston, Ill.:
Northwestern University Press, 1969), esp. Chap. 9.

[52] Dorr's speech to the People's Convention, November 1841, in *Burke's
Report*, pp. 376–378; *Nine Lawyers' Opinion*, p. 71.

[53] *Nine Lawyers' Opinion*, p. 73.

ception of how the people might legitimately act to frame a constitution. They distinguished the "supreme and ultimate" power of the state, residing "in the People themselves," from the inferior legislative power, which was said to be the creature and not the master of the popular will.[54] From its inception, the Rhode Island Suffrage Association insisted that a state constitution be drafted by "the people in their primary capacity," not by the secondary power of the General Assembly.[55] This echoed earlier expressions of radical views in the state,[56] which were in turn reflections of eighteenth-century revolutionary principles. R. R. Palmer has pronounced the theory and practice of "the people as constituent power" to be America's unique contributions to the eighteenth-century Democratic Revolution.[57] When Association adherents applied these doctrines, hallowed now by the blood of patriots, to Rhode Island, the conclusion seemed inescapable: the framing and ratification of the People's Constitution were completely consistent with America's sacred revolutionary past. It was inconceivable to them that anyone could draw different lessons from 1776.[58]

This doctrine of Popular Constituent Sovereignty—the preeminent right of the people at large to draft constitutions—not

---

[54] *Ibid.,* pp. 68, 71, 74.

[55] *Preamble and Constitution of the Rhode Island Suffrage Association . . . March 27, 1840* (Providence: B. T. Albro, 1840), p. 6.

[56] See pp. 10–11.

[57] R. R. Palmer, *The Age of the Democratic Revolution,* 2 vols. (Princeton, N.J.: Princeton University Press, 1959–1964), I, 213–235. Cf. Elisha P. Douglass, *Rebels and Democrats: The Struggle for Equal Political Rights and Majority Rule During the American Revolution* (Chapel Hill, N.C.: University of North Carolina Press, 1955), p. 126 and *passim;* Gordon S. Wood, *The Creation of the American Republic: 1776–1787* (Chapel Hill, N.C.: University of North Carolina Press, 1969), esp. Chap. 8.

[58] The Rhode Island radicals were unaware, of course, that the principles they cherished were those of the losing faction in 1776–1787. See Douglass, *Rebels and Democrats,* esp. Chaps. 3, 4, 5, and Wood, *Creation of the American Republic, passim,* on the defeat of the extreme democrats in the American Revolution. Soon, however, the Rhode Island conservatives would show the radicals that other conclusions could be drawn from the American revolutionary experience.

only legitimized the People's Constitution, it also disposed of the claims of the rival Landholders' Constitution. Conservatives stressed that the convention which framed the People's Constitution had not been called by any act of the General Assembly. But the Nine Lawyers replied that constitutions were expressions of the people's will and as such did not depend on prior legislative authorization.

> This doctrine of a necessary permission, authority or request, from the General Assembly to the People, before they can rightfully proceed to form a Constitution, is . . . [a doctrine] borrowed from the Parliament of England, in which body the sovereignty is lodged by the theory of the English Constitution. It is a doctrine which has no application in this country, where the sovereignty resides in the people.[59]

According to the Nine Lawyers, not only were the people in their sovereign capacity entitled to draft constitutions in Rhode Island, where under the Charter there was no established mode of constitutional change or amendment, but even where such provisions existed, the sovereign people could "rightfully proceed in the mode and manner which they deem most proper." [60] To some Rhode Island radicals, developments in their own tiny state seemed to be a model for political change elsewhere.

Despite these claims of wide application for the principles of Popular Constituent Sovereignty, the Association was not advocating "revolution" or frequent meddling by the populace in political affairs. Its middle-class spokesmen feared conflict almost as much as did their conservative opponents. Dorr had proclaimed the previous year that the People's Convention, far from being "irregular or revolutionary," was "strictly in order." [61] He continued to placate (and mislead) his supporters with assurances that they were not participating in any mere insurrection.[62]

---

[59] *Nine Lawyers' Opinion,* pp. 73, 76.

[60] *Ibid.,* p. 78. See also the Address of the State Suffrage Association Committee, June 1841, in *Burke's Report,* p. 263. Some out-of-state supporters believed that on this point the Rhode Island radicals had pushed their doctrines too far. See Senator Silas Wright, Jr., to Dorr, April 25, 1842, Dorr MSS.

[61] Speech to the People's Convention, *Burke's Report,* p. 863.

[62] Dorr's message to the People's Legislature, May 4, 1842, *ibid.,* p. 720.

He repeatedly maintained that the reformers did not intend to overthrow the Charter Government, but merely wanted to succeed it.[63] This was a nice distinction, but one that conservatives could scarcely accept. Issuing a similar disavowal of radical intent, the Nine Lawyers conceded in March that "Sovereign power from its nature can and ought to be but rarely exercised." [64] Dorr subsequently explained the implications of this usually "latent and invisible" character of Popular Constituent Sovereignty. The people, he wrote, were often unaware of the popular power underlying the state, since they customarily saw only the operation of government officials, who represented the derived, secondary authority. It was therefore necessary to make each generation of Americans aware of "the true doctrine of original imperscriptible [sic] sovereignty," either by actual exercises of such power, as in Rhode Island, or by frequent invocation of its tenets.[65]

This doctrine of an Invisible Hand in politics [66] implied a muted but continuously operating set of democratic safeguards,

---

[63] See Dan King, The Life and Times of Thomas Wilson Dorr; With Outlines of the Political History of Rhode Island (Boston: published by the author, 1859), p. 53.

[64] Nine Lawyers' Opinion, p. 71.

[65] Dorr to Estwick Evans (aspiring author of a book on popular rights), April 12, 1842, Misc. MSS., LC; Dorr, Address to the People of Rhode Island, August 1843, in Burke's Report, pp. 744–745; Dorr's argument at his 1844 treason trial, ibid., p. 945. (For this 1843 Address and the trial, see below, Chapter 6.)

[66] Dorr did not use the term "Invisible Hand," but some such idea of a "mighty hand" whose operation is "latent and invisible" is frequently found in his statements. Dorr's usage invites comparison with Adam Smith's classic formulation of a beneficent, self-regulating mechanism controlling the capitalist marketplace in An Inquiry Into the Nature and Causes of the Wealth of Nations, Edwin Canaan, ed. (New York: Modern Library, 1937), p. 423. Both ideas derived from Enlightenment beliefs in automatic social processes (see Karl Polyani, The Great Transformation [Boston: Beacon Press, 1957]), but there were important differences. Smith purported to have discovered the unconscious, beneficent consequences of individual, selfish actions, whereas Dorr stressed conscious reverence for Popular Constituent Sovereignty and fully realized the need for political organization to uphold these salutary principles. Dorr's beliefs did retain a large measure of faith in the automatic operation of principles presumably imbedded in the American political system since 1776. This faith was to be sorely tried by the events of 1842.

which, once the citizens were sufficiently enlightened, would operate almost automatically. Dorr explained:

> When these principles [of Popular Constituent Sovereignty] are carefully guarded and maintained, and enter into the apprehension and imbue the sentiments of the community, the political state will not fail to conform . . . to the standard of equality and justice. The hand is withdrawn. Its use is suspended. The certainty that it exists, and can and will be used in the last resort, prevents the necessity of using it all all.[67]

Defending himself from charges of treason a year later, Dorr stated that although a majority of citizens could "intervene without forms" to change their political system at any time, "this is a work which can rarely be done."

> [C]onstitutions are made to last, and, like the planetary system, are set in motion, with inherent sustaining powers, which cannot often require the intervention of the hand that created them.[68]

It was the tenacious grasp on unjust power by the Charter authorities, Dorr reflected in 1843, that prompted the Invisible Hand to become manifest, when the people drafted and ratified "a republican constitution, which rightfully became the paramount and supreme law of the State." [69]

Ungenerous critics had already attacked the notion of the Invisible Hand as mere bluff raised to the level of political philosophy.[70] But these hostile critics were less than fair to the reformers who obviously were not consciously trying to carry on any deception. Dorr and his followers firmly believed in their doctrines, and if they deceived anyone by the notion that their

---

[67] Dorr, Address to the People of Rhode Island, August 1843, in *Burke's Report,* pp. 744–745.

[68] Dorr's argument at his 1844 treason trial, *ibid.,* p. 945.

[69] Dorr, Address to the People of Rhode Island, August 1843, *ibid.,* pp. 732, 736, 745.

[70] In his anonymous pamphlet *To the Members of the General Assembly,* John Pitman restated the principle of the Invisible Hand: "They [the radicals] only require that you should suffer them to put you down *peacably,* and then they will act as peaceable citizens;—otherwise you are to be charged with all their guilt, if you compel them to put you down by force."

victory could be gained without bitter conflict, it was themselves.

The Association's ideology not only harkened back to 1776 for its debilitating optimism,[71] but also looked toward the future, albeit with apprehension. If the people had to wait for official authorization before exercising their rightful sovereignty, then the "boast that American institutions differ in their basis from the monarchies of the old world" was, Dorr warned, "empty and fallacious." Denied the right "as a principle of government itself" to carry out constitutional change, the people would have "no remedy in the last resort but direct and *unauthorized* force for inveterate evils in the body politic." The consequence was in-evitable, Dorr believed: "Force will become the arbiter of right, as it now is in the countries of the old world." The Invisible Hand of Popular Constituent Sovereignty, as Association spokesmen saw matters, was "the true conservative element" in the American political system.[72]

Having convinced themselves, if no one else, that they were not radicals,[73] the reformers went on to attack "aristocracy" as the great danger of America's future. Such attacks had long been a standard feature of Rhode Island political rhetoric,[74] and the

---

[71] Karl Marx was thinking of the shortcomings of the French revolutionary tradition, not of American radicalism, when he wrote that "The tradition of all the dead generations weighs like a nightmare on the brain of the living. And just when they seem engaged in revolutionising themselves and things, in creating something entirely new, precisely in such epochs of revolutionary crisis they anxiously conjure up the spirits of the past to their service and borrow from them names, battle slogans and costumes in order to present the new scene of world history in . . . time-honoured disguise and . . . borrowed language." *The Eighteenth Brumaire of Louis Bonaparte* (New York: International Publishers, n.d.), p. 13. But Marx's observation applies with uncanny accuracy to the Rhode Island radicals of the 1840s. Cf. Aileen Kraditor, "Radical Historians."

[72] Dorr, Address to the People of Rhode Island, August 1843, in *Burke's Report,* pp. 743–744. It should be remembered that outside the United States democratic and republican doctrines and practices were still widely abhorred at the time.

[73] Actually, many historians have denied that the Dorrites were authentic radicals. For my criticism of this antiradical historiography, see the bibliographical essay, pp. 246 ff.

[74] See pp. 18–19; Marvin E. Gettleman and Noel P. Conlon, eds., "Responses to the Rhode Island Workingmen's Reform Agitation of 1833,"

term "aristocracy" had a variety of meanings. Most often it was used as a synonym for oligarchy, or minority rule; thus the *New Age* urged voters to reject the Landholders' Constitution and thus bring the "numbered hours of [the] Rhode Island aristocracy . . . to a close." [75] Dorr applied the term "aristocrat" to the person, rich or poor, desiring to possess or retain the political rights of others, such as the haughty Rhode Island freemen who refused for so long to share political power. He believed this concentrated political power would pose a great danger in the future, when "the relative decrease of the [rural] population," coupled with "increase of wealth and luxury" and "the growth of monopoly" would further concentrate political power in a new aristocracy in Rhode Island and elsewhere. Unless the power of the majority were augmented by victories for the principles of Popular Constituent Sovereignty, the liberties of all Americans would be threatened. [76]

Although there may have been a sound basis for some of these fears of aristocratic resurgence, [77] reform ideologists were unable to distill from their principles any realistic strategy that squarely faced the probability of armed conflict. Wrapping their measures in the sacred mantle of 1776, they mistakenly assumed that no sustained opposition could appear, since to disagree with them would be to repudiate the American Revolution and to embrace the decadent political outlook of monarchical Europe. Naïvely counting on their opponents to "cave in" rather than

---

Rhode Island History, XXVIII (August 1969), 75–94; Anne Mary Newton, "Rebellion in Rhode Island: The Story of the Dorr War" (M.A. Thesis, Columbia University, 1947), p. 2.

[75] *New Age,* March 18, 1842.

[76] Dorr, Address to the People of Rhode Island, August 1843, in *Burke's Report,* pp. 732, 745.

[77] See the description of the "aristocratic" tendencies in the Age of Jackson in Douglas T. Miller, *Jacksonian Aristocracy: Class and Democracy in New York, 1830–1860* (New York: Oxford University Press, 1967), and Edward Pessen, "The Egalitarian Myth and the American Social Reality: Wealth, Mobility and Equality in the 'Era of the Common Man,'" *American Historical Review,* LXXVI (October 1971), 989–1034, which neglects to deal with Rhode Island. Cf. Lee Benson, "Middle Period Historiography: What is to be Done," in George Athan Billias and Gerald N. Grob, eds., *American History: Retrospect and Prospect* (New York: Free Press, 1971), pp. 174–190.

put up any serious resistance to their measures,[78] the radicals neglected to prepare for the eventuality of intensified struggle. Also, seeking a political victory by exclusively political means, they never dealt directly with the social and economic grievances that rankled among the plebeians,[79] and therefore never aroused popular elements for protracted struggle. By projecting an easy, almost effortless victory, radical leaders helped ensure their eventual defeat.

IV

In the struggle over ratification of the Landholders' Constitution, Rhode Island conservatives demonstrated that a plausible and defensible counterideology could be derived from America's eighteenth-century revolutionary experience. Conservative lawyers and jurists responded to the radicals' ideological challenge by subjecting the doctrines of Popular Constituent Sovereignty to withering criticism and by striking at the philosophical assumptions underlying their opponents' measures.

Federal Judge John Pitman had laid down the broad outlines of the conservative argument in his January 1842 pamphlet, *To the Members of the General Assembly.*[80] In Pitman's view the People's Constitution had been "framed without law; put out to the people without law, [and] . . . voted upon, without law, by persons who in no legal sense are the people of this state." Thus radicals in the Rhode Island Suffrage Association were trying to bluff the state authorities into capitulating to a great show of popular force. Pitman ridiculed the notion that the broad mass of the populace could at pleasure change and revise the funda-

---

[78] Dorr's correspondence in the early spring of 1842 is full of expressions of naïve optimism. See, for examples, Dorr to Aaron White, Jr., April 4, 1842, Dorr Mss.; Dorr to [Duttee J. Pearce], March 23, 1842, Pearce Papers, Newport Historical Society.

[79] For expressions of these grievances, see pp. 19–21. Neither Dorr nor any of the middle- and upper-class radical spokesmen wove working-class ideas such as the communitarianism of Seth Luther into their major statements of suffrage principles. This led conservatives to believe that nothing but a visionary individualism, corrosive of all community ties, was behind the Association's efforts.

[80] See pp. 57–58, 175.

mental law. "In the original formation of society," he conceded, "every man may have an equal voice" in determining who should make the basic political decisions in a community. But once the choice has been made, "those who are excluded have no right to complain . . . , much less have they a right to force themselves on the body politic." Implying that there had been no dissolution of the social contract in 1776 to justify the making of a popular constitution, Pitman denied any need for basic political change.[81] Persons and property, he stated, were better protected in Rhode Island than in places like New York, where a wider suffrage obtained.

> [W]hat is complained of as a grievance may in truth, be a benefit. This often happens in regard to the government of God—what we deem a curse turns out a blessing—and it is often so in human governments.[82]

Only those who were already convinced were likely to accept this equating of political privilege with divine justice. The conservatives needed a more persuasive refutation of the *Nine Lawyers' Opinion* and radical ideological claims.

Job Durfee, Chief Justice of Rhode Island's Supreme Judicial Court, undertook the responsibility. The convening of a state grand jury in mid-March gave him the opportunity to frame the definitive reply to the adherents of free suffrage. Durfee's charge to the jury was also delivered widely throughout Rhode Island as a political speech in behalf of the Landholders' Constitution.[83] Apologizing for expressing partisan "feelings not usual to the bench," he explained that there were certain occasions when "humanity" could be excused "for raising [*sic*] above the petty

---

[81] Privately, however, Pitman admitted: "we shall have to give up our freehold qualification." See Pitman to Joseph Story, January 24, 1842, Pitman-Story Correspondence, William L. Clements Library, University of Michigan, Ann Arbor.

[82] [Pitman], *To the Members of the General Assembly*, pp. 4, 9–10, 14–15.

[83] For a frank admission of partisanship, see Durfee to Elisha R. Potter, Jr., March [14] 1842, Potter Collection, RIHSL. Unable to fathom the appeal of Durfee's arguments, Dorr dismissed the Chief Justice's "furioso-bombastical" advocacy of "ultra-slavish doctrines" as actually having converted people to the rebel side. See Dorr to Duttee J. Pearce, March 18, 1842, Pearce Papers, Newport Historical Society.

etiquette of official dignity." The revolutionary outburst in the state, he said, was one of these occasions, demanding of magistrates and all citizens the strongest and most energetic denunciation.[84]

Durfee's main task was to refute the radicals' interpretation of the American Revolution. Without minimizing the achievements of the Founding Fathers, he dismissed as "preposterous" the idea that there had been some kind of lapse into a state of nature in 1776, with sovereignty passing directly to the people. Rhode Island, he argued, had been a "corporate" entity long before the American Revolution, and her citizens had resisted the "aggressions and claims of the king of Great Britain . . . as a corporate people." Rhode Islanders in 1776 had not been a random, unordered collection of mere "individuals, isolated, independent and bound together by no common law, as the natural state supposes." If they had been, Durfee observed cleverly, they would have been incapable of collective action against England in association with twelve other corporate entities during the Revolution.[85]

Conservatives like Durfee framed the convincing argument that the American Revolution was so great an achievement, and the society it fostered so excellent, that no further need for revolutionary measures existed. This argument required a stress on the purely anticolonial aspects of the Revolution and a minimization of the domestic struggles in the states.[86] Accordingly, Durfee distinguished the American war for independence, a mere contest "between the colonies and the mother country," from an event such as the French Revolution, which released all the low and brutal passions of Man. He predicted that the Association's sinister program would have the latter results, the

---

[84] *Charge of the Hon. Chief Justice Durfee, Delivered to the Grand Jury at the March Term of the Supreme Judicial Court, at Bristol, Rhode-Island . . .* (n.p., [March 1842]), p. 15.

[85] *Ibid.,* pp. 4–6.

[86] In Rhode Island there was indeed little struggle over "who would rule at home" during the Independence movement (even though the legislature had to depose Tory Governor Joseph Wanton in May 1776). See Allan Nevins, *The American States During and After the Revolution, 1775–1789* (New York: Augustus M. Kelley, 1969), pp. 46–47, 79–80; Lovejoy, *Rhode Island Politics and the American Revolution, passim.*

prospect of which should, he said, send a thrill of terror "through the heart of every man, woman and child in this State." Departing from argument for theatrics, he deigned to "whisper a few questions" to his audience about the abundance of "combustible material in this wide-spread union." He invoked folk beliefs about "certain birds of the air, and beasts of the desert, who are endowed with something like a prescience or foreknowledge of the coming banquet which human strife is to provide." He held out the prospect of untold horrors should the human counterparts of these creatures descend upon Rhode Island, as they were sure to do if the radicals had their way. Durfee called upon the "sainted spirits" of the Founding Fathers to join sensible Rhode Islanders "in a prayer to the Almighty Father of all spirits" to save the state from its current revolutionary delusions.[87]

The Chief Justice, expressing a major theme of antebellum conservatism, also directly attacked the radical individualism of the suffrage movement as distorting the true nature of political institutions.[88] To Durfee the state was a continuous entity,

> a legally organized people, subsisting as such from generation to generation, without end, giving through forms of law, the wills of the many, to become one sovereign will. [The state] . . . is a body politic, qualified to subsist by perpetual succession and accession. It is a self-subsistent corporation resting upon its own centre.

Willfully ignoring these weighty and profound truths, the Rhode Island rebels, Durfee said, succumbed to the "strange infatuation" of visionary theories about creating new constitutions and new political communities by whim and will.[89]

Central to Durfee's appeal was the idea that there was no grievance great enough in Rhode Island to justify the radicals'

---

[87] *Charge of Durfee,* pp. 4–6, 13–15.

[88] In his *Inner Civil War: Northern Intellectuals and the Crisis of the Union* (New York: Harper Torchbooks, 1968), Chap. 2, George M. Fredrickson shows how some New England antebellum conservatives developed an elitist "doctrine of corporate authority" in response to what they believed were the anti-institutional beliefs of reformers in the era. Durfee's attacks on the reformist ideology is another example of this antebellum intellectual dispute. But see pp. 20 n, 73 n.

[89] *Charge of Durfee,* pp. 13–15.

agitations. Their demand for an enlarged electorate and equality of representation was "the merest trifle compared with the calamities through which we must pass, in order to redress it in the mode which this movement has proposed." He challenged them where their ideology was most ambiguous and vulnerable—on the question of whether force would be necessary to achieve their ends. For Durfee shrewdly perceived that their disavowals of revolutionary intent contained a hidden premise: that the Charter Government would simply fade away at some appropriate time. He pressed the radicals to declare themselves on precisely the point they had not thought through. Were they prepared to use force and violence if the Charter Government (or its successor regime, should the Landholders' Constitution be ratified) refused to capitulate? Mercilessly exposing the fallacy of the Invisible Hand, Durfee warned that they would not be permitted to enjoy the fruits of revolution without having to suffer its "calamitous consequences." Revolution may be called for, he conceded, "where a people, by the oppression and violence of their rulers, are thrown back upon the natural right of self preservation. . . ." Addressing himself particularly to "those gentlemen who have engaged in this [radical] movement—for many of whom a personal acquaintance enables us to cherish sincere respect and esteem," he inquired whether they really intended to continue on what was clearly the road to revolutionary conflict. "[And] . . . for what? can any one tell us?" [90] Questions like these would soon occur to many within the Association, especially to that class of "gentlemen" likely to have the acquaintance of the Chief Justice.

The ideological debate in the spring of 1842 was not simply an interchange between radical lawyers (or lawyers who gave expression to radical ideas) and conservative jurists. It raged through every level of Rhode Island society, and it took the form of fiery newspaper editorials,[91] bitter personal disputes and even religious quarrels.[92] At stake were rival constitutions,

---

[90] *Ibid.*, pp. 14–16 and *passim.*

[91] Compare, for example, the conservative *Providence Journal*, March 15, 1842 with the pro-suffrage *Providence Express*, March 18, 1842.

[92] On the personal disputes that rent families in 1842, see Catherine R. Williams, "Recollections of the Life and Conversation of Thomas W.

competing political fortunes and clashing political philosophies. To the radicals, a victory for the principles of Popular Constituent Sovereignty would purify the state and elevate American politics generally. Some may have been believed that a democratic social and economic transformation would result. For the conservatives, social stability and tradition seemed to hinge on the Landholders' Constitution. The immediate fruit of this stirring political dispute was a vast outpouring of votes for and against ratification, exceeding the previously unprecedented total cast for the People's Constitution three months earlier.

V

The radicals, knowing that Rhode Island's elite—"the money-power . . . , the lawyers, the clergy"—were against them,[93] were nonetheless confident of victory at the polls. "We shall drub the tories soundly," Dorr wrote to one of his associates a few days before the ratification election.[94] In deciding to waive the landholding qualification for voting, the Charter authorities had placed a potent weapon in the hands of their opponents.[95]

Dorr, First Governor of Rhode Island Under the People's Constitution" (unpublished draft, n.d.), Dorr MSS., p. 32. For disputes among Baptists over whether church members could advocate suffrage measures, see Elias Smith, "The Civil War in Rhode-Island," *Liberator,* July 22, 1842, p. 115; *New Age,* September 23, 1842; J. G. Sherman to E[lisha] R. Potter [Jr.], December 18, 1842, Potter Collection, RIHSL.

[93] Dorr to Duttee J. Pearce, March 18, 1842, Pearce Papers, Newport Historical Society. An electoral broadside, *Circular* (n.p., [March 1842]), WLHU, listed the names of distinguished Rhode Islanders, including former governors James Fenner, John Brown Francis and William C. Gibbs, who urged their fellow citizens to beat back the radical threat to peace and legality by voting against the People's Constitution. Leading merchants such as Edward Carrington, Isaac Brown and Moses Brown Ives also supported the appeal. This elite was soon to become the core of the conservative Law and Order Party in Rhode Island.

[94] Dorr to Duttee J. Pearce, March 18, 1842, Pearce Papers, Newport Historical Society.

[95] With their own frame of government already ratified, leaders of the suffrage movement hoped that defeat of the Landholders' Constitution would facilitate acceptance of the People's Constitution. Therefore they did not call for a boycott of the March 1842 ratifying election. This

Many enemies of the Landholders' Constitution could thus cast ballots against it. Staunch upholders of the Charter of 1663, who opposed any change whatever, also voted against ratification,[96] although it is impossible to discover what proportion of the negative vote these ultraconservatives cast. The Landholders' Constitution was defeated by the narrow margin of 676 votes out of a total of 16,702 ballots cast.[97] Advocates of suffrage reform

> rejoice[d] in that defeat the more because it was effected by an orderly exercise of the right of suffrage, against the tremendous influence of wealth, talent, official dignity and judicial authority all combined, and exerting their utmost energy against [them].

For the Rhode Island Association, the balloting in March was a triumph of the true "sovereignty of the people" over the spurious "sovereignty of corporations." [98]

The reformers' pleasure over the outcome of the election was qualified by a decline in their own electoral strength since the December 1841 voting for the People's Constitution and by the consequent rise of a numerous and distinguished conservative opposition. Twenty percent fewer eligible voters had cast ballots against the Landholders' Constitution than had voted to ratify the People's Constitution, with the falling off about the same in the industrial as the agricultural towns.[99] The total suffrage vote was down by approximately five thousand after three months of bitter political struggle.[100] Evidently increasing numbers of

---

tactical decision seemed to have been obvious to them, since there is no record of any internal debate or discussion on the matter.

[96] John Brown Francis to Elisha R. Potter, Jr., M[arch] 12, 1842, Potter Collection, RIHSL; John Pitman to Joseph Story, March 30, 1842, Pitman-Story Correspondence, William L. Clements Library, University of Michigan, Ann Arbor; Mowry, *Dorr War,* p. 124.

[97] The vote was 8,689 opposed to 8,013 in favor of the Landholders' Constitution. See *Burke's Report,* pp. 105–106; Appendix B.

[98] Resolutions of a Providence Suffrage Association meeting, March 25, 1842 in *Providence Express,* March 29, 1842.

[99] See Table V, p. 88.

[100] The voting frequencies are given in Appendix B.

Rhode Islanders had come to believe that the Charter Government would offer reasonable concessions and that the Association was drifting into unwarranted radicalism. By the spring of 1842 an automatic triumph of Popular Constituent Sovereignty began to appear less and less likely.

4

The Drift Toward
Radicalism
Spring 1842

I

During the struggle over the Landholders' Constitution two opposing political groups took shape. One of these, the Rhode Island Suffrage Association, had assumed by the early spring of 1842 many of the characteristics of a political party. It had developed and propagated what anguished conservatives perceived as a revolutionary ideology. Its own internal structure had coalesced, its State Central Committee had been in operation for almost a year, and Thomas Dorr had begun to emerge as the party's leader.[1] His efforts in drafting and managing the ratification of the People's Constitution had made him the chief

[1] On the characteristics and functions of American political parties, see William Nisbet Chambers, *Political Parties in a New Nation: The American Experience, 1776–1809* (New York: Oxford University Press, 1963), Chap. 5; Paul Goodman, "The First American Party System," in Chambers and Walter Dean Burnham, eds., *The American Party Systems: Stages of Political Development* (New York: Oxford University Press, 1967), esp. pp. 60, 72–73. Robert A. Dahl, "The American Oppositions: Affirmation and Denial" in Dahl, ed., *Political Oppositions in Western Democracies* (New Haven: Yale University Press, 1966), pp. 34–69, and Richard Hofstadter, *The Idea of a Party System: The Rise of Legitimate*

advocate of the political transformation of Rhode Island. Appreciative supporters conferred on Dorr the "Title of the Political *Mentor* of the Suffrage Party." [2] Meanwhile, the opponents of this radical party had begun to shake off their lethargy and organize themselves in a conservative coalition, the Law and Order Party. In defending established authority from the radical threat, the Law and Order Party was virtually coextensive with the Charter Government in Rhode Island.[3] Far from viewing each other with equanimity as legitimate rivals for power, the Suffrage Party and the Law and Order Party, having advanced irreconcilable claims, were on a collision course. Some contemporaries had a vivid perception of the confrontation looming. Wrote a contributor to the *New Age:*

> This was a controversy of no ordinary kind. It was not between rival candidates, or parties in ordinary political warfare, but between two opposing principles—that of *Popular Sovereignty,* on the one hand, and of *Aristocracy* on the other. It was a contest for right—the right of the people to make and establish a government for themselves—against the claim of a few arrogant dictators, to set up a government for *themselves,* and for their own special purposes, at war with the opinions, the feelings and the interests of the common People of this State.[4]

The first logical step for the Suffrage Party after the defeat of the Landholders' Constitution was to arrange for the election of a new government to replace the Charter regime.[5] According to the People's Constitution, April 18 would be the day for this election. The task of nominating candidates fell to

Opposition in the United States, 1780–1840 (Berkeley: University of California Press, 1970), show how political parties blunt radicalism and how they positively revel in the fact. Rhode Island in the era of the Dorr Rebellion provides a unique opportunity to study the interaction of radicalism and party development, which appears in that context more complicated than recent writers have supposed.

[2] The accolade is found in a letter from Suffrage Party men in North Scituate, Alexander Allen, Harley Luther, Simon Mathewson to Dorr, February 22, 1842, Dorr MSS.

[3] See pp. 89–98 for Law and Order strategy.

[4] *New Age,* March 23, 1842.

[5] *Ibid.,* April 14, 1842. The feverish preelectoral activity of the early spring belies Anne Mary Newton's judgment that the period was a

a committee of the People's Convention. As an active member of this committee, Dorr worked hard to obtain agreement from leading men in the state to run for office. This was not an easy task; prominent Suffragists and others scrambled to escape the responsibilities of leadership. Two of the Nine Lawyers declined to run for Governor.[6] Only after ardent pleading was Dorr able to convince Wager Weeden, a Whig judge from South Kingston, to head the Suffrage Party ticket, which also included William C. Barker, a Providence merchant, as candidate for Lieutenant Governor; Walter S. Burges and John P. Knowles, two of the Nine Lawyers, for Secretary of State and Attorney General, respectively; and John Sterne, a Newport Whig, for State Treasurer.[7] In the towns, nearly one hundred men, mostly country lawyers, tradesmen or merchants, stood for election to the People's Legislature.[8]

"blank" in the reform struggle. Cf. her "Rebellion in Rhode Island: The Story of the Dorr War" (M.A. Thesis, Columbia University, 1947), p. 68.

[6] These were two Providence attorneys, Walter S. Burges and Thomas F. Carpenter.

[7] Wager Weeden to Dorr (February 17), Dorr to Weeden, (February 19 [draft], Weeden to Dorr (February 19), E. D. Campbell to Dorr (Febuary 18), Dorr MSS.; Arthur May Mowry, *The Dorr War: Or, The Constitutional Struggle in Rhode Island* (Providence: Preston and Rounds, 1901), pp. 134–135. From an old Providence family, Barker was listed as a merchant-tailor in the *Providence City Directory* (Providence, 1841), p. 24. He later enjoyed federal patronage as a customs official through his connection with Dorr. He served in the Landholders' Constitutional Convention. See *Providence Journal,* August 27, 1841; Charles Carroll, *Rhode Island: Three Centuries of Democracy,* 4 vols. (New York: Lewis Historical Publishing Co., 1932), IV, 542. The *Providence Journal* in mid-March charged that Barker had abandoned the Suffragist cause. For his indignant denial, see *New Age,* March 19, 1842. Barker, along with all these other candidates for major office under the Suffrage Party, did later withdraw his candidacy. Walter S. Burges, Dorr's closest associate throughout the upheaval in Rhode Island, was also a former Whig who switched, but he was a somewhat wavering supporter of the Suffragist cause. After graduating from Brown University and beginning his law practice, Burges married a daughter of Senator James Burrill. Appointed United States District Attorney by President Polk in 1845, Burges later served as Associate Justice of the Rhode Island Supreme Court. See Carroll, *Rhode Island,* IV, 134; Richard M. Bayles and others, *History of Providence County,* 2 vols. (New York: W. W. Preston, 1891),

Dorr was not at first a candidate for any post under the People's Constitution. In early April he drafted a letter to fellow members of the state nominations committee, declaring his intention to avoid the responsibilities of an officeholder. But Dorr nevertheless reiterated his devotion to Suffrage Party principles and voiced his abhorrence of the arrogant minority in Rhode Island that "had refused Time and again to divide their power with non-freeholders and thereby reconcile the practice of the government [of this state] to the first and plainest notions of a free republic." Recent threats by the Charter Government to arrest anyone who ran for office in the forthcoming unauthorized election made it clear to Dorr that "sacrifices . . . of a most terrific character" would have to be made if the people's cause were to be kept alive.[9] By the end of this letter (which was apparently never sent) Dorr may have convinced himself of the necessity of what he had denied at its beginning—namely, that he would stand as a candidate. When Wager Weeden and all the other Suffrage Party candidates for major office withdrew in face of government threats,[10] Dorr decided to take the risks others shrank from.

A scant week before the election Dorr's name stood at the head of a revised "People's Constitutional and State Rights" ticket. The slate also included Amasa Eddy of Glocester, a staunch and determined Suffragist militant, as candidate for Lieutenant Governor; [11] William H. Smith, a Woonsocket at-

---

I, 53. Knowles also graduated from Brown; he went on to study law at Harvard. In 1869 Knowles became federal district judge for Rhode Island. See *Representative Men and Old Families of Rhode Island,* 3 vols. (Chicago: Beers, 1908), I, 356. Sterne was earlier considered as a candidate deserving of Constitutional Party support. See Asahel Johnson to Dorr, March 24, 1837, Dorr MSS.

[8] See Table IV, p. 85, for data on the social composition of the Suffrage Party and its leading men.

[9] Dorr to "Gentlemen of the State [Suffrage Party] Nominating Committee," April 2, 1842 (draft), Dorr MSS.

[10] See pp. 89–98.

[11] See *New Age,* April 8, 12, 1842; *Chepachet Memorial* (n.p., September 28, 1844), Broadside Collection, John Hay Library, Brown University. See Plate 4.

TABLE IV   OCCUPATIONAL PROFILE OF THE
RHODE ISLAND SUFFRAGE ASSOCIATION,
1842 *

Lawyers	9	Stonecutters	1
Tailors	3	Watchmakers	1
Grocers	3	Silversmiths	1
Jewelers	2	Auctioneers	1
Carpenters	2	Brewers	1
Mechanics	2	Manufacturers	1
Merchants	2	Ministers	1
Cordwainers	2	Teamsters	1
Factory directors	2	Storekeepers	1
Textile workers	2	Physicians	1
Farmers	2	Tavernkeepers	1
Blacksmiths	1		

* Sources: *Providence Directory, 1841* (Providence, 1841), *passim; Burke's Report, passim;* "Records of the Commissioners Appointed by the General Assembly of Rhode Island in June, 1842, to Examine the Prisoners Arrested During the Late Rebellion" (MSS., Providence, 1842), in John Hay Library, Brown University; J. R. Cole, ed., *History of Washington and Kent Counties, Rhode Island* (New York: W. W. Preston, 1889), *passim; Biographic Encyclopedia of Representative Men of Rhode Island* (Providence: National Biographic Publishing Co., 1881), *passim;* Dorr MSS., *passim.* I have chosen for inclusion in this table only those Suffragists who played some leadership role in the Association. There is only minimal overlap with Table VI, p. 120 (Dorr; Otis Holmes, brewer; Charles W. Carpenter, blacksmith). I was unable to find a complete list of members of the People's Legislature, let alone occupational or social data on this group.

torney and former clerk of the Rhode Island Supreme Court, for Secretary of State; [12] Joseph Joslin, a minor Newport lawyer, for State Treasurer; [13] and Jonah Titus, a reformist attorney from Scituate, for Attorney General.[14]

---

[12] See Papers of William H. Smith, Dorr MSS.; *Docket of the Court of Common Pleas for the County of Providence, December Term, A.D. 1841* (Providence: B. Cranston, 1841), p. [3], copy in RIHSL; Smith to Dorr, September 3, 1842, Dorr MSS.

[13] See John Brown Francis to Elisha R. Potter, Jr., December 20, 1842, Potter Collection, RIHSL; Joseph Joslin to Governor [Samuel Ward] King, March 3, 1843, Dorr MSS.

[14] See Charles Randall to Dorr, May 8, 1837, Dorr MSS.; *Docket of*

A few days before this ticket appeared publicly, Dorr's parents got advance news of it,[15] and they were aghast. Pleading with their son to retire before he became engulfed in political crimes that would bring "disgrace and ruin," they wrote:

> If your heart is sensible to parental anguish you will renounce your present course and restore us to a peace of mind which has for a long time been a stranger to us.
> May God in his infinite mercy prompt you to a decision which can only restore you to the good opinion of your friends and fellow citizens whose esteem is worth the cultivation, and will preserve our grey heads from that shame and disgrace which will attend us if you persist, and which will hurry us sorrowing to the grave.
>
> Your affectionate parents
and best friends
Sullivan Dorr
Lydia Dorr [16]

But Dorr, aware that withdrawal at this time would expose him to charges of cowardice and to ridicule, would not submit to parental entreaty. Himself a champion of political rights for mechanics and other common folk, Dorr could hardly endorse the patrician contempt for the Suffrage Party and its membership that was expressed in his parents' letter. In the crusade for popular rights he seemed to have found the purpose in life he had been seeking for the last decade.

On election day there was no candidate to oppose Dorr or any of the other candidates under the People's Constitution. Conservatives tried to dissuade Rhode Islanders from balloting by circulating what the *New Age* called "aristocratic hand-

---

the *Providence Court of Common Pleas* . . . , *1841,* p. [3]; Jonah Titus, *Sensible Conclusion* (Scituate, April 15, 1842), Broadside Collection, John Hay Library, Brown University; Abraham Payne, *Reminiscences of the Rhode Island Bar* (Providence: Tibbits & Preston, 1885), p. 41.

[15] Dorr lived at home until early April. Then, perhaps because of political conflicts within the Sullivan Dorr household, he took up residence at the Franklin House in Providence. See W[ilkins] Updike to Elisha R. Potter, Jr., April 6, 1842, Potter Collection, RIHSL.

[16] Sullivan and Lydia Dorr to Thomas Dorr, April 8, 1842, Dorr MSS.

bills." [17] Whether because of this Law and Order pressure, bad weather on April 18,[18] the absence of competition, or a falling off of reformist enthusiasm after the ratification of the People's Constitution three and a half months earlier, the overall vote for the Suffrage Party was about 6,400, less than half of what it had been in December.[19] This was a less spectacular decline in Dorrite support when compared with the March balloting on the Landholders' Constitution, although the latter comparison is somewhat complicated by the fact that not all opposition to that constitution arose from Dorrite commitment.[20] Table V shows that rebel strength fell off most precipitously in the agricultural regions of the southern part of the state, while the northern towns remained the more solid centers of rebel sentiment. Commenting derisively on the April votes, conservatives noted a "wonderful falling off" of radicalism in the state.[21] But Governor-elect Dorr and many others in the Suffrage Party did not seem discouraged by the results of the canvass and continued to uphold their cause.

By mid-April 1842 the Suffrage Party was at a crossroads. In over a year of active organizing and propagandizing the Suffragists had become a major political force in Rhode Island, challenging the traditional party structure. Compared with the

---

[17] *New Age,* April 19, 1842. Probably the Suffrage Party organ was referring to the Broadside Proclamation of April 14, containing a letter from President Tyler purporting to support the established government of Rhode Island (copy in WLHU). For the campaign to win the support of the President and other Washington officials, see pp. 98 ff.

[18] *Providence Express,* April 22, 1842.

[19] For the voting returns, see *Burke's Report,* pp. 452–453. Dorr received 6,359 votes, although 6,457 Rhode Islanders cast ballots for Senatorial candidates (no list of voting returns is available for members of the People's Legislature's lower house).

[20] For the March vote, in which the Landholders' Constitution failed of ratification, see pp. 78–80. I have found no way to estimate how many of the 8,689 negative votes in March were cast by supporters of the People's Constitution and how many by upholders of the Charter of 1663.

[21] Newport *Herald of the Times,* April 21, 1842; *Providence Journal,* April 21, 1842; *The Mountain Labored and Brought Forth a Mouse* (Providence, April 19, 1842), Broadside Collection, John Hay Library, Brown University.

TABLE V   PROPORTIONS OF ELIGIBLE
ELECTORATE CASTING BALLOTS, 1841–1842 *

	Ratification of People's Constitution, December 1841	Votes Against Landholders' Constitution, March 1842	Votes for Dorrite Senators, April 1842
Senate districts 1–6 (Industrial towns)	64%	45%	36%
Senate districts 7–12 (Agricultural towns)	41%	21%	11%
Totals	55%	34%	25%

* Source: voting frequencies in Appendix B.

ill-fated efforts of the Constitutionalists of the mid-1830s, or even the Anti-Masons in Rhode Island,[22] the Suffrage Party had achieved spectacular success. But so far this success had been won outside the authorized and legitimate political process. The Suffrage Party could not continue much further on this path without coming into conflict with state and perhaps even federal

---

[22] Anti-Masonry was a burning political issue in the early 1830s in Rhode Island, which vexed and frustrated Whig politicians who were unable to comprehend the "witchery" of the movement or to conceive of what was to be done with "that miserable affair called antimasonry." N[athan] Dixon to James F. Simmons, March 3, 1831, Simmons Papers, LC. Rhode Island Democrats, however, were able to use anti-Masonry more successfully as a means to bring Democratic politicians into office without requiring voters to endorse the "hated Jackson" party. John Brown Francis to Elisha R. Potter, Jr., January 4, 1843, Potter Collection, RIHSL. The conjunction of anti-Masonry and Democracy in Rhode Island, as well as elsewhere in New England, casts some doubt on the significance of Lee Benson's "test case," in which he finds an anti-Mason–Whig connection in New York State. See Benson, *The Concept of Jacksonian Democracy: New York as a Test Case* (New York: Atheneum, 1964), Chap. 2. There is no adequate account of Rhode Island anti-Masonry, although some

authorities, in which event it would have to shift its tactics, shedding some of its mock legalism and becoming more openly and explicitly radical. Although this impending change was implicit in Suffrage Party ideology, much also depended upon the actions of the Law and Order antagonists who in the spring of 1842 had shaken off their initial lethargy and begun to move decisively.

II

Closely watching and reacting to each other, the Suffrage and Law and Order parties drifted closer to collision in April. The protracted interaction of these contending groups, extending over several months before armed conflict erupted, reenforced mutual bitterness and hostility. Law and Order members' denunciations of their opponents' radical and revolutionary measures incensed Suffrage adherents, who leaped to increasingly angry and militant defense of their party. Incredulous at first that there could be any quarrel with their literal interpretation of the Declaration of Independence, the radicals began to be aware that conservative opposition would not be silenced by pious invocations of the spirit of 1776. The Invisible Hand alone would not be effective, and a reform party nourishing a latent radical ideology began to transform itself into something more closely approximating the image held by its opponents.[23]

discussion of the subject may be found in Edward Field, *State of Rhode Island and Providence Plantations at the End of the* [Nineteenth] *Century: A History,* 3 vols. (Boston and Syracuse: Mason Publishing Co., 1902), I, 318–329, III, 508–515 and in Peter J. Coleman, *The Transformation of Rhode Island, 1790–1860* (Providence: Brown University Press, 1963), pp. 246 ff. The Simmons Papers, LC, are a rich source for study of the political impact of anti-Masonry in Rhode Island.

[23] This hypothesis of a dynamic interaction between the parties in the insurrectionary confrontation, according to which each began to conform to the worst image held by the other, derives from the insights of Charles Horton Cooley and Robert Merton, who conceive of the development of the self as a process of responding to images held by significant others, as in a looking glass. See Cooley, *Human Nature and the Social Order* (Glencoe, Ill.: The Free Press, 1964), pp. 183–184. Merton generalizes this concept more widely in his celebrated essay "The Self-Con-

In early April, a few weeks before the election of Dorr as Governor, the Law and Order Party also went beyond propaganda appeals, broadsides, and theoretical arguments to fashion more potent weapons for the impending struggle. The General Assembly, again brushing aside reformist proposals from Samuel Y. Atwell,[24] passed an "Act in Relation to Offenses Against the Sovereign Power of the State," directed against "certain designing persons . . . now endeavoring to carry through a plan for the subversion of our government." Though carried out "under assumed forms of law," Suffrage Party measures—framing an illegal constitution and attempting to bring a government into being—were said to have violated "the first principles of constitutional right." Dominated by the Law and Order members, the legislature decreed harsh penalties for those who persisted in upholding these measures. Clerks, wardens or moderators who presided at meetings to elect officers under the People's Constitution would risk stiff fines and six months' imprisonment. Anyone presuming to run for unauthorized office was subject to heavier fines and longer imprisonment, and those who actually dared to exercise such office were deemed guilty of treason and could be jailed for life. The State Supreme Court, consisting exclusively of Law and Order judges, had sole jurisdiction over cases arising under this law. Furthermore, although jury trial was provided for, these cases were not required to be tried in the county where the allegedly criminal acts occurred—

---

firming Prophecy," *Social Theory and Social Structure* (Glencoe, Ill.: The Free Press, 1949), pp. 421–436. By means of this concept of how members of a group respond to the conceptions of themselves held by others (especially those others with whom they are locked in conflict), we can understand the emergence of radicalism in formerly nonradical groups. This process of radical self-definition was no mere instantaneous adoption of the label "radical" by Suffragist reformers; it resulted from the extended and intense interaction narrated in previous chapters. Of course, not all members of the predominantly reformist early Suffrage Party went along with the new radical phase. For a discussion of defectors, see pp. 92–93 and Chapter 5.

[24] Atwell had again proposed that the General Assembly authorize the People's Constitution, but his efforts in the spring to head off conflict between the Suffrage Party and the government by means of the latter's concessions was no more successful than his earlier attempts. See *New Age*, April 1, 5, 1842. Cf. pp. 42, 50, 58; Mowry, *Dorr War*, pp. 131–133.

a provision that radicals suspected was included to ensure pliant juries willing to convict.[25] Suffragists promptly dubbed this act the "Algerine Law," so as to associate it with a notorious contemporary tyrant, the Dey of Algiers.[26]

Suffrage Party members publicly responded to the Algerine Law with a blithe insouciance that barely concealed their apprehension. Suffragist orators and newspapers attacked the law as the futile "expiring throes" of the Charter Government. "It is an exhibition of impotent wrath, signifying nothing," concluded the *New Age*.[27] In the northern village of Chepachet, later the scene of a rebel military encampment, the radicals ridiculed the authorities for passing "such a foolhardy act," and pledged to maintain the sovereignty of the people "till the strong arm of superior force" compelled them to yield.[28] A Suffrage Party meeting at the Providence Town House received the news about the Algerine Law with "much mirth." Dorr struck a more somber note of concern, characterizing the law as "a daring assumption of despotic power," a transparent "device to overawe and intimidate the People." But even he merely urged that Suffragists disregard the law and proceed to elect a strong ticket at the April 18 elections.[29] Excited knots of Suffragist militants, gathering in the squares of towns and villages to plan their opposition to the Algerine Law, consciously acted as their ancestors had in opposing British tyranny more than half a century earlier.[30] Who would dare to enforce the repressive law? the radicals asked defiantly. Let the militia officers muster "their several regiments and brigades, and order them to fire on their unarmed fellow citizens, their neighbors, their friends." The vote-

---

[25] *Ibid.*, p. 133. For the text of this act, see *Burke's Report*, pp. 133–135.

[26] *Providence Express*, April 5, 1842, quoted in Mowry, *Dorr War*, p. 134. Even conservatives accepted the name "Algerine Law." See Jacob Frieze, *Concise History of the Efforts to Obtain an Extension of Suffrage in Rhode Island From the Year 1811 to 1842* (Providence: B. Moore, 1842), p. 63.

[27] *New Age*, April 5, 1842.

[28] *Ibid.*, April 8, 1842.

[29] *Ibid.*, April 5, 1842; Dorr, notes for a speech in early April 1842, Dorr MSS.

[30] *New Age*, April 8, 1842; Boston *Bay State Democrat*, April 15, 1842.

less common folk who made up the bulk of the militia would surely refuse. The *New Age* predicted:

> they would turn on their blood thirsty commander, and tell him it was their duty to protect, not to destroy the persons of their fellow citizens [as] it was their duty to protect their rights as men not to prostrate them at the foot of military power.[31]

As one segment of the Suffrage Party responded to Law and Order menacing with revolutionary fervor, another promptly collapsed. As previously noted, all candidates for major office resigned rather than risk prosecution under the Algerine Law. Except for Dorr, the Nine Lawyers, who in March had written bravely of the right of the people to frame constitutions, were unwilling to uphold the People's Constitution a few weeks later. Even Samuel Y. Atwell, the Suffrage Party's gadfly in the General Assembly, dissociated himself from the radical cause after passage of the Algerine Law.[32] The precise social composition of this defecting group is impossible to assess, but contemporaries believed that the more wealthy and respectable professional and mercantile elements, wary of hazarding career and fortune, tended to split off from the Suffrage Party in April.[33]

---

[31] *New Age,* April 8, 1842.

[32] Atwell's defection was, according to one Dorrite chronicler, the "first direct blow that the Suffrage Party received." [Frances H. (Whipple) McDougall], *Might and Right by a Rhode Islander,* 2nd ed. (Providence: A. H. Stillwell, 1844), p. 183. See also *New Age,* April 19, 29, 1842; Walter Simmons to James F. Simmons, April 2, 1842, Simmons Papers, LC. Cf. Mowry, *Dorr War,* p. 118. Atwell regretted and retracted his disavowal of Suffrage Party measures (*New Age,* April 26, 1842), but not before they had a deleterious impact on the April 18 elections.

[33] On the class factors in the defections, see Catherine R. Williams, "Recollections of the Life and Conversation of Thomas W. Dorr, First Governor of Rhode Island Under the People's Constitution" (unpublished draft, n.d., Dorr MSS.), p. 39; Frieze, *Concise History,* pp. 61–63, 125; [McDougall], *Might and Right,* pp. 183–184, 231; [Francis C. Treadwell], *The Conspiracy to Defeat the Liberation of Gov. Dorr; Or, The Hunkers and Algerines Unveiled; To Which is Added, a Report on the Case Ex Parte Dorr . . .* (New York: John Windt, 1845), p. 4; Dan King, *The Life and Times of Thomas Wilson Dorr, With Outlines of the Political History of Rhode Island* (Boston: published by the author,

Those remaining were for many reasons more determined to uphold the People's Constitution; Dorr mainly because of his tenacious belief in the movement's democratic ideology and others, of more humble origins, because of their hope for a vague adjustment and equalization of conditions in Rhode Island under the People's Constitution.[34] Thus the effect of the Algerine Law was to drive moderates out of the Suffrage Party and give it a more radical cast.

The Law and Order authorities, unwilling to rely simply on the Algerine Law, called on the Federal Government for assistance in putting down the radicals. The impetus for this appeal apparently came from John Pitman, who had been one of the first conservatives to take alarm over the radical threat in January. A few days after the defeat of the Landholders' Constitution Judge Pitman sent a letter to Joseph Story, United States Supreme Court justice, calling upon him to bring the Rhode Island question to the attention of Secretary of State Daniel Webster. Prompt action by the Federal Government would "open [the] eyes of the deluded among us," Pitman stated, and such action should not wait until violence had actually broken out.[35] Less than a week after Pitman's letter, Samuel

---

1859), p. 288; Payne, *Reminiscences of the Rhode Island Bar,* p. 274; Almon D. Hodges, Jr., ed., *Almon Danforth Hodges and his Neighbors: An Autobiographical Sketch of a Typical Old New Englander* (Boston: privately printed, 1909), p. 178. Cf. Lamar Middleton, *Revolt U.S.A.* (New York: Stackpole Sons, 1938), p. 17; Joseph Brennan, *Social Conditions in Industrial Rhode Island, 1820–1860* (Washington, D.C.: Catholic University of America Press, 1940), pp. 170–171; Newton, "Rebellion in Rhode Island," p. 71.

34 See the reminiscences of Charles W. Trescott of Providence, a journeyman shoemaker in 1842, in Rhode Island Historical Society Scrapbook, Vol. 7 (1903), p. 113. Law and Order stalwart William G. Goddard (writing under the pesudonym "Town Born" in the *Providence Journal,* September 21, 1842) referred sarcastically to the shoemakers and house carpenters among the Suffrage Party who propagandized extravagantly about democratic rights. See also William M. Bailey to his mother, June 14, 1842 (copy), Dorr MSS.

35 Pitman to Story, March 30, 1842, Pitman-Story Correspondence, William L. Clements Library, University of Michigan, Ann Arbor. Pitman's opinion that the federal power should act in Rhode Island was the reverse of his view expressed in the anonymous pamphlet *To the Mem-*

Ward King, Charter Governor of Rhode Island, formally requested military aid from the Federal Government under the clause in the United States Constitution guaranteeing each state protection "against domestic Violence." Like Pitman, King called for preventive federal action, lest the insurrection in Rhode Island get out of hand.[36] To impress upon President John Tyler the need for immediate action, King dispatched three leading Law and Order men to Washington: John Brown Francis, Elisha R. Potter, Jr., and John Whipple.[37]

---

bers of the General Assembly of Rhode Island (Providence: Knowles and Vose, [January] 1842), p. 24, where he stated that the issues raised by the Dorrites should be resolved in Rhode Island without interference by the government in Washington. Story did write Webster within the month urging anticipatory action. Story to Webster, April 26, 1842, Webster Papers, New Hampshire Historical Society.

[36] Samuel Ward King to the President of the United States, two letters of April 4, 1842, in Burke's Report, pp. 656–657. Mowry's treatment of this episode (Dorr War, pp. 140–142) is biased and inaccurate. Using evidence of hostile witnesses who testified later in the month to the radicals' allegedly warlike intentions, Mowry attempts to show that the Suffrage Party was actively plotting armed insurrection early in April. Aside from the suspect evidence, this judgment makes no sense. Although they were later to contemplate military measures, the Suffragists at midmonth still hoped to elect their ticket, and by the strict observance of the forms of political propriety to cow their opponents into submission, as their ideology dictated. On the "Guarantee Clause" as a factor in the Dorr Rebellion, see William M. Wiecek, The Guarantee Clause of the U.S. Constitution (Ithaca, N.Y.: Cornell University Press, 1972). (I have benefited from studying portions of this work in early draft through the courtesy of Professor Wiecek of the University of Missouri.)

[37] Francis had been Governor of Rhode Island in the 1830s. Potter was a leading Law and Order Democrat from the southern part of the state. Whipple, in whose office Dorr had read law, was a distinguished Whig attorney in Providence. See Biographical Directory of the American Congresses, 1775–1949, Document No. 607, 81 Cong., 2 Sess., 1950, pp. 914, 1474; I[rving] B. R[ichman], "Francis, John Brown," in Allen Johnson and Dumas Malone, eds., Dictionary of American Biography, 22 vols. (New York: Charles Scribner's Sons, 1928–1958), VI, 579–580; Sidney S. Rider, Historical Research and Educational Labor, Illustrated in the Work of Elisha Reynolds Potter (Pawtucket, R.I.: Press of the Chronicle Printing Co., 1905); Representative Men and Old Families of Rhode Island, I, 53, 454; Payne, Reminiscences of the Rhode Island Bar, pp. 12–13, 33–37.

"His Accidency" John Tyler [38] was placed in an awkward position by the Law and Order delegation's request for an armed force. A conservative Virginian, Tyler had accepted second place on the Whig ticket of 1840 and found himself President after William H. Harrison's death. Distrusted by both Whigs and Democrats, Tyler was busy in the spring of 1842 attempting to build an independent base of electoral support in advance of the 1844 Presidential election.[39] Thus he had potential sympathy for a conservative bipartisan political grouping such as the Rhode Island Law and Order Party. Moreover, facing a revolt in his native state, Tyler was under some pressure (despite his states' rights views) to uphold the right of the Federal Government to suppress insurrection.[40] But he experienced countervailing pressure also. The Suffrage Party had not yet done anything illegal; its elections, forbidden by the Algerine Law, were not scheduled to take place until later in the month. A Suffrage delegate, following close upon the heels of the Law and Order trio, met with Tyler on April 10 and received what he believed were assurances that the Administration would not meddle with Rhode Island.[41]

Seeing no need to act precipitously by sending an armed

---

[38] The hostile reference is from the Boston *Bay State Democrat* (a paper supporting the Dorr rebels), May 13, 1842.

[39] Democratic leaders in Congress had little "confidence in his [Tyler's] stability or patriotism." Levi Woodbury (United States Senator from New Hampshire) to Dorr, April 17, 1842, Dorr MSS. For similar Whig dislike of Tyler, see Charles Simmons to James F. Simmons, May 17, 1842, Simmons Papers, LC.; Josiah Quincy to Robert Winthrop, February 13, 1843, Winthrop Papers, Massachusetts Historical Society; Theodore Sedgwick to Charles Sumner, September 10, 1842, Sumner Papers, Houghton Library, Harvard University. Mainly, the Whigs objected to Tyler's banking and tariff policy. See Oliver P. Chitwood, *John Tyler: Champion of the Old South* (New York: D. Appleton-Century, 1939), p. 326; Robert Seager, *And Tyler Too* (New York: McGraw-Hill, 1963), Chaps. 3–9.

[40] On the situation Tyler faced in Virginia, see Charles Henry Ambler, *Sectionalism in Virginia from 1776–1861* (Chicago: University of Chicago Press, 1910), pp. 254–255 (I am indebted to Professor Norman Dain of Rutgers University for calling this reference to my attention).

[41] "Dr." John A. Brown, botanical physician and manufacturer of root beer in Providence, was the Suffrage Party delegate to President Tyler. A naïve and credulous man, Brown interpreted Tyler's vague and

force to crush an as yet nonexistent rebellion, Tyler on April 11 drafted a forceful letter that he hoped would calm the turmoil in Rhode Island. He declared that the obligations of the Chief Executive were clear. Though he had no power "to anticipate insurrectionary movements," he had a duty to intervene should revolt actually threaten the government of any state. In such a case Tyler would "not be found to shrink from the performance of a duty, which, while it would be the most painful, is, at the same time, the most imperative." Tyler denied that the President

> could . . . look into real or supposed defects of the existing government, in order to ascertain whether some other plan of government proposed for adoption was better suited to the wants, and more in accordance with the wishes, of any portion of her citizens.

To exercise power to choose between the various factions in a state would render the President an "armed arbitrator . . . , and might lead to a usurped power, dangerous alike to the stability of the State governments and the liberties of the people." But he was obliged "to respect the requisitions of that [Rhode Island] government which has been recognized as the existing government of that State through all time past." Tyler hoped the occasion would not present itself when he would have to apply federal power in that little state whose people had been "too long distinguished for their love of order and of regular government." Though he urged the authorities there to redress promptly all legitimate grievances and to conciliate the agitated citizenry, he clearly indicated that in the eventuality of armed conflict he would intervene on the side of the established authorities.[42]

---

guarded statements as firm endorsement of Suffrage Party measures. He reported to Dorr that the President had given "short shrift" to the Law and Order delegation and was preparing a letter which would "give no encouragement of meddling with Rhode Island." Brown to Dorr, (n.d., postmarked April 11 [1842]), Dorr MSS. The *New Age* echoed these optimistic sentiments, assuring its readers that the Suffrage Party had "nothing to fear" from the Federal Government. *New Age,* April 8, 12, 15, 1842; Boston *Daily Advertiser and Patriot,* April 14, 1842.

[42] Tyler to "his Excellency the Governor of Rhode Island," April 11, 1842, in *Burke's Report,* pp. 658–659; also in a broadside edition, April 14, 1842, Broadside Collection, WLHU.

The effect of Tyler's letter, made public at once, four days before the Suffrage Party elections, was the opposite of that intended by its author. Law and Order members, privately furious at the President's unwillingness to take forceful preventive action,[43] nevertheless flaunted Tyler's letter in a broadside edition clearly intended to influence the canvass. Incensed that a threat of federal intervention should be hurled at them for the inoffensive and peaceful act of going to the polls, those Suffrage members who had not defected after passage of the Algerine Law became even more militant and defiant. Troubled conservatives noted that the radicals "were not at all alarmed" by Tyler's letter, and that they were "going on and elect[ing] their officers as was always talked by them." [44] Suffrage Party spokesmen blithely dismissed "Uncle Sam's men" as no danger to the people's cause; if federal troops should arrive, the *New Age* declared, "they will be well received here. They will doubtless fire *above* the heads of the common people to whom, in feeling and interest, they belong." [45] Tyler's letter thus fell short of promising the sort of decisive action wanted by Law and Order conservatives, and although it may have diminished the radical vote in April, it did not prevent the election at which Dorr was chosen Governor of Rhode Island.[46]

In addition to passing the repressive Algerine Law and asking

---

[43] W. C. Simmons to James F. Simmons, April 9, 1842, Simmons Papers, LC; H. A. S. Dearborn to John Davis, June 6, 1842, Dearborn Writings, New York Public Library; William Sprague to John Brown Francis, July 29, 1842, Francis Collection, RIHSL; Hodges, *Hodges,* p. 182.

[44] W. C. Simmons to James F. Simmons, Simmons Papers, LC; John Brown Francis to Elisha R. Potter, Jr., April 20, 1842, Potter Collection, RIHSL.

[45] *New Age,* April 12, 1842. In its April 19 issue the *New Age* admitted that it had not even reprinted the text of President Tyler's April 11 letter.

[46] Lacking sufficient familiarity with the Rhode Island background of Tyler's maneuvers, and omitting mention of the political motives (building a national Tylerite electoral coalition) that contemporaries plainly perceived, those of Tyler's biographers who touch upon the Dorr Rebellion have nothing but praise for his political finesse. See Chitwood, *Tyler,* pp. 327–328; Robert J. Morgan, *A Whig Embattled: The Presidency Under John Tyler* (Lincoln, Neb.: University of Nebraska Press, 1954), p. 104.

for federal military support, Rhode Island conservatives formed a Board of Councillors "to advise with the Governor as to the executive measures proper to be taken in the present emergency of the State." This seven-man council consisted of prominent Law and Order politicians, six of whom were Whigs. The exception was former Democratic Governor James Fenner.[47] None of these measures was successful in heading off confrontation; after ratification of the People's Constitution the Suffrage Party was fixed on a collision course with its Law and Order opponents, whose every move reenforced radical determination among Dorr and his shrinking band of increasingly desperate followers.

III

Despite increased Dorrite militancy, the Suffrage Party leadership was not yet ready to risk forcible measures. The government elected on April 18 was not scheduled to assume power until early the next month. In the interim, the threat of Presidential intervention impelled the Dorrites into feverish action. They mobilized the support in Washington they hoped would be sufficient to forestall the appearance of federal troops in Rhode Island.

Dorr warned leading Congressional Democrats of Tyler's plans and challenged them to respond with appropriate vigor. To New Hampshire Senator Levi Woodbury he described how U.S. soldiers might come "upon this State, in the case that the People should proceed to put into operation their constitution recently adopted and ratified by a large majority of the citizens." Law and Order members had arranged this threatened federal intervention, Dorr believed, because they simply lacked enough local popular support to contest Suffrage Party measures by fair means. He asked:

---

[47] Fenner later served as Law and Order Governor, 1843–1845. See Chapter 6. The other members of the council were: Richard K. Randolph, Benjamin Hazard's successor as conservative leader of the General Assembly; Edward Carrington, a leading merchant; Lemuel H. Arnold, also a former governor; Nathan F. Dixon, later a Whig member of Congress; Peleg Wilbur, another Whig dignitary; and Byron Diman, Lieutenant Governor of the state. See Mowry, *Dorr War*, pp. 147–148.

Will the friends of American Democracy in the two houses
of Congress permit such a proceeding to take place in violation of the rights and expressed opinions of the Sovereign People of a State—however small its territorial dimensions, without one word of remonstrance? We are without advice from
any friend in Congress. . . . Will any friend of States Rights
in either house do us the favor of saying by letter what we are
to expect? [48]

In the letters to Woodbury and others Dorr restated the basic
ideology of the Suffrage Party: since the people were sovereign
and the government merely their creature, the people could
frame fundamental law at their pleasure. This could be done,
Dorr somewhat recklessly asserted, even when another authorized procedure for constitutional revision was specified in a
written constitution.[49]

The replies to these urgent missives, although expressing sympathy for the Suffragists,[50] supplied little concrete help. Senator
Woodbury at first assured Dorr that the "rumours" of Tyler's
interference in Rhode Island affairs "are not . . . entitled to the
slightest confidence, but are circulated by your opponents for
stage effect." [51] But when Woodbury actually saw Tyler's letter,
he confessed "surprise," and could offer only stale homilies by
way of advice: "keep calm – cool – yet resolute in right. Shun
violence – insubordination – civil war but move onward . . . and
not only will all true democrats and patriots be with you in heart
and prayer, but God himself will speed your exertions." He as-

---

[48] Dorr to Woodbury, April 13, 1842, Levi Woodbury Papers, LC.

[49] Dorr to Ohio Senator William Allen, April 14, 17, 1842 (drafts); Silas
Wright, Jr. (Senator from New York) to Dorr, April 16, 25, 1842; Edmund Burke (New Hampshire Congressman) to Dorr, May 8, 17, 19,
1842, Dorr MSS.

[50] The sympathy did not, however, extend to Dorr's extreme claim that
Popular Constituent Sovereignty provided a mechanism to bypass existing procedures for constitutional amendment. See Allen to Dorr, April
15, 1842; Wright to Dorr, April 16, 1842, Dorr MSS.

[51] Woodbury to Dorr, April 15, 1842, in John B. Rae, ed., "Democrats
and the Dorr Rebellion," *New England Quarterly,* IX (September 1936),
476–477. This collection of correspondence contains some of the replies
to Dorr's letters, but it leaves out important sections of some of the
letters (the originals of which are in the Dorr MSS.) and fails to place
them in the context of subsequent Congressional action.

serted that the President, already shunned by Democrats in Washington, would alienate even the Whigs by any threat to "intermeddl[e] by *force* in the civil affairs of one of our sovereign States." [52]

One Congressional sympathizer who offered the Dorrites more than mere advice that spring was Senator William Allen, an ardent Democrat from Ohio. On April 18, the same day Suffrage Party elections were held in Rhode Island, Allen introduced a resolution demanding that Tyler explain to Congress why he had interfered with "the proceedings which have taken place, or are in contemplation in Rhode Island with a view to the establishment of a constitutional republican form of government . . . in the place of the land company Charter granted by King Charles II of England." [53]

Allen's resolution, which was not acted upon at once, led to hectic Senate maneuvering in the weeks that followed. The opposition was led by Senator William C. Preston of South Carolina, who held that the resolution was improper because it served no legislative purpose. It was the President, this former Nullificationist argued, who had the sole power to act "in such emergencies as the one which has arisen . . . according to [his] sense of what is right under the constitution. . . . Congress could predicate no action at all upon it." Voting along fairly sharp party lines, a majority of the Whig-dominated Senate supported Preston's move to table.[54] Allen's subsequent attempts to revive his resolution failed as Senate Whigs, including James F. Simmons and William Sprague of Rhode Island, voted solidly and repeatedly to close off debate. So unrelenting was Preston's op-

---

[52] Woodbury to Dorr ("confidential"), April 17, 1842, Dorr MSS. (emphasis in original). Some years later Woodbury was appointed to the Supreme Court by President Polk and so had an opportunity to sit in judgment on the celebrated *Luther v. Borden* case, which arose out of the Dorr Rebellion. For Woodbury's views at that later time (1849), see Chapter 7.

[53] *Congressional Globe,* 27 Cong., 2 Sess., April 18, 1842, p. 430; Mowry, *Dorr War,* p. 145.

[54] *Congressional Globe,* 27 Cong., 2 Sess., pp. 431, 438, 449, 459; on Preston, see *Biographical Directory of American Congresses,* p. 1418. Some Dorrites believed that New York Senator Nathaniel P. Tallmadge was their chief opponent in the Congress. See Aaron White, Jr., to Dorr, May 25, 1842, Dorr MSS.

position that it took a full month for Allen to make a pro-Dorrite speech on the Senate floor.[55] There was no discussion of the Rhode Island situation in the lower house of Congress at this time,[56] and the skirmishes on Capitol Hill had little effect in heading off conflict in that state.

IV

The new regime in Rhode Island, elected on April 18, was scheduled to take office on the first Tuesday in May. Until that time, the Suffragists graciously permitted "the present government [to] exercise all the powers with which it is now clothed." [57] On the appointed day, May 3, 1842, thousands of people flocked into Providence to join or witness the festivities accompanying the inauguration of Dorr and the deliberations of the new legislature. A gala procession, including armed militia companies, contingents of artisans, shopkeepers and mechanics, and visitors from other states, wound its way through the narrow streets of the city to the accompaniment of a brass band.[58] Dorrites found the pageant imposing and inspiring. "There they were, the hard-handed mechanics and the sun-burnt farmers walking . . . erect" in the consciousness of their new political dignity.[59] On the other hand, conservative onlookers noted with alarm the armed enthusiasts in the procession, and some sent their families out of town for safety.[60] The hostile *Providence Journal* maliciously reported that pickpockets circulating in the crowd found mostly empty purses among the supporters of the People's Government.[61] For Suffragists it was a day of euphoria,

---

[55] For the roll call votes, see *Congressional Globe,* 27 Cong., 2 Sess., pp. 446, 479, 511; for Allen's speech, see *ibid.,* p. 459, and *Burke's Report,* pp. 1059–1063.

[56] For later (1844) discussion of the Rhode Island question in the House of Representatives, see Chapter 6.

[57] People's Constitution, Article 14, Appendix A.

[58] *New Age,* May 7, 1842; *Providence Journal,* May 4, 5, 1842; Providence *Evening Chronicle,* May 5, 7, 1842; Mowry, *Dorr War,* p. [151].

[59] [McDougall], *Might and Right,* p. 231.

[60] John Pitman to Joseph Story, May 4, 1842, Pitman-Story Correspondence, William L. Clements Library, University of Michigan, Ann Arbor.

[61] *Providence Journal,* May 5, 1842.

climaxing two years of political organizing. The *New Age* triumphantly celebrated the radicals' determination "to place the keystone in the arch of the proud fabric of [Rhode Island] independence." [62]

The pageantry of inauguration day, in which the sovereign people celebrated their power, contrasted with the tawdry circumstances in which the new legislature was forced to meet. The Suffrage Party had unsuccessfully petitioned Charter Government officials for permission to use the State House in Providence. Rebuffed, the rebel legislators and their spectators withdrew to the drafty hall of an unfinished foundry building nearby, where the new government organized itself despite the rain dropping on the heads of the speakers. Agile youngsters scrambled for seats on the crossbeams and rafters to witness the unprecedented spectacle.[63]

The deliberations of the People's Legislature were productive, sedate, and brief. During the two-day session the delegates chose officers, swore in state officials, divided into committees, and enacted a number of statutes—such as acts regulating the voting in town and ward meetings and the choosing of militia officers.[64] In addition, they repealed a number of obnoxious laws of the Charter regime, including the Algerine Law and the resolution establishing the Board of Councillors.[65] The new legislature, considering itself merely the successor of the Charter Government, tacitly assumed that legislation not repealed continued in force.[66] With a view to public opinion in the nation's capital and

---

[62] *New Age,* May 7, 1842.

[63] *Ibid.;* Frieze, *Concise History,* pp. 70–71; King, *Life and Times of Dorr,* pp. 99–100; Mowry, *Dorr War,* pp. [151]–155; testimony of Jeremiah Briggs, in Report of Treason Trial of Dorr, in *Burke's Report,* p. 874; John H. Keinyon to Sidney S. Rider, March 13, 1895, Dorr MSS.

[64] Proceedings and Journals of the People's Legislature, in *Burke's Report,* pp. 462–466.

[65] *Ibid.,* p. 464.

[66] Unlike the Confederate legislature, which in 1861 explicitly reenacted "all the laws of the United States of America . . . not inconsistent with the Constitution of the Confederate States," the Dorrites of 1842 did not think they had broken sharply with past tradition. On the Confederacy, see Jefferson Davis, *The Rise and Fall of the Confederate Government,* 2 vols. (New York: D. Appleton and Co., 1881), I, 243.

elsewhere, the legislators empowered Governor Dorr to notify the President of the United States, both houses of Congress and the governors of the other states that the new government had been instituted in Rhode Island.[67]

Before adjourning until July, the two houses of the People's Legislature sat together to hear Dorr deliver his inaugural address. The People's Governor offered what the unfriendly *Providence Journal* called a mere "patchwork of his own [earlier] speeches and the articles in the New Age." [68] Restating the ideology of the suffrage movement, Dorr failed to take into account the rising tide of conservative opposition and the necessity (which he recognized privately) for forceful measures. Again he vehemently denied revolutionary aims, dismissing any "idea of imposing a government on the people of this State by mere power." His party, he said, simply acted on the basis of self-evident "axioms," which were "too late to call into question." He contrasted the manly yet restrained struggle for liberty in Rhode Island with the mean-spirited behavior of the Charter authorities and the members of the Law and Order Party who jealously guarded the exclusive political rights of the landholders and who only made minimal concessions under pressure. But now, Dorr stated, the people had expressed their irrevocable will, the Invisible Hand in all its awesome majesty had become manifest, and the opposition had no choice but to stand aside.[69] He omitted any mention of what might have to be done if the authorities did not give way and allow the new government to take over state power.

Despite Dorr's disavowal of "mere power" in his formal inaugural and his continued invocation of the peaceable doctrine of the Invisible Hand, he was working quietly in early May to get his followers to endorse more forceful measures. A few blocks from the foundry building where the People's Legislature was meeting stood the Rhode Island State House, containing the archives, the state seal, and other symbols of sovereignty. Dorr

---

[67] Resolution of the People's Legislature, May 4, 1842, in *Burke's Report,* pp. 457–458, 469.

[68] *Providence Journal,* May 5, 1842. Cf. Newton's observation ("Rebellion in Rhode Island," p. 96) that "In essence, Thomas Dorr had only one speech," which he delivered over and over again.

[69] Dorr, Inaugural Address, May 3, 1842, in *Burke's Report,* pp. 720–731.

proposed that the delegates simply go and seize it. Since the People's Government was the lawful one, it was fully entitled to assume control of public property "and proceed to the work of legislation in the place occupied by [its] . . . predecessors." Dorr later wrote:

> Prompt use of the moderate degree of force necessary at this critical point of affairs would have rendered greater force unnecessary, would have removed the danger of subsequent violence and of bloodshed. . . . Had this step been taken, right would have been confirmed by possession, the law and fact would have been conjoined, and the new order of things would have been acquiesced in by all. . . .[70]

But just as he had been unable the previous fall to persuade delegates to the People's Constitutional Convention to endorse suffrage for blacks, so he was unable on May 4 to convince enough legislators to take "active measures." [71] Some of them objected to "breaking bars and bolts." If the State House could not be had without fighting for it, one of them said, "let us adjourn and go home." [72] Both at the time and in retrospect Dorr considered such timidity at a "critical moment" disastrous for the Suffragist cause, costing it "the accession of all the doubtful and wavering," as well as weakening the confidence of its friends "by exciting a doubt" as to whether Suffragists themselves "felt

---

[70] Dorr, Address to the People of Rhode Island, August 1843, in *Burke's Report*, p. 738.

[71] *Ibid.,* p. 750.

[72] Nathaniel Mowry, representative from Smithfield, quoted in Dexter Randall, *Democracy Vindicated and Dorrism Unveiled* (Providence: H. H. Brown, 1846), p. 30 (copy in New York Public Library). For Nathaniel Mowry's earlier opposition to black suffrage in the People's Constitution, see above, pp. 46–47. Insufficient data does not permit systematic correlation between opposition to black rights and opposition to force, but if there were some, like Mowry, who opposed both, there were others, like Dorr, who supported both. It is curious to note that Arthur Mowry, author of *The Dorr War,* who may have been a descendant of Nathaniel Mowry, endorses both decisions—to avoid abolitionist taint and to forgo forcible measures for quiet agitation (pp. 99, 299). But the later Mowry is somewhat ambivalent about force, agreeing with Dorr (p. 155) that the "vacillating and retreating disposition" of legislators in early May cost the Suffrage Party the struggle in Rhode Island.

confident of being in the right. . . ." Using seafaring imagery appropriate to maritime Rhode Island, Dorr concluded that by not seizing state property the radicals "lost the tide" and saw their enterprise "cast among shoals and quicksands." [73]

Since no roll call votes were taken or recorded on the proposition to occupy the State House, it is impossible to pinpoint the groups in the People's Legislature that favored forcible measures and those that did not. The most prominent opponent was Duttee J. Pearce, the wily lawyer and former Democratic Congressman from Newport who later boasted that if it had not been for him, Dorr and his men would have taken possession of the public property.[74] No doubt Pearce magnified his own role, for a considerable number of the legislators in May shunned the use of force.[75]

Many members of the Dorrite rank and file, on the other hand, pledged armed defense of the People's Constitution, and some actually proved willing to fight in May and June. This cleavage on the issue of strategy may have had a class basis, for the members of the legislature were often professionals and tradesmen, whereas most of the Suffragists who later supported Dorr's forcible measures were humble farmers or mechanics.[76]

The People's Legislature barely compensated for its faint-

---

[73] Dorr, Address to the People of Rhode Island, August 1843, in *Burke's Report*, p. 739.

[74] See Pearce's testimony in Report of Treason Trial of Dorr, in *Burke's Report*, p. 875. Cf. John H. Keinyon to Sidney S. Rider, March 13, 1895, Dorr MSS.

[75] In a neglected journalistic account of American radicalism by Lamar Middleton (*Revolt U.S.A.*, pp. 14–17 and *passim*) the proposition is advanced that rebellious rank and filers "desert . . . their leaders and capitulate . . . to the government the instant that an armed clash becomes probable." Middleton ascribes this behavior to national character, and however unsatisfactory such an explanation is, the existence of defectors is an undeniable fact that no student of American radicalism ought to overlook. In the case of the Dorr Rebellion, no simple rank and file vs. leadership interpretation is adequate. If anything, the Dorr Rebellion is an example of leaders abandoning their following, although even this dualism is too simple. See Chapter 5.

[76] For an analysis of the social composition of the Dorrites who participated in armed struggle, see Chapter 5. On the People's Legislature and middle-level Dorrite leadership, see Table IV, p. 85.

heartedness by leaving Dorr to execute a resolution, introduced by Pearce, that required all persons to turn over public property to the new government. The Governor himself was charged with the ominous responsibility of taking over "arms and cannon" belonging to Rhode Island.[77] Some Suffragist legislators, anxious to dissociate themselves from Dorr's advocacy of violence, later declared they did not imply that the Governor should use force to achieve compliance with these resolutions.[78] But Dorr himself understood the legislature's action as a mandate to defend the People's Constitution by all necessary means, which did not rule out exertion of force at some later time.[79]

The hasty adjournment of the People's Legislature after a brief two-day session marked the beginning of the Suffrage Party's downfall. An ambiguous ideology fostered the illusion of easy victory by the almost effortless operation of the Invisible Hand and ill prepared adherents for sustained and forcible conflict. The unwillingness of the opposition and the authorities to accept as self-evident the principles of Popular Constituent Sovereignty puzzled and infuriated Suffragists. When opponents went further, organizing against the Dorrites and even threatening them, a crisis was reached. Some Suffragists, unable to endorse even the most minor forcible actions to uphold the People's Constitution, defected from party ranks. Others reluctantly accepted the designation "radical" and began to assay desperate measures. These remaining Dorrites thus drifted into a radicalism that may have been latent in their ideology but that neither they nor their opponents wished to actuate. Radicals despite themselves, plagued by defections and indecisive leadership, the Dorrites had already begun to founder when the People's Government deliberated in early May, and their prospects did not look good as the inevitable confrontation approached.

---

[77] Journals and Resolutions of the People's Legislature, May 3–4, 1842, in *Burke's Report,* pp. 457–459, 464–467.

[78] Testimony of Levi Salisbury, former clerk of the People's Legislature, at Dorr's treason trial, 1844, *ibid.,* p. 875.

[79] Dorr, Address to the People of Rhode Island, August 1843, *ibid.,* p. 738.

5

Onset of Conflict
Spring and Summer
1842

I

The failure of the People's Legislature to take decisive action in early May prompted the Dorrites to seek outside help again. Before adjournment the rebels had authorized another expedition to the nation's capital, in which "suitable persons" would "make known to the President of the United States that the people of this State have formed a written constitution, elected officers, and peaceably organized the government under the same; and that said government is now in full operation." The People's Legislature empowered Dorr to choose and dispatch the delegation to Washington; he was also instructed to convey the same information to Congress and to the governors of the several states.[1]

Mindful of the fiasco that had resulted when the naïve "Dr." John A. Brown represented the Suffrage Party in Washington a few weeks earlier, Dorr took greater care in assembling the May delegation. He sent Burrington Anthony, who previously had been United States Marshal in Providence and had been

[1] Resolutions nos. 1 and 17 of the People's Legislature, May 3–4, 1842, in *Burke's Report*, pp. 461, 469.

elected Sheriff of Providence County that April on the People's ticket,[2] and Duttee J. Pearce. Both these men had experience in the nation's capital and could presumably counteract a second Law and Order delegation headed there.

Hardly had Pearce and Anthony left when Dorr, bearing a letter to President Tyler,[3] rushed to join them. Dorr later claimed that he left Rhode Island at this crucial moment on the advice of friends, in order "to present our cause to our democratic brethren abroad" and to "ascertain, on the spot, what were the springs of the movement against us in Washington, and whether there was a final determination to suppress our constitution by force." [4] A rally in Providence on May 5 or 6 had resolved that Dorr "be requested personally to represent at the seat of Government the cause of the People of Rhode Island." [5] But his enemies insinuated that he had merely fled Rhode Island to avoid imprisonment, a charge he was hard put to refute.[6]

Whatever Dorr's motivation, his hasty trip resulted in little augmented support for the radicals; it merely increased the confusion and disarray in his party. The authorities had begun to make arrests under the Algerine Law even before he left,[7] and "excited multitudes" of Suffragists milled about aimlessly, seek-

---

[2] See Providence *Republican Herald,* April 17, 1841; Arthur May Mowry, *The Dorr War: Or, The Constitutional Struggle in Rhode Island* (Providence: Preston & Rounds, 1901), p. 160.

[3] For Dorr's (undated) letter to Tyler, accompanying the resolutions of the People's Legislature, see *Burke's Report,* p. 675. The Governor's letter bore the Seal of Rhode Island, which the rebels had forged, since the original lay undisturbed in the Providence State House.

[4] Dorr, Address to the People of Rhode Island, August 1843, *ibid.,* p. 750.

[5] Providence *Evening Chronicle,* May 7, 1842.

[6] *Providence Journal,* May 9, 1842. Dorr's difficulties in countering the charge of cowardice were compounded when he actually did flee Rhode Island, not once but twice later that spring and summer, after the two failures of armed action. See below, pp. 120–122, 135–138.

[7] Some writers have stated that the first arrests came only after Dorr left the state. W. S. Reynolds, "The Dorr War," typescript, 1938, in John Hay Library, Brown University; Dan King, *The Life and Times of Thomas Wilson Dorr, with Outlines of the Political History of Rhode Island* (Boston: published by the author, 1859), p. 127. But Mowry (*Dorr War,* p. 162) established the correct chronology for the events of early May.

ing instructions from their absent governor on how to respond. The Law and Order forces spread rumors that Dorr had left for good, while Suffragists anxiously waited and even demanded his return.[8] The Governor meanwhile proceeded to Washington, dimly perceiving the chaos he had left behind, urging his supporters to "stand firm," and asking them to refuse to give bail if arrested, even if doing so meant a jail sentence.[9] But by hastily leaving Rhode Island himself, Dorr hardly presented his followers with any model of brave and decisive action. Instead, it appeared as if well-to-do, respectable gentlemen reformers were leaving their less distinguished followers behind to take the consequences of the radical Suffragist measures.

As Dorr saw things, the danger of federal intervention was the major threat to the suffrage movement in early May, and to head it off he paid a personal visit to the President. Tyler professed great sympathy for the people's cause in Rhode Island, but Dorr distrusted him, suspecting that the President was "a very good natured weak man, unequal to his situation, and having his mind made up for him by others." [10] Nor did Dorr find any sign of positive Congressional action. While he was in Washington,

---

[8] John S. Harris to Dorr, two letters of May 9, 1842; W[alter] S. B[urges] to Dorr, May 9, 1842, all in Dorr MSS.

[9] Dorr professed to be sure that any confinement would be short, for the rising tide of popular indignation would soon bring about a speedy release from prison. Writing from Jersey City, New Jersey, en route to Washington, he claimed that he would submit to Algerine imprisonment rather than confer recognition on the Charter Government by giving bail. He also predicted that "It may be expedient to strike a blow as soon as I return." Dorr to Crawford Allen, May 8, 1842, Dorr MSS. But such promises and assurances were not systematically transmitted to his followers, and Dorr's behavior in leaving Rhode Island counterbalanced his intentions, leaving his hapless supporters leaderless and foundering at a key moment. See Mowry, *Dorr War*, p. 166.

[10] Dorr's account of his interview with President Tyler appears in two letters written from New York City on May 12, 1842, to Walter S. Burges and Aaron White, Jr. (Mowry's treatment of the episode [*Dorr War*, pp. 161–162] was written before MSS. sources were available.) Prominent among the "others" whom Dorrites suspected of dominating Tyler was Secretary of State Daniel Webster. "The President is a weak and vacillating man," Dorr heard from one of his supporters in Congress, "completely under the influence of Webster." Edmund Burke to Dorr, May 8, 1842. Dorr MSS.

Senator Allen of Ohio continued his futile efforts to push his pro-Dorr resolution through the upper house, but no action was pending at all in the lower house. Dorr could only send back the vaguest of assurances. "We have the moral & intellectual weight of Congress on our side," he wrote, "and perhaps the numerical weight, after a full & fair discussion, but this I will not positively expect." [11]

The rival Law and Order delegation that visited Washington in early May enjoyed a somewhat different, but by no means completely satisfying, reception.[12] Bearing an urgent request that President Tyler "forthwith . . . interpose the authority and power of the United States" to suppress the "insurrectionary and lawless assemblages" in Rhode Island, they met with unwillingness on the part both of the President and his Cabinet to use federal force. Tyler told the delegation that despite his unchanged opinions on the obligations of the Federal Government to aid the established authorities in Rhode Island, he hoped to avoid such an unpleasant exigency. New information led the

---

[11] Dorr to Aaron White, Jr., May 12, 1842, Dorr MSS. Dorr's efforts to generate support in Washington were clearly intended to head off hostile Presidential action. They were not, as George Marshel Dennison erroneously wrote ("The Constitutional Issues of the Dorr War: A Study in the Evolution of American Constitutionalism, 1776–1849" [Ph.D. Thesis, University of Washington, 1967], pp. 6–7, 262), the result of some Dorrite "strategy" to send a rival Congressional delegation to Washington. Nor was there any factional split in the Suffrage Party over this particular question, as Dennison states. It is true that in 1840 the suggestion to submit the suffrage dispute to Congress was raised (see above, p. 31), but nobody acted upon it then or later. From time to time someone casually suggested electing Congressmen to contest Rhode Island's seats in the national legislature. See *New Age,* April 12, 1842; Edmund Burke to Dorr, May 8, 1842; Dorr to Aaron White, Jr., June 1, 1842, the last two in Dorr MSS. But they let pass a major chance in the early spring of 1842 when they could have appointed someone to fill the unexpired Senate term of Nathaniel Dixon. Apparently it never occurred to the Dorrites to take this step. There is no record of any such proposal being made at the early May sessions of the People's Legislature.

[12] The May delegation included two men: Elisha R. Potter, Jr., who had been to see President Tyler with April's Law and Order delegation, and Richard K. Randolph, member of Governor King's council, Whig speaker of the General Assembly, and transplanted Virginia gentleman. See Abraham Payne, *Reminiscences of the Rhode Island Bar* (Providence: Tibbitts and Preston, 1885), p. 51.

President to believe that turmoil there had already begun to subside, and he urged conciliation.[13] Privately he even suggested a course of action to Rhode Island Governor Samuel W. King:

> [I]f the General Assembly would authorize you to announce a general amnesty and pardon for the past, without making any exception, upon the condition of a return to allegiance, and follow it up by a call for a new convention upon somewhat liberal principles . . . , all difficulty would at once cease. And why should this not be done? A government never loses anything by mildness and forbearance to its own citizens; more especially when the consequences may be the shedding of blood. . . . If you succeed by the bayonet, you succeed against your own fellow-citizens . . . ; whereas, by taking the opposite course, you will have shown a patient care for the lives of your people . . . [A]doption of [conciliatory] measures will give you peace, and insure you harmony. A resort to force, on the contrary, will engender, for years to come, feelings of animosity.

"Try the experiment" of conciliation, Tyler added; "and if it fails, then your justification in using force becomes complete." [14] In a subsequent meeting with the Cabinet, the Law and Order delegation met the same reluctance to commit federal troops. Secretary of State Daniel Webster was openly annoyed that the Rhode Island authorities should attempt to dump their internal political problems in the lap of the Federal Government and not solve them on their own.[15]

Neither the most influential Law and Order representatives nor the radical Dorrites welcomed Tyler's counsel of conciliation. John Whipple, after meeting secretly on the President's suggestion with some of Dorr's lieutenants, drafted a compromise agreement that would have involved suspension of the Algerine Law and complementary concessions by the rebels until the conflict could be submitted to the federal courts.[16] In an alternate

---

[13] Governor King to Tyler, May 4, 1842; Tyler to King, May 7, 1842, in *Burke's Report,* pp. 674–675.

[14] Tyler to King ("Private and Confidential"), May 9, 1842, *ibid.,* p. 676.

[15] See Elisha R. Potter, Jr., "Memo of a Visit to Washington, D.C.— May 6, 1842," Potter Collection, RIHSL.

[16] For the text of Whipple's suggested compromise agreement, see

plan for securing a judicial resolution, Elisha R. Potter, Jr., suggested that Dorr "allow himself to be arrested peaceably, and give bail," so that his case could reach the courts.[17] But Dorr was already unalterably opposed to giving bail, since to do so would concede the legitimacy of the Charter regime. The Providence *Express* declared that the radicals would accept no agreement

> that has not for its basis an acknowledgement that the ultimate source of all political and sovereign power does rest in the whole adult male citizens of the State; and that no action of the legislative authority is or of right can be necessary to say when or how that ultimate sovereign power may be exercised.[18]

Neither would conservatives relent and offer conciliatory terms while the radicals "continu[ed] their threats." [19] The positions of both parties had become so antagonistic by the spring of 1842 that there was no longer (if indeed there ever had been) any realistic basis for compromise.

[Frances H. (Whipple) McDougall], *Might and Right by a Rhode Islander,* 2nd ed. (Providence: A. H. Stillwell, 1844), pp. 258–259. The agreement was drafted at a meeting in New York on May 13 in which Daniel Webster represented the Tyler Administration, Whipple the Law and Order Party. Dorr reluctantly attended and was repelled by what he considered Webster's cynicism. But Burrington Anthony, believing that compromise was still possible, flaunted the news of imminent agreement when he arrived back in Providence. Anthony may have wished to act as great peacemaker, but one effect of his actions was to sow confusion in the Dorrite ranks. See *ibid.,* p. 259; Daniel Webster to John Whipple, May 9, 1842; W. Channing Gibbs to Webster, May 12, 1842, both in Webster Papers, New Hampshire Historical Society. See also Dorr to Walter S. Burges, May 12, 1842, Dorr MSS.; *Providence Journal,* May 26, 1842.

[17] Potter to Tyler, May 15, 1842, in *Burke's Report,* pp. 677–678.

[18] Providence *Express,* May 13, 1842.

[19] Potter to Tyler, May 15, 1842, in *Burke's Report,* pp. 677–678. Potter to John Brown Francis, [May 16, 1842], Francis Collection, RIHSL; [McDougall], *Might and Right,* p. 259; *Letter from Hon. Lemuel Arnold, in reply to the Letter of John Whipple, Esq.* (broadside, n.p., May 1, 1845), Broadside Collection, WLHU. Mowry's conservative bias leads him far beyond the evidence in his assertion (*Dorr War,* pp. 174–175) that Law and Order members were prepared to offer Dorr some genuinely conciliatory proposal in mid-May.

Dorr, disappointed with Tyler's feeble efforts to arrange a compromise and disheartened by Congressional inaction, began to transfer his hopes for outside aid to "the People of the States," to whom, he was "happy to say, we shall not look in vain." [20] This search for out-of-state support, which drew him away from Rhode Island in the crucial early weeks of May, stemmed in part from what seemed to be clear indications of sympathy in scattered quarters. Democratic governors of nearby states indicated they might come to the aid of Rhode Island if the state proved "unable to contend singly against the forces of the United States" in a struggle that involved "the great principles of American Freedom and the clearest principles of a Sovereign People." [21] New York was a main center of Dorrite sympathy, even though its Whig governor, William H. Seward, was no friend of rebellious movements within or without the Empire State.[22] New York City Democrats, who earlier had called for Tyler's impeachment because he threatened intervention on the Law and Order side in Rhode Island,[23] greeted Dorr with gala festivities in mid-May. Welcomed as "His Excellency Governor T. W. Dorr of Rhode Island," Dorr enjoyed two days of public acclaim in the metropolis and conferred with local Democratic leaders, who assured him of their support.[24]

Before he returned to Rhode Island, Dorr received an even more explicit sign of support: two New York militia officers volunteered to accompany him to Providence with a military

[20] Dorr to Aaron White, Jr., May 12, 1842, Dorr MSS.

[21] Dorr to Governor John Fairfield of Maine, May 13 1842; Dorr to Governor Chauncey Cleveland of Connecticut, May 13, 1842 (drafts), Dorr MSS. Mowry (*Dorr War*, p. 172), relying on newspaper accounts, misdates one of these letters.

[22] Seward was Governor during the antirent agitation in upstate New York, calling out the Militia to suppress the rebels. For Seward's attitude toward the Rhode Island upheaval, see Frederick W. Seward, ed., *Autobiography of William H. Seward*, 3 vols. (New York: D. Appleton and Co., 1877–1891), I, 599–609.

[23] See Mowry, *Dorr War*, p. 168.

[24] Jacob Frieze, *Concise History of the Efforts to Obtain an Extension of Suffrage in Rhode Island from the Year 1811 to 1842* (Providence: B. Moore, 1842), pp. 83–84; A[aron] White, Jr., to Dorr, May 15, 1842, Dorr MSS.

escort.[25] He gratefully declined, acknowledging "the fraternal interest" with which New Yorkers regarded the "struggle for their just rights of the people of Rhode Island":

> While I should not feel justified at the present moment in withdrawing you from your homes and business, on the expedition contemplated, allow me to say that the time may not be far distant, when I may be obliged to call upon you for your services in that cause to which you would so promptly render the most efficient aid—the cause of American citizens contending for their sovereign right to make and maintain a republican Constitution [even when] . . . opposed by the hired soldiers of the General Government.

"In this unequal contest" Dorr welcomed aid from sympathetic outsiders; he was even prepared to "rely on them in the last resort to defend our rights from . . . arbitrary aggression." [26]

Dorr miscalculated the seriousness of the expressions of sympathy and support he received in his travels outside Rhode Island. Although there is no reason to suspect that the offer to escort Dorr back to his home state was insincere, many of the other promises and assurances were inflated bravado. For Tammany Democrats, noisy endorsement of the Rhode Island rebels at public rallies [27] provided a relatively effortless way to wrap their own partisan appeals in the mantle of Dorrite principle.

---

[25] Alexander Ming, Jr., and A. G. Crasto to Dorr, May 13, 1842. In his printed version of this letter (*Dorr War*, pp. 172–173, copying the *Providence Journal* of May 19), Mowry mistook Ming for a nonexistent Col. "Wing," not recognizing that this militia officer, who made the offer of armed escort, was a leading New York Locofoco (see Glyndon G. Van Deusen, *The Jacksonian Era, 1828–1848* [New York: Harper & Row, 1959], p. 95).

[26] Dorr to Ming and Crasto, May 14, 1842, in Mowry, *Dorr War*, p. 173.

[27] After Dorr left New York, his well-wishers in that city staged a great outdoor rally in which, according to one hostile observer, Democrats "high and low" expressed readiness to "espouse openly the cause of the Rhode Island rebels, and respond to the call to send men and arms to support them in their opposition to the laws." Allan Nevins, ed., *The Diary of Philip Hone, 1828–1851* (New York: Dodd, Mead and Co., 1936), p. 602 (diary entry for May 14, 1842). For the May 17 New York City meeting, which involved all segments of the local Democracy, from patricians Aaron Vanderpoel and Samuel J. Tilden to labor radicals Ely Moore, Levi Slamm and Mike Walsh, see Mowry, *Dorr War*, pp. 170–171.

But Dorr, desperately striving to maintain his belief in the eventual triumph of free suffrage principles, placed great faith in these ambiguous expressions. Even the casual courtesy of a Jersey City policeman who helped "Governor Dorr" with his baggage symbolized to him the rising tide of support throughout the country.[28] An ideology that stressed faith in the efficacy of an Invisible Hand confirmed the Dorrites in their compulsive optimism and led them to believe that people outside Rhode Island, whose own freedom was presumably at stake in the struggle for suffrage, would flock to their aid. Although reliance on outside aid was consistent with Dorrite ideology,[29] it permitted Suffragists to overlook the growing weakness of their position in the state and to rest in the illusion that they would not have to fight their way to victory. When Dorr assured his followers that a thousand armed volunteers would come to Rhode Island from New York alone if they were needed,[30] he was attempting to cow the Law and Order opposition into submission, but more significantly, he was bluffing himself and his movement.[31]

II

Once state authorities had been alerted to the danger of a radical takeover,[32] they showed little willingness to bow before the mighty force of popular power. The news from New York made conservatives even more vigilant and determined, for they discerned "a horrible plot" to import bands of "lawless and ferocious ruffians" from New York City to "butcher" peaceful and

---

[28] Dorr to [Crawford] Allen, May 8, 1842, Dorr MSS.

[29] Irving B. Richman's conclusion that Dorr was a "reformer" until his early May trip to Washington and New York and that he "returned to Providence a fanatic" (*Rhode Island: A Study in Separatism* [Boston and New York: Houghton, Mifflin and Co., 1905], p. 299), which echoed Mowry's similar judgment (*Dorr War*, pp. 168, 260), is unfounded.

[30] Dorr to Arron White, Jr., May 12, 1842, Dorr MSS.

[31] Misled by their ideology, the Dorrites who believed that their opponents' appeal to Washington for aid was an admission of weakness seemed unable to understand that their own reliance on outside support also indicated weakness.

[32] See above, p. 89.

innocent Rhode Islanders.[33] State property, including the Providence arsenal, was placed under armed guard.[34] Sobered by President Tyler's reluctance to send troops to Rhode Island in anticipation of rebellion, conservatives were prepared "to meet the worst" with their own forces. "If we had a man for a pres-[iden]t," one of them wrote, conflict could be avoided. He continued:

> It is too bad that our men should go out to fight these [Dorrite] rowdies. One of our mens lives are [sic] worth ten of theirs and one mans life on either side is worth more than the whole suffrage of the state yet we go for the right and we do not think of compromising or holding council with men engaged in treason.[35]

At this time, many wavering and moderate Rhode Islanders, alarmed by fears of outside intervention, went over to the Law and Order side and prepared for active opposition to Dorrite measures.

Dorr's return to Providence on May 16 [36] did little to allay fears of imminent conflict. According to one eyewitness, "He was escorted into the city by a procession numbering about twelve hundred—three hundred of whom were under arms—preceded by a band of music." To many fearful citizens, this bold pageant insulted civil order and challenged duly consti-

---

[33] Broadside, *A Horrible Plot Discovered* (Providence, May 14, 1842), Broadside Collection, WLHU.

[34] The almost daily letters from Providence by Charles Simmons addressed to his father, James Fowler Simmons, U.S. Senator in Washington, in May 1842, Simmons Papers, LC, give a good account of how the Law and Order forces organized themselves. See esp. letters of May 6 and 17. Official vigilance occasionally failed, as when on the afternoon of May 17 Dorrites seized artillery pieces dating from the Revolutionary War. The captors neglected to take the balls and shot for these artillery pieces, but when they returned later that afternoon, they found that the Charter authorities had removed the ammunition. See Mowry, *Dorr War,* pp. 181-182.

[35] Charles Simmons to James F. Simmons, May 17, 1842, Simmons Papers, LC.

[36] He had arrived in Rhode Island the previous morning via the ferry from New York to Stonington, Connecticut, a town near the state line. A train was dispatched to Stonington to bring the Governor to Providence. See Mowry, *Dorr War,* p. 175.

tuted authority.³⁷ Dorr also issued a fiery manifesto the same
day, proclaiming readiness to call for military aid, which he said
would be "immediately and most cheerfully tendered . . . from
the city of New York and from other places" if any soldier of
the United States were "set in motion by whatever direction,
to act against the people of this State" in support of the Charter
Government. Dorr regretted that "the constitutional question in
this State cannot be adjusted among our own citizens. . . ."

> [B]ut, as the minority have asked that the sword of the na-
> tional Executive may be thrown onto the scale against the peo-
> ple, . . . [t]hey who have been the first to ask assistance from
> abroad, can have no reason to complain of any consequences
> which may ensue.³⁸

Dorr amplified the ominous tone of his proclamation with an
extemporaneous address delivered from the carriage which
brought him to his headquarters in Providence. He began his
speech to the large, enthusiastic throng of supporters ³⁹ with
regrets that he had left Rhode Island ten days before. Had he
been in the state, Dorr boasted, he "would not have counte-
nanced the arrest of any Free Suffrage man." But he claimed his
trip had been profitable. Masses of volunteers were now ready
to march into Rhode Island if federal troops should be used
against the People's Government, he said, probably as much

---

³⁷ [Charles C. Jewett], *The Close of the Late Rebellion in Rhode-Island:
An Extract from a Letter by a Massachusetts Man Resident in Providence* (Providence: B. Cranston, 1842), pp. [3]–4. Jewett, whose anonymous pamphlet in late May or early June somewhat prematurely celebrated the "Close" of the Rebellion, was librarian at Brown University,
a center of anti-Dorr sentiment. University President Francis Wayland
and William G. Goddard, Professor of Moral Philosophy, were both
ardent anti-Dorrites. See Wilson Smith, *Professors and Public Ethics:
Studies of Northern Moral Philosophers before the Civil War* (Ithaca,
N.Y.: Cornell University Press, 1956), pp. 128–146. For other expressions of conservative fears when Dorr returned to Rhode Island, see
Charles Simmons to James F. Simmons, May 17, 18, 19, 1842, Simmons
Papers, LC; Henry Storms to William H. Seward, May 18, 1842, Seward
Papers, Rush Rhees Library, University of Rochester.

³⁸ Dorr's proclamation, May [1]6, 1842, in *Burke's Report,* pp. 679–680.

³⁹ The Sheriff of Providence, who had in hand a warrant for Dorr's
arrest, understandably did not serve it at the time. See Mowry, *Dorr War,*
p. 175, and Plate 5.

to encourage his followers as to intimidate conservatives. Then, according to most accounts of the speech, Dorr unsheathed a sword, which he said had belonged to an officer slain in the Florida Indian wars. "It has been already dyed in blood and if necessary, would again be in blood should the suffrage cause demand it," the People's Governor declared.[40] After these sanguinary anticipations, he retired for strategy discussions to Burrington Anthony's house near the state arsenal in Providence, his headquarters for the next few decisive days.

There is little doubt that the discussions centered on the question of force. Dorr had long been convinced of the necessity "to strike a blow" to uphold the claim that the People's Government was legitimate.[41] His reception in New York only reenforced this feeling. The People's Legislature, though it had declined to act on its own, had empowered Dorr to take possession of state property. The milling, armed throngs in Providence, which had given him such an enthusiastic welcome, revived the hope that forcible measures might succeed. Artillery standing outside Dorr's headquarters gave added meaning to the discussions, while discouraging any attempt by the authorities to disperse the rebels.

No secret revolutionary cabal debated strategy in Anthony's house; rather, a group of divided, indecisive and desperate men strove to formulate plans of action in an atmosphere of rumor, excitement and crisis. No attempt was made to exclude spies or enemies of the suffrage cause. Many of these, including Dorr's

---

[40] Providence *Evening Chronicle,* May 16; *Providence Journal,* May 17; *Boston Daily Advertiser and Patriot,* May 17; *Boston Bay State Democrat,* May 17, 1842. On May 18 the bitterly hostile *Providence Journal* ridiculed Dorr's speech, saying the sword had belonged to some soldier who died of dysentery, "and all the blood that was ever upon it would not wet the point." Mowry's discussion of the conflicting testimony on Dorr's "sword" speech (*Dorr War,* pp. 176–178) failed to distinguish adequately between contemporary testimony and the recollections of witnesses who testified at Dorr's treason trial three years later. It would have been more appropriate had Dorr brandished a Revolutionary War sword on May 16, but the one presented to him on the ferry from New York was apparently the only weapon at hand.

[41] Dorr to [Crawford] Allen, May 8, 1842, Dorr MSS. (It is important to note that Dorr was thinking along the lines of forcible action before his reception in New York. See note 29, p. 115.)

own relatives, came to headquarters to plead for compromise.[42] A significant group of his own followers, almost the entire stratum of petty professionals and tradesmen, offered like counsel, refusing to endorse armed measures and urging virtual abandonment of the struggle. Dorr, who knew that his Law and Order antagonists could not offer any satisfactory compromise, resolved instead to take drastic action. In this he had the support of many of the lower-class members of the Suffrage Party —the farmers, housewrights, shoemakers, blacksmiths, stonemasons and factory hands who had loudly demanded equal political rights in Rhode Island and were now ready for action.[43]

Despite the risks, Dorr decided to attack the arsenal. He had available to him considerable armament, some of it stolen from the Charter Government but most probably the bulk from militia units such as the Woonsocket Infantry, whose sympathies were with the rebels.[44] Dorr explained that such solid backing, along with feelings of "Duty and fidelity," motivated him at the arsenal. He later wrote:

> To surrender my post, and to retire from the responsibility which it imposed upon me, was a thought not likely to occur to me. To submit to an arrest, and to the [consequent] breaking up of the [People's] government, without an effort in its behalf, and in the face of the strong pledge of nearly 800 men in arms assembled at the inauguration, that they would respond to all lawful commands proceeding from me as chief magistrate, . . . would have been in the general opinion and in fact a dishonorable abandonment of the means apparently placed at my disposal, to maintain my own, and the rights intrusted to my keeping.[45]

Why he chose the arsenal as a target is not clear. The People's Legislature did charge the Governor with the task of taking over the "arms and cannon" belonging to the state, but these

---

[42] For the events and discussions at Dorrite headquarters in mid-May, see Frieze, *Concise History*, pp. 93–94; [McDougall], *Might and Right*, pp. 242–246; King, *Life and Times of Dorr*, p. 128.

[43] See Table VI, p. 120.

[44] For the militia connections of many of the Dorrite soldiers at the arsenal, see "Records of Commissioners" (cited in Table VI, p. 120).

[45] Dorr, Address to the People of Rhode Island, August 1843, in *Burke's Report*, p. 753.

TABLE VI OCCUPATIONS OF DORRITES WHO CAME OUT BOTH AT THE ARSENAL AND AT FEDERAL HILL, 1842 *

Farmers	5	Painters	2
Shoemakers	4	Laborers	1
Carpenters	4	Storekeepers	1
Innkeepers	2	Brewers	1
Physicians	2	Jewelers	1
Factory workers	2	Seamen	1
Factory overseers	2	Bakers	1
Hired hands	2	Lawyer (Dorr)	1

Total for whom occupational data is available   32

* Source: "Records of the Commissioners Appointed by the General Assembly of the State of Rhode Island in June, 1842, to Examine the Prisoners Arrested During the Late Rebellion" (MSS., Providence, 1842), in John Hay Library, Brown University.

were not the only items of public property he was instructed to sequester. Perhaps Dorr believed that seizing the military resources of the state would instantly revive the waning fortunes of the Suffrage Party, or that the forces guarding the arsenal would voluntarily surrender when they saw that he seriously meant to assert his claims of legitimate authority. The notion of the Invisible Hand encouraged Dorr systematically to underestimate his opponents. The Charter authorities were not prepared to hand over public property, especially the arsenal, without a fight.

After midnight on May 18 an armed rebel contingent moved out from Dorrite headquarters against the arsenal.[46] The attack force was composed of over two hundred men, many of them members of various militia groups favorable to the rebel cause. Few if any of the more respectable Dorrites joined in the assault, except, of course, the People's Governor himself. Dorr bitterly resented the absence of men who formerly had sustained the People's Constitution "and the sovereignty from which it sprang with their ability, their zeal, and means—some with the elo-

---

[46] See Plate 7 for the attack route.

quence of the lips and pen." [47] Even some militant working sympathizers prudently declined to participate in the attack. One of these, a Providence journeyman shoemaker, was told by his militia captain of the plan to assault the arsenal; the captain warned his men "to keep the news a profound secret." But as he was en route to the staging place, the militiaman later recalled, he met a friend who called out:

> "So Charlie, you've got to go up to the Arsenal tonight?" I passed on, wondering how he knew. When I entered Jim Slocum's shop, one of my fellow journeymen let on he knew about the raid on the Arsenal. Well, that night before the hour of the proposed attack, the bells of the city rang, and I concluded that if the men in charge of the venture wouldn't keep the secret, and if everybody knew about it, I had better stay away—and I did.[48]

In the foggy, moonless night Dorr may not have noticed the thinness of his forces, as he apparently did not notice that they had left behind some of their artillery pieces. Despite the disorganization and disarray, he ordered his forces drawn up in the field in front of the arsenal.[49]

The two-story stone building was well defended. Loyal militiamen and volunteers had responded to a Charter Government broadside issued earlier that evening.[50] Among the defenders were Dorr's father; his younger brother; his brother-in-law, Samuel Ames (who was in charge at the arsenal that night); and his former legal mentor, John Whipple. The rebel attackers, under a flag of truce, sent a demand to the arsenal for surrender. The reply came. The commandant of the arsenal knew no "Governor Dorr" and would not surrender. "It can't be possible," said one of the defenders to young Sullivan Dorr, "that your brother intends to fire on this building when he knows

---

[47] Dorr, Address to the People of Rhode Island, August 1843, in *Burke's Report,* p. 754.

[48] See the recollections of Charles W. Trescott, June 21, 1903, in RIHS Scrapbook, Vol. VII, p. 113, RIHSL.

[49] On the preparations for the arsenal attack, see Dorr's account in Boston *Daily Advertiser and Patriot,* May 31, 1842; [Jewett], *Close of the Late Rebellion,* pp. 5–8.

[50] *To the Citizens of Providence ! ! !* (Providence, May 17, 1842), broadside issued at 6:00 P.M., printed in Mowry, *Dorr War,* p. 183. See Plate 6.

that you, his father and his uncles are all in it." Sullivan looked at his questioner and calmly replied, "I guess you are not acquainted with the breed." [51] Thomas Dorr greeted the refusal to surrender with the firmness his brother had anticipated; he issued the order to fire the two cannons, and according to some accounts applied the torch himself. But the guns had been plugged or had otherwise become unserviceable, for neither fired. In the ensuing confusion, most of Dorr's soldiers fled. Daylight was approaching, and Dorr managed with thirty or forty of his men to bring his artillery off the field. They returned to their headquarters and hastily erected fortifications on adjoining Federal Hill.[52]

Disarray in rebel ranks was aggravated by Dorr's flight from Providence to avoid arrest at the hands of Charter authorities. On May 19, the day after the arsenal fiasco, the rebel leader was in the village of Woonsocket, in the extreme northern part of the state, still urging his military forces to maintain their fortified position. So out of touch with reality was he that despite the events of the previous day he still entertained hopes of capturing the arsenal and expressed hope that he would soon rejoin his militant supporters on Federal Hill.[53] But instead of returning to the battlefield, Dorr soon left Rhode Island altogether, amid

---

[51] Obituary of Sullivan Dorr, Jr., in RIHS Scrapbook, Vol. VIII, p. 57, RIHSL.

[52] Dorr's own accounts of the arsenal adventure appear in Boston *Daily Advertiser and Patriot,* May 31, 1842; and in his Address to the People of Rhode Island, August 1843, in *Burke's Report,* p. 753. See also [Jewett], *Close of the Late Rebellion,* pp. 6–9; Address of Zachariah Allen (an eyewitness and a relative of Dorr) before the RIHS, reprinted in the Providence *Morning Star,* April 20, 1881; Charles Simmons to James Fowler Simmons, May 19, 1842, Simmons Papers, LC; Mowry, *Dorr War,* pp. 184–188; Anne Mary Newton, "Rebellion in Rhode Island: The Story of the Dorr War" (M.A. Thesis, Columbia University, 1947), Chap. 14.

[53] Dorr's communication from Woonsocket was in a letter to "Col" [Henry] D'Wolf (draft), May 19, 1842, Dorr MSS. This letter repeated verbal messages that Dorr had relayed to Federal Hill some hours before. Later Dorr regretted that the verbal message was not delivered and that the written communication, probably a version of this letter to D'Wolf, arrived after the Dorrite camp on Federal Hill had been abandoned. See Dorr, Address to the People of Rhode Island, August 1843, in *Burke's Report,* p. 754. D'Wolf is a shadowy figure. A resident

conservative jeers that out of cowardice he had "absquatu-
lated." [54] Dorr claimed that he had made only a temporary retreat and would soon return to press Suffrage Party claims.[55]
But many men defected outright after the arsenal attack. A
group of tradesmen and small manufacturers who represented
Providence in the People's Legislature publicly resigned their
positions the morning after,[56] an act Dorr sensed would have
a demoralizing effect on the men still devoted to the suffrage
struggle.[57] These "reckless desperadoes," as one hostile observer called the largely working-class defenders of Federal
Hill,[58] made a brave show of resistance before the Charter

---

of Uxbridge, Massachusetts, D'Wolf arrived at the scene of combat after
the arsenal attack and was then chosen commander. No source describes
what qualification D'Wolf had or how he was chosen. He remained in
Dorr's favor until early in June, when he went over to the Law and
Order forces and earned denunciation by rebels as another Benedict Ar-
nold. See Dorr to [Jedediah] Sprague, D'Wolf and others, June 6, 1842;
Charles E. Newell to Dorr, June 13, 1842; A[aron] White, Jr., to Dorr,
June 12, 1842, all in Dorr MSS.; [Jewett], *Close of Rebellion*, p. 12;
[McDougall], *Might and Right*, p. 255.

[54] *Diary of Philip Hone*, p. 602 (entry of May 19, 1842). Especially
after his suspicious flight earlier that month, Dorr's behavior in mid-
May provided additional evidence for charges of cowardice laid against
him.

[55] Dorr to [Henry] D'Wolf (draft), May 19, 1842, Dorr MSS.; Dorr,
Address to the People of Rhode Island, August 1843, in *Burke's Report*,
p. 754.

[56] Samuel Wales, Eli Brown, William Coleman, F. L. Beckford, and
John A. Howland to Dorr, May 18, 1842, Dorr MSS. Wales was a
watchmaker, Brown a dyer, Coleman a blockmaker, Howland a tinplate
manufacturer, each with his own shop. Beckford, admitting a "mechanical
profession" (*Providence Journal*, September 14, 1841), like a gentleman
did not list his occupation in the *Providence Directory, 1841* (Providence,
1841). See *Resignation of Officers Under People's Constitution* ([Provi-
dence], May 18, 1842, 9:00 A.M.), Broadside Collection, John Hay Library, Brown University. Samuel Wales, who organized this wave of
defections, took the liberty of putting the names of Suffragists to this
broadside without their approval. Mowry's account (*Dorr War*, p. 190)
is inaccurate. See Dorr's remarks in Boston *Daily Advertiser and Patriot*,
May 31, 1842; John S. Harris to Dorr, May 25, 1842, Dorr MSS.

[57] See Dorr to [Henry] D'Wolf (draft), May 19, 1842, Dorr MSS.

[58] [Jewett], *Close of Rebellion*, p. 11. On the working-class status of those
defenders of Federal Hill for whom data is available, see Table VI, p.
120.

militia massed around the rebel encampment. Despite the tense confrontation, armed conflict was avoided for the time. But the defiant rebel soldiers could not hold out long in the face of abandonment by their leaders and defections among the middle strata of the Suffrage Party. After a day or two they meekly retreated from the encampment,[59] some of them yet determined to fight for the People's Constitution.[60]

III

Though some observers believed that the attack on the arsenal marked the close of the Rhode Island rebellion,[61] Dorr and some of his followers remained passionately committed to the struggle. They would not concede that the principles for which they strove had in any way been invalidated by the poorly conceived, badly mounted venture of May 18. Actually, defections from the Suffrage Party made further struggle more likely,

---

[59] Jewett, a rabid anti-Dorrite, described the men on Federal Hill as "ferocious by nature, desperate in circumstances and infuriated by liquor. They brandished their lighted matches within a few inches of their heavy-loaded cannon, and were several times prevented from firing [at the Charter militia Jewett implied were in range at the foot of the hill] only by one of them, less drunk, who struck off the match with a sword just as it was descending upon the powder. . . . They worked [on fortifications] all night, and drank deeply of rum—but the cold dew and hard labor had a wonderful effect in sobering them down, so that towards morning [May 19], finding that they were not reinforced as they expected to be, they brought back the cannon and dispersed." *Close of the Late Rebellion,* pp. 11–12. But another eyewitness observer who served in the Charter militia reported nothing about drunkenness among the rebel soldiers on Federal Hill and wrote that the militia drew up soldiers at the foot of Federal Hill well out of the range of Dorrite guns. See Charles Simmons to James F. Simmons, May 19, 1842, Simmons Papers, LC. Cf. [McDougall], *Might and Right,* pp. 254–256, a Dorrite account in which the rebel soldiers on Federal Hill are portrayed as brave patriots and the Charter militia are denounced as mercenary cowards. McDougall also wrote that spirits were banned at the Federal Hill encampment.

[60] For the renewal of armed struggle in June, see below, pp. 135–138.

[61] Philip Hone, a conservative New York diarist, closed what he thought would be a final diary entry on the Rhode Island Rebellion with the couplet: "And Governor Dorr/Was Seen no More." *Diary of Hone,* p. 603 (entry of May 19, 1842). See also [Jewett], *Close of the Late Rebellion.*

for the remaining Dorrites were more militant and radical than those who abandoned the cause.

Dorr was haunted by the memory of the thousands who had voted for the People's Constitution half a year earlier, for whose political rights he was trustee. Surely he owed them a better opportunity to sustain their cause than the attempt to take the arsenal had provided. "[Y]our Constitution," Dorr wrote to his supporters from temporary exile in New York, "being founded in right and justice, cannot be overthrown by a *failure* of arms, or by the resignation of those elected to office under it; . . . the duty to maintain it has not been effaced by recent events." [62] Dorr still hoped that those who had once supported Suffrage Party measures by their votes would render more substantial aid should armed conflict again break out.[63] The rebels, he believed, would be instantly augmented by out-of-state volunteers if the Federal Government entered the contest. Aware of the factors behind Dorrite persistence, some local conservatives in May fearfully predicted that Rhode Island might "have another rumpus yet." [64]

But the Dorrites were not able to stage another "rumpus" for many weeks after the arsenal attack. Their main problems were internal divisions and weak leadership. As working-class Suffragists clamored for renewal of the struggle,[65] almost the entire leadership of the party collapsed. Defections earlier in the year in face of the Algerine Law and the unwillingness of many middle-class Dorrites to endorse forcible seizure of public property presaged the wholesale abandonment of the Suffrage Party by its more respectable elements. Some defected with public fanfare, as in the case of the Providence delegates to the People's Legislature. Most just quietly disengaged when it became clear

---

[62] Dorr, quoted in Boston *Daily Advertiser and Patriot,* May 31, 1842.

[63] Dorr, Address to the People of Rhode Island, August 1843, in *Burke's Report,* p. 755.

[64] E[lisha R.] P[otter, Jr.] to John Brown Francis, May 25, 1842, Francis Collection, RIHSL.

[65] Few of Dorr's working-class supporters enjoyed direct access to the People's Governor. One who did was shoemaker David Parmenter, who was a popular free suffrage orator of the day. In Parmenter to Dorr, May 30, 1842 (second letter of that date), Dorr MSS., are articulated some of the dissatisfactions rankling among working-class Suffragists.

that it would take a bitter fight to sustain the People's Constitution. These defections, especially when coupled with Dorr's own suspicious absence from Rhode Island, confused and demoralized working-class Suffragists.

Dorr, indignantly denying personal cowardice in leaving his followers after the arsenal attack, remained outside Rhode Island for over a month.[66] Never able to exercise strong leadership over the Suffrage Party, he further weakened his control by this absence.[67] He went primarily in search of the military assistance that had been promised to him by sympathizers in neighboring states. But news of the rebel fiasco at the arsenal and the subsequent defections preceded him to New York.[68] Those who had pledged aid earlier in the month were understandably reluctant to help a movement that had demonstrated its ineptitude so clearly. Also, Dorr was unable to satisfy a major condition attached to the offers of aid he had received in New York—that only if federal troops appeared in Rhode Island would the volunteers come. He suspected that the United States soldiers in disguise had joined the Charter militia at Federal Hill, but he could not prove this.[69] Although, according to him, he again received the "heartfelt sympathy" of New York Democrats,[70] only a small number of these were willing to accompany him on his return to Rhode Island for an almost assured renewal of armed conflict.

The Charter authorities, as part of their preparation for any new Dorrite maneuver, again applied to President Tyler for military aid. Governor King claimed that the rebels were plotting a fresh attempt "to subvert, by open war, the government of this State." [71] Tyler, who after his great reluctance to believe that the Rhode Island dispute would actually result in

---

[66] Dorr, Address to the People of Rhode Island, August 1843, in *Burke's Report,* p. 755.

[67] Charles Simmons to James Fowler Simmons, May 26, 28, June 11, 1842, Simmons Papers, LC; A[aron] White, Jr., to Dorr; J[ohn] S. Harris to Dorr, both June 12, 1842, Dorr MSS.

[68] New York *Tribune,* May 21, 1842.

[69] For expression of this suspicion, see Dorr to [Henry] D'Wolf (draft), May 19, 1842, Dorr MSS.

[70] Dorr to Aaron White, Jr., June 1, 1842, Dorr MSS.

[71] King to Tyler, May 25, 1842, in *Burke's Report,* p. 681.

armed conflict, now admitted that "Mr. Dorr's recent proceedings, have been of so extravagant a character as almost to extinguish the last hope of a peaceable result." [72] Yet the President still remained "slow to believe" rumors that Dorr was about to invade the little state at the head of an army of foreign interlopers.[73] Tyler enjoyed confidential reports on the Rhode Island situation gathered by Secretary of State Webster, which suggested that "Governor King and his council alone, of all the intelligent persons" in the state, "fear an inruption upon them of an armed force to be collected in other States." Sensible people knew, Tyler was assured, that all these threats were mere Dorrite bluster.[74] But the President did take certain precautionary measures,[75] and the Charter Government got arms and ammunition from the sympathetic officials in neighboring Massachusetts.[76]

---

[72] Tyler to Elisha R. Potter [Jr.], May 20, 1842, in *Burke's Report*, p. 678.

[73] Tyler to King, May 28, 1842, *ibid.*, p. 682.

[74] Webster to Tyler, June 3, 1842, enclosing an anonymous report on "the Rhode Island business," *ibid.*, pp. 685–686.

[75] Tyler prepared a Presidential Proclamation ordering "all insurgents" to "disperse and retire" in case "intruders of a dangerous and abandoned character" should invade the state. Tyler also alerted United States Army officers at Newport to stand by in case they were needed to suppress an insurrection. See Presidential Proclamation (undated) and other documents, *ibid.*, pp. 683–687. Through June, Tyler's attitude toward pleas for intervention from the Rhode Island authorities was unreceptive. For example, even when there was palpable evidence of another Dorrite armed encampment late in June and Governor King despatched another fervent appeal to Washington, Tyler replied evasively and legalistically, pointing out that King had "unintentionally overlooked the fact" that the legislature of Rhode Island was then in session and that under the Act of Congress dated February 28, 1795, any request for federal aid had to come officially from the legislature. King to Tyler, June 23; Tyler to King, June 25, 1842, *ibid.*, pp. 688–690. At this time Tyler also moved troops to Fort Adams, Newport, and other localities in and around Rhode Island in case they might be needed. See U.S. Congress, House, *U.S. Troops in Rhode Island: Message from the President, April 10, 1844*, Dec. No. 225, 28 Cong., 1 Sess., 1844, pp. 44–59; *Burke's Report*, pp. 283–288, 652–655, 682–687, 693–695, 700–705.

[76] Whig Governor John Davis was at first reluctant to send help to Rhode Island, believing that the Charter authorities were placing undue reliance on "floating rumors." See John Davis to an unidentified correspondent, June 3, 1842, Peck MSS., RIHSL. But soon, under the enthusiastic di-

While organizing their forces for a second military confrontation with the Dorrites, the Rhode Island authorities sought to undercut the radicals in other ways as well. Knowing that if Dorr could be taken captive the rebels would surely crumble, Governor King posted a $1,000 reward and encouraged adventurers to search for the People's Governor in New York City and elsewhere.[77] The Whig governors of New York and Massachusetts agreed to arrest Dorr if he could be found within their authority and return him to Rhode Island.[78] In addition, the Charter Government purged the state militia of Dorrites and even commissioned new loyal militia units. Arrest and harassment of suspected Dorrites under the authority of the Algerine Law increased in tempo.[79] This spurt of vigorous repressive action culminated in the promulgation of martial law throughout Rhode Island in late June. Governor King's proclamation of martial law warned "all persons against any intercourse or connexion with the traitor Thomas Wilson Dorr, or his deluded adherents, now assembled in arms against the laws and authorities of this State." He promised "condign punish-

---

rection of Massachusetts' Adjutant General Henry A. S. Dearborn, a vigorous Whig partisan, the Bay State complied with Governor King's request for arms and ammunition. See Dearborn to Governor John Davis, June 26, 1842, in Dearborn, "Writings on Many Subjects," Vol. II (1846), MSS. Division, New York Public Library. Later the Massachusetts Whigs would suffer politically for their aid to the Charter Government in Rhode Island as Bay State Democrats in 1843 waged a successful electoral campaign in part on this issue. See the materials in Dearborn's "Writings" (*ibid.*) and Arthur B. Darling, *Political Changes in Massachusetts, 1824–1848: A Study of Liberal Movements in Politics* (New Haven: Yale University Press, 1925), pp. 286–288.

[77] See Boston *Advertiser and Patriot,* June 9, 1842; William J. Harris to William M. Bailey, February 25, 1888, Dorr MSS., RIHSL (containing the reminiscences of a man who tried to hunt Dorr in Connecticut); Frieze, *Concise History,* pp. 99–100.

[78] In New York Dorr was protected by Mike Walsh's Spartan Band of political toughs, who moved the People's Governor from place to place to elude capture. See Dorr to [Aaron White, Jr.], May 27, 1842, Dorr MSS.; Elias Smith, "The Civil War in Rhode-Island," *Liberator,* July 22, 1842, p. 115; Frieze, *Concise History,* pp. 99–100.

[79] For these Charter Government actions of late May and June 1842, see W. C. Simmons to James F. Simmons, June 20, 21, 22, 1843. Simmons Papers, LC; *Providence Journal,* June 9, 1842; A[aron] White, Jr., to Dorr, June 3, 5, 1842; Mowry, *Dorr War,* p. 205.

ment [to] all engaged in said unholy and criminal enterprise against the peace and dignity of the State." [80]

Although the authorities met the Dorrite challenge mainly with threats of repression, they also ventured to make some cautious concessions. Over the objection of some diehard conservatives who were unwilling to be conciliatory until the rebellion was fully crushed,[81] the Charter Government offered to liberalize the suffrage. Senator William Sprague argued that concessions, however distasteful, were necessary to undercut the radicals' appeal. "I know that there are many on both sides opposed to an arrangement of this kind," Sprague admitted, "but I fear we shall have no peace unless we go as far as I have suggested." [82] Such considerations of prudence apparently swayed a majority at the June sessions of the General Assembly, which called a new constitutional convention to meet at the earliest opportunity. The conservatives had learned by the defeat of the Landholders' Constitution that spring to give advance assurance of their commitment to reform; hence they permitted all adult males in the state, landholders and nonlandholders alike, to vote for convention delegates.[83]

On one issue—black suffrage—the Law and Order coalition went further than the Dorrites were willing to go. Rhode Island's blacks, clustered in a cohesive, tightly knit community in Providence,[84] had been distressed by the Suffrage Party's refusal to grant them the franchise in the People's Constitution. The blacks' desire for political rights coincided with the conservatives' need for allies in the impending armed clash with the

---

[80] Broadside, *State of Rhode Island and Providence Plantations: Martial Law* ([Providence], June 26, 1842), Broadside Collection, John Hay Library, Brown University; W. C. Simmons to James Fowler Simmons, June 25, 1842, Simmons Papers, LC; Mowry, *Dorr War,* pp. 225–226.

[81] Boston *Daily Advertiser and Patriot,* June 10, 1842; Edwin Noyes to [Elisha R.] Potter, Jr., June 23, 1842, Potter Collection, RIHSL.

[82] Sprague to E[lisha] R. Potter, Jr., June 10, 1842, Potter Collection, RIHSL.

[83] Mowry, *Dorr War,* p. 204. The liberality of the Charter authorities in June had its strict limits. The apportionment of delegates remained practically the same as for the Landholders' Convention the previous year, underrepresenting the northern industrial regions. See Appendix C.

[84] Julian Rammelkamp, "The Providence Negro Community, 1820–1842," *Rhode Island History,* VII (January 1948), 20–33.

rebels. A bargain was struck whereby blacks gave support to the authorities, joining loyal militia companies in exchange for the right to vote for delegates to the new constitutional convention.[85] "There is not so much scolding about letting the blacks vote as was expected," wrote one prominent Law and Order member. "They pass it off in this way, that they would rather have the negroes vote than the d——d *Irish.*" [86]

Patrolled and virtually pacified by the newly strengthened loyal militia units,[87] Providence was no longer available to the radicals as an organizing center.[88] After the arsenal fiasco the locus of rebel power shifted to the industrial districts in the northern part of the state that had long been strongholds of Suffrage Party electoral strength.[89] In the spring of 1842 the Charter Government's writ hardly extended to villages like Chepachet or Woonsocket, where the Algerine Law could not be enforced. When a Charter sheriff attempted to arrest Welcome B. Sayles, speaker of the lower house in the People's Legislature, a Suffragist mob in Woonsocket "amid groans and hurras" forced his release.[90] The shift to the northern villages was not simply

---

[85] The black negotiator of this bargain apparently was William J. Brown, an independent Providence carpenter who, according to his own account, received money from the Law and Order Party for delivering black votes. See William J. Brown, *The Life of William J. Brown of Providence, R.I. with Personal Recollections of Incidents in Rhode Island* (Providence: Angell & Co., 1883), pp. 156, 171–173. Cf. J. Stanley Lemons and Michael A. McKenna, "Re-enfranchisement of Rhode Island Negroes," *Rhode Island History,* XXX (February 1971), 10–13.

[86] Elisha R. Potter, Jr., to John Brown Francis, July 22, 1842, Francis Collection, RIHSL.

[87] Under the bargain between the black community and the Law and Order Party, nearly two hundred black men volunteered to patrol the streets against the danger of Dorrite attack. See Lemons and McKenna, "Re-enfranchisement of Rhode Island Negroes," p. 12.

[88] The Suffrage Party organ *New Age,* published in Providence until June, succumbed to Law and Order pressure and harassment. On this see J[ohn] S. Harris to Dorr, June 2, 1842; William P. Miller to Dorr, June 15, 1842, Dorr MSS.; Elias Smith, "The Civil War in Rhode-Island," *The Liberator,* July 22, 1842, p. 115; *Burke's Report,* pp. 309–312. The paper resumed publication in the fall.

[89] See Appendix B.

[90] *Providence Journal,* May 10, 1842; J[ohn] S. Harris to Dorr, May 9, 1842; W[alter] S. B[urges] to Dorr, May 9, 1842, both in Dorr MSS.

geographical. It reflected the retreat of respectable Providence professional men and small manufacturers from the Suffrage Party and thus had a class character as well. By late June the composition of what was left of the party had become far more plebeian as Suffragists again began to gather for a confrontation with their enemies.

IV

With the little success he was having in rounding up military aid in New York, Dorr welcomed the news that his supporters were again stirring in Rhode Island. Without his prior knowledge or authorization a group of Dorrite militia officers, including some who had been at the arsenal and Federal Hill in May, chose the village of Chepachet for an armed encampment where Suffragist troops could train for their next encounter with the Charter authorities.[91] Dorr naïvely hoped that the People's Legislature would also reconvene at Chepachet, and that what he saw as two divergent wings of his party would draw together. The moderate "no-force constitutionalists," as he called them, could rally to the People's Legislature, while the militants could have a better opportunity to display their courage than had been possible the previous month at the arsenal.[92] Whether Dorr thought that a concentration of his forces at Chepachet would make such a stunning military array that his opponents would be cowed into submission, or that his reconstituted militia, if attacked, would defeat the Charter forces, or that the reconvening of the People's Legislature would recall to militant action all those who voted for the People's Constitution, is hard to say. Dorr's political viewpoint always had a large component of fantasy, and his

---

[91] A[aron] White, Jr., to Dorr, June 3, 1842, Dorr MSS; Charles Simmons to James Fowler Simmons, June 1, 1842, Simmons Papers, LC; Frieze, *Concise History*, pp. 101–102.

[92] The fullest expression of Dorr's own hopes in early June are in Dorr to "Brig. General Sprague" and others, June 6, 1842, Dorr MSS. Dorr was writing to Jedediah Sprague (1803–1889), an innkeeper at Chepachet whose premises served in late June as Dorrite headquarters in the little village. See Sprague's reminiscences of the Dorr War in Frank H. Potter, "Chepachet and Thereabouts in the Town of Glocester" (MS., 1939), in RIHSL. For Sprague's early activism in the suffrage cause, see Providence *Republican Herald*, January 9, 1841.

desperation after the arsenal defeat brought no new sobriety of outlook. Away from the situation in Rhode Island, Dorr was in no position to exercise decisive leadership or critically weigh various courses of action. Instead he eagerly clutched at any possibility that his movement might yet be vindicated.

He was not alone in hoping for a renewal of suffrage radicalism at Chepachet. In mid-June, before his return to Rhode Island, men began to gather at that little village. Arriving in groups, fathers with their sons, friends and fellow workers, they were mainly "sons of the soil," "rugged, hard-handed people, farmers and mechanics." [93] Available data, summarized in Table VII,[94] corroborates observers' impressions that the militants at Chepachet were drawn from the lower-class adherents of the Suffrage Party. Some walked to the encampment from the nearby towns of Johnston and Scituate. Others came by horse or wagon from the bustling towns of Providence County.[95] Hundreds of volunteers came to Chepachet, tethering their animals at Jedediah Sprague's tavern, seeking food and places to sleep, and awaiting Dorr's imminent return.[96]

---

[93] Dorr, Address to the People of Rhode Island, August 1843, in *Burke's Report,* pp. 758–759; Testimony of Caleb E. Tucker at Dorr's treason trial, 1844, *ibid.,* p. 894.

[94] The arrests in late June were on a farily random basis, and although the precise occupational proportions in the table might not hold true for the entire Dorrite contingent at Chepachet, the overwhelming preponderance of mechanics, workingmen and farmers cannot be doubted.

[95] Of 149 Dorrites arrested in late June for whom data is available, 110 came from the expanding towns of Cranston (4), Johnston (16), Providence (27), North Providence (18), Cumberland (5), Smithfield (26) and Warwick (14); 37 from the four static towns of Glocester, (22), Scituate (4), East Greenwich (2), and Coventry (9); and only 2 from the declining town of Foster. Residence locations are from "Records of Commissioners" (see Table VI, p. 120). Distinctions between Rhode Island towns are developed in Peter J. Coleman, *The Transformation of Rhode Island, 1790–1860* (Providence: Brown University Press, 1963), *passim.* When divided into age categories, the Dorrite militants who were captured in June range from under eighteen to seventy-two, with most twenty to forty years old. See "Records of Commissioners," *passim.*

[96] The precise number of volunteers at Chepachet is difficult to specify. Men had been gathering since the middle of June, but many left before Dorr arrived on June 25 (see below, p. 135). Estimates ranged from 400 to 700 men, but many of these included spectators and stragglers along

TABLE VII SOCIAL PROFILE OF DORRITES
AT CHEPACHET, JUNE, 1842 *

Farmers	23	Merchants and	
Factory workers		professional men	
(unspecified)	15	(including Dorr)	5
Carpenters	12	Stonecutters	4
Textile workers	11	Painters	3
Shoemakers	9	Laborers	3
Store or tavern		Miscellaneous	
keepers	8	mechanical occu-	
Hired hands	6	pations	19

Total for whom occupational data is available   118

* Souce: "Records of the Commissioners" (see Table VI, p. 120), listing occupations of over two thirds of the prisoners in June 1842.

What brought these men to Chepachet is not easy to gauge. Most of the surviving documents deal with the ideas, considerations, and beliefs of the middle- and upper-class leaders of the Suffrage Party; disappointingly little is available on the motivations of their inarticulate followers.[97] Some of these men later testified to Charter Government inquisitors that they came to the rebel camp only to avoid impressment into the Charter militia or simply "to see the place." [98] But these subsequent disavowals of radicalism were obviously intended to

---

with Dorrite militants. See Mowry, *Dorr War,* p. 208. For the situation found in Chepachet by the arriving volunteers, see testimony in "Records of Commissioners," *passim.*

[97] For the Dorr Rebellion, as for other antebellum radical and reform movements, as David Brion Davis has pointed out, "[l]ittle is known of the rank and file members, to say nothing of the passive supporters. . . ." "Introduction," in Davis, ed., *Ante-Bellum Reform* (New York: Harper & Row, 1967), p. 10. On problems of writing about the history of the inarticulate, see Jesse Lemisch, "The American Revolution Seen from the Bottom Up," in Barton J. Bernstein, ed., *Towards a New Past: Dissenting Essays in American History* (New York: Pantheon, 1968), pp. 3 ff.

[98] See "Records of Commissioners," *passim.*

deceive the Charter officials and bring about dismissal of criminal charges.[99] A few of the Chepachet volunteers, however, risking long prison terms, forcefully expressed the convictions and attitudes that were probably widespread among the rebels: that the People's Government was the rightful one in Rhode Island; that Governor Dorr and its other officials [100] must be protected; and that the landholders must give way before the majority.[101] One staunch Dorrite, a blacksmith by trade, proudly stated his willingness "to march to [the] cannon's mouth" for free suffrage principles. He would do this even if "the great folks" were to run away.[102]

For these Dorrite common people, some of whom had exercised political rights for the first time under Suffrage Party auspices, the doctrine of Popular Constituent Sovereignty was a sacred political creed. Under that creed power had apparently been wrested from the haughty landholding aristocracy of Rhode Island and the state had at long last been brought into line with the democratic spirit of the age. But the aristocrats, instead of bowing to the popular will, had reasserted their power, frightening some timid souls into abandoning the struggle. For radicals who viewed matters in this way, threats of Charter Government repression and talk of concession could not lessen the primary obligation that had fallen on a saving remnant—to uphold, by force if necessary, the authority of the People's Constitution.

*   *   *

---

[99] Newton, the first scholar to use the "Records of Commissioners," read the testimony in this valuable source far too literally. See her "Rebellion in Rhode Island," Chap. 14.

[100] One of the ironies in the situation was that the only two officials of the People's Government (besides Dorr) who seem to have been present at the Chepachet encampment—Benjamin Nichols, Representative of East Greenwich and Duttee J. Pearce of Newport—were there to persuade Dorr and his cohorts to give up the struggle. See "Records of Commissioners," p. 105; Pearce's testimony at Dorr's 1844 treason trial, in *Burke's Report,* pp. 897–898.

[101] "Records of Commissioners," testimony of Oliver Ballou, Charles W. Carpenter and Seth Luther, pp. 101–105, 164.

[102] *Ibid.,* testimony of Charles W. Carpenter, p. 105. The reference to "great folks" was probably meant to apply to Dorr.

V

While a determined core of radical Suffragists, mainly common folk, were preparing at Chepachet to renew the struggle, Dorr was slowly returning to Rhode Island.[103] He had with him no vast horde of New York volunteers, but a dozen or so men from one of that city's least respectable political organizations—Mike Walsh's Spartan Band of "Bowery bhoys." [104] Claiming to have come to Rhode Island in order to help destroy the "Algerine despotism" there, Walsh probably also aimed to expose his local political enemies in Tammany Hall, who promised Dorr "abundant aid . . . , and then entirely abandoned him." [105] Arriving in Chepachet in the early morning of June 25, Dorr was dismayed to find fewer than 250 men. Arms had been collected, and some fortifications had been erected on nearby Acote's

---

[103] Dorr never gave any satisfactory explanation of either his long absence, May 19 to June 25, or his slow progress back to Rhode Island once he had heard that his forces were gathering at Chepachet. He lingered for some days in Connecticut until, as he later wrote, he had heard that an attack by the Charter authorities was imminent. Dorr, Address to the People of Rhode Island, August 1843, in *Burke's Report,* p. 756. But that makes no sense, because once he was at Chepachet and heard for sure that Charter troops were on the way, he fled Rhode Island again. What is more likely, given Dorr's indecisiveness, is that he was waiting for the rallying of his forces in sufficient numbers for him to make a triumphant reentry but had little understanding that his own absence from the state was among the factors preventing such a rallying.

[104] On Mike Walsh and the Spartans see Robert Ernst, "The One and Only Mike Walsh," *New-York Historical Society Quarterly,* XXXVI (January 1952), 42–65. Walsh was not, as Chilton Williamson asserts ("The Disenchantment of Thomas Wilson Dorr," *Rhode Island History,* XVII [October 1958], 103) a "leader" of Tammany Hall. On the contrary, Walsh was an anti-Tammany demagogue, a sympathizer with the Calhounites and with the expansionist Southerners. See Edward Pessen, *Most Uncommon Jacksonians: The Radical Leaders of the Early Labor Movement* ([Albany]: State University of New York Press, 1967), p. 96n; Mike Walsh to John A. Quiteman, September 6, 1854, quoted in Philip Foner, *A History of Cuba and Its Relations With the United States,* 2 vols. (New York: International Publishers, 1962–1963), II, 87. Dorr left a lengthy character sketch of Walsh in his "Daily Memos," March 1849, p. 48, Dorr MSS.

[105] Walsh in his *Subterranean,* III, July 26, 1845.

Hill,[106] but clearly these were inadequate for a determined last-ditch defense of the People's Constitution.

Dorr issued two proclamations from the rebel camp that day. One of these called upon the legislators of the People's Government to assemble in Glocester on the Fourth of July. In the case of towns "in which vacancies may have occurred, by the resignations of Representatives or Senators," Dorr blandly advised them "to proceed forthwith to supply the same by new elections." The second proclamation called for armed volunteers to rally at once to defend the People's Constitution.

> The only alternative is an abject submission to a despotism . . .
> without parallel in the history of the American States. I call
> upon the people of Rhode Island to assert their rights, and to
> vindicate the freedom which they are qualified to enjoy in
> common with the other citizens of the American republic. I
> cannot doubt that they will cheerfully and promptly respond
> to this appeal to their patriotism and to their sense of justice;
> and that they will show themselves in this exigency to be
> the worthy descendants of those ancestors who aided in achiev-
> ing our national independence.[107]

Dorr waited impatiently for a day and a half after issuing his proclamations. He cut a strange figure, this portly, well-dressed man, in a frock coat with pistols strapped about his waist. Men

---

[106] Dorr later stated that the military preparations taken previous to his arrival put the rebel force at Acote's Hill in an "untenable position" (Address to the People of Rhode Island, August 1843, in *Burke's Report*, p. 757), but he did little to improve that position beyond posting scouts and taking some of the elementary security measures that had not been taken the month before (see above, pp. 118–119). Dorr's later defenders argued that his military blunders at the arsenal and at Chepachet were the natural result of his lack of soldierly experience and interest. King, *Life and Times of Dorr*, p. 130; [McDougall], *Might and Right*, p. 269.

[107] It is unlikely that these proclamations got very wide circulation, since the authorities had suppressed the Dorrite newspapers in Rhode Island, and there seem to have been no printing facilities at Chepachet. I have seen no newspaper or broadside editions of the Chepachet proclamations, which are reprinted in [McDougall], *Might and Right*, p. 265. Dorr mentions them in his Address to the People of Rhode Island, August 1843, in *Burke's Report*, p. 764. See Plate 10.

Thomas Wilson Dorr

Rhode Island, 1842

AUGUST 1837.

Constitutional Ticket.

Representatives to the Twenty-Fifth Congress
of the United States:

THOMAS W. DORR,

OF PROVIDENCE.

DAN KING,

OF CHARLESTOWN.

Constitutional Party Electoral Ticket, 1837

PEOPLE'S

Constitutional and State Rights'

TICKET.

[*Election Monday, April 18th, 1842.*]

—

FOR GOVERNOR,

THOMAS W. DORR,
OF PROVIDENCE.

FOR LIEUTENANT GOVERNOR,

AMASA EDDY, JR.
OF GLOCESTER.

WILLIAM H. SMITH, *Secretary of State.*
JOSEPH JOSLIN, *General Treasurer.*
JONAH TITUS, *Attorney General.*

For Sheriff of the County of Providence,
BURRINGTON ANTHONY.

Suffrage Party Electoral Ticket, 1842

Dorr Returns to Providence, May, 1842

Defenders of the Arsenal, May, 1842

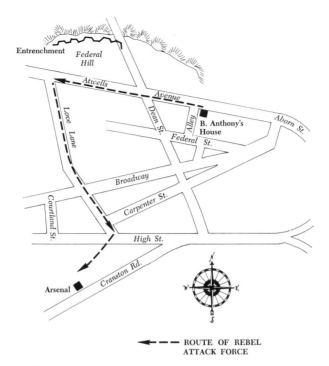

Rebel Headquarters in Providence and the May 18 Attack on the Arsenal

Attempt to Take the Providence Arsenal, May, 1842

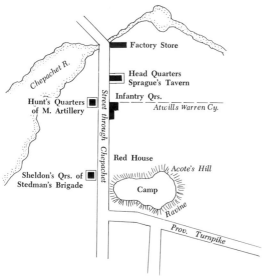

Factory Store

Head Quarters
Sprague's Tavern

Chepachet R.

Infantry Qrs.

Hunt's Quarters
of M. Artillery

Atwills Warren Cy.

Street through Chepachet

Red House

Acote's Hill

Sheldon's Qrs. of
Stedman's Brigade

Camp

Ravine

Prov. Turnpike

*Chepachet: Showing Dorrite
Headquarters, Encampment, an
Charter Militia Quarters, 1842*

Charter Troops at Chepachet, June, 1842

Dorr Liberation Stock, 1844

DORR LIBERATION STOCK.

I HEREBY CERTIFY,

that _____ has

contributed Ten Cents to the Dorr Liberation Fund, for the purpose of carrying, by Writ of Error, the Case of The State of Rhode Island against Thomas Wilson Dorr, to the Supreme Court of the United States. *F. C. Treadwell*

Counsel for sundry Citizens of Rhode Island.

Countersigned,

_____

President of the Dorr Lib. Soc.

Providence, R. I Oct. 28, 1844.

The Four Traitors,*

Who most infamously sold themselves to the Dorrites, for Office and Political Power.

Let us not reward Traitors, but with just indignation abandon them as " Scape- Goats," to their destiny—forever.

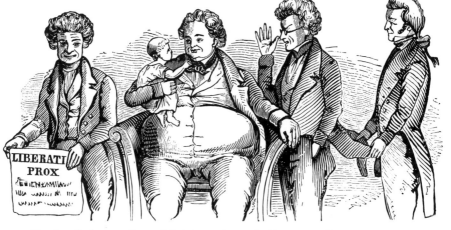

Charles Jackson.   **Samuel F. Man.**   **James F. Simmons.**   **Lemuel H. Arnold.**
Providence.   *Cumberland.*   *Johnston.*   *South Kingston.*

"O, heaven, that such companions thou'dst unfold;
And put in every honest hand a whip
To lash the rascals naked through the world"

The Four Traitors, Broadside, 1845

remembered him striding about on Acote's Hill, giving words of encouragement to his troops, meeting anxiously with his military advisers, and periodically scanning the horizon for the expected arrivals.[108] But the only information that came in was bad news: declarations from members of the People's Legislature calling it "the height of folly" for that body to reconvene; defections of former Suffragists who had helped draft the *Nine Lawyers' Opinion;* widespread acceptance by former rebels of the Charter Government's intention to draft a new reformed constitution.[109] Most ominous was the news that a four-thousand-man Charter militia force, including some of Dorr's former adherents, was advancing on Chepachet.[110] Dorr's anxious vigil was over. It had become painfully clear that the very people for whose rights he was contending had deserted him.[111]

Despite the willingness of some of the men at Chepachet to face the Charter force, Dorr and his chief advisers decided to abandon the encampment. On the afternoon of June 27 he sent a notice of surrender to the *Providence Express.* "Believing that a majority of the People who voted for the Constitution are [now] opposed to its further support by military means," he stated, "I have directed that the military here assembled be dispersed." [112] Whereupon Dorr again fled the state, compulsively reenacting his disastrous maneuvers after the arsenal fiasco. But this time he left his troops at the mercy of the Charter forces, who were in no mood to comply with Dorr's lame request

---

[108] Testimony of various witnesses at Dorr's 1844 treason trial, *ibid.,* pp. 881, 884, 885, 887, 891, 894.

[109] See declaration of Duttee J. Pearce and others, June 24, 1842, *Newport Mercury,* June 25, 1842; *Providence Journal,* June 25, 1842. Cf. Mowry, *Dorr War,* pp. 219–220.

[110] Mowry, *Dorr War,* pp. 212–215.

[111] See Dorr's gloomy conclusion in his Address to the People of Rhode Island, August 1843, in *Burke's Report,* p. 758.

[112] Dorr to W[alter] S. Burges, June 27, 1842, Dorr MSS. Sending this letter to the *Express* via his friend Burges, Dorr was unaware in Chepachet that the *Express* had ceased publication. Mowry (*Dorr War,* pp. 215, 221) makes too much of the Charter Government's delay in permitting publication of Dorr's letter.

that "no impediments . . . be thrown in the way of the return of our men to their homes." [113]

The rebellion was apparently at an end. When the militia reached Chepachet, they found the insurgent camp abandoned, but they rounded up as many of Dorr's supporters as they could find in the vicinity.[114] Relieved conservatives, gladdened by the Dorrite defeat, began to treat the whole episode with jocularity.

[T]he camp was taken quiet possession of with the arms and ammunition, powder and pumkins, guns and geese, pikes and potatoes. . . . This was the way to treat rebellion.[115]

Soon verses and broadsides began to appear in which the struggle was pictured as a comic-opera episode, fit only for ridicule.[116] Although in retrospect there was ample material for satire in this almost bloodless [117] rebellion, it had looked like serious enough business when the cannons were trained on the arsenal in May and when rebel troops were gathered at Chepachet in June. Even after the "taking" of Chepachet, conservatives would still be plagued by the strange persistence of Dorrism. Although it no longer took the form of armed uprising, Dorrism nevertheless remained an unsettling force in Rhode Island years after the dramatic if slightly comical events of the spring and summer of 1842.

---

[113] Dorr to W[alter] S. Burges, June 27, 1842, Dorr MSS. For the arrests, conviction and brutal mistreatment of Dorrite prisoners captured in and around Chepachet, see Chapter 6.

[114] Later these prisoners were interrogated by Charter Government commissioners, whose records (see Table VI, p. 120) constitute a major datum on the social composition of the rebel movement. None of Mike Walsh's Spartan Band seem to have been captured.

[115] *Diary of Hone,* pp. 606, 607 (entries of June 27 and 30, 1842). See Plate 9.

[116] See *Gov. King's Extra* (n.p., 1842), Broadside Collection, WLHU; Henry B. Anthony, "The Dorriad," in Mowry, *Dorr War,* pp. 390–399; and, most savagely satirical of all, [Samuel Kettel], *Daw's Doings, Or the History of the Late War in the Plantations* . . . (Boston: William White & H. P. Lewis, 1842), copy in WLHU.

[117] Actually, one man was killed during the June events—a Massachusetts supporter of the Dorrites who was shot during a demonstration by a Charter militiaman. See *Burke's Report,* pp. 292–307.

6

Rebel Defeat and the Revival of Party Politics 1842 to 1845

I

Despite defeat, humiliation and exile, Dorr was not yet ready to relinquish the struggle.[1] From exile in New Hampshire[2] he

---

[1] In justification for carrying the story of the Dorr Rebellion beyond Chepachet (where previous writers have generally been content to stop), I would like to suggest that perhaps as much can be learned about the nature of radicalism by studying how a radical movement such as the Rhode Island suffrage crusade faced and accommodated to its defeat as by studying its causes and high tide. Other radical movements may profit by such treatment, including the apparently waning New Left radicalism of the 1960s.

[2] There is no direct evidence I can find on why Dorr chose New Hampshire. It was unlikely that he was attracted simply by the beauty of the fall countryside there. Decades earlier he had been a secondary school pupil at Phillips Exeter, and by 1842 there was a hospitable Democratic political climate in the state. New Hampshire's two Democratic Senators supported the Dorrite cause on Capitol Hill; Representative Edmund Burke, also from the Granite State, was perhaps Dorr's strongest Congressional supporter. Also, Governor Henry Hubbard publicly rejected the request that Dorr be handed over to the Rhode Island authorities. Dorr may have had advance notice of Hubbard's attitude. See *Letters of the Hon. C[hauncey] F. Cleveland, and Hon. Henry Hubbard, Governors*

soon began to communicate with his political friends in Rhode Island, confounding the hopes of many that his absence would be complete and permanent.[3] His former political associates assured him that although forcible measures were no longer appropriate, "the cause was not extinct," and that they "had hopes of accomplishing something at the ballot-box." [4] Dorr fervently seized on these assurances, and on expressions of sympathy from outside Rhode Island,[5] as encouraging signs warranting

of Connecticut and New Hampshire, to Samuel Ward King, the Charter Governor of Rhode Island, Refusing to Deliver Up Thomas Wilson Dorr, the Constitutional Governor of the State, to the Usurping Authorities Thereof. Also, the Letters of the Hon. Marcus Morton, and Others, to the Suffrage Clam-Bake . . . (Fall River, Mass.: Thomas Almy, [September] 1842), pp. 8–12. (This pamphlet, hereafter cited as *Letters of Cleveland, Hubbard and Morton,* is in WLHU; the original letters are in the Dorr MSS.)

[3] For these hopes, see William Sprague to John Brown Francis, June 12, 1842, Francis Collection, RIHSL; S[amuel] Blatchford to William Henry Seward, July 1, 1842, Seward Papers, Rush Rhees Library, University of Rochester; Boston *Daily Advertiser and Patriot,* July 11, 1842; Jacob Frieze, *Concise History of the Efforts to Obtain an Extension of Suffrage in Rhode Island from the Year 1811 to 1842* (Providence: B. Moore, 1842), p. 97.

[4] Dorr, Address to the People of Rhode Island, August 1843, in *Burke's Report,* p. 762.

[5] Not only did the New Hampshire Governor publicly refuse to deliver Dorr to Rhode Island authorities, but the Democratic Governor of Connecticut, Chauncey Cleveland, did likewise. See *Letters of Cleveland, Hubbard and Morton,* pp. 3–12. The Connecticut Governor's letter was apparently drafted by Gideon Welles, then a minor state officeholder. See Welles Papers, Box 97, LC. Some later writers have criticized the refusal to deliver up Dorr as noxious "intermeddling" in Rhode Island affairs. See Charles T. Congdon, *Reminiscences of a Journalist* (Boston: James R. Osgood, 1880), pp. 114–115; Arthur May Mowry, *The Dorr War: Or, The Constitutional Struggle in Rhode Island* (Providence: Preston and Rounds, 1901), pp. 302–303. In neighboring Massachusetts, Marcus Morton, the Democratic candidate for Governor, framed his successful campaign against the Whig incumbent John Davis in part as a defense of Dorrite principles. Morton's letter in support of Dorr, August 27, 1842, was printed as a *Republican Herald* broadside (copy in the WLHU) and in *Letters of Cleveland, Hubbard and Morton,* pp. 12–16. For Massachusetts Governor Davis' aid to the Rhode Island Charter forces, see above, pp. 127–128. For the impact of the Dorr Rebellion on Massachusetts politics, see Arthur B. Darling, *Political Changes in Massachusetts,*

optimism and continued action in behalf of the People's Constitution.[6]

The Charter Government itself inadvertently contributed to Dorrite persistence in the weeks after Chepachet. The official declaration of martial law unleashed savage feelings on the part of some government adherents. Dorrite prisoners captured around Chepachet in late June were treated brutally, not only by the authorities, but by anti-Dorr crowds as well. One particularly cruel example was the mock execution of a hapless rebel soldier; he was blindfolded by a Charter militia company, whereupon the firing squad raised its guns and fired blank bullets.[7] Over a hundred other captives were led back to the state capital on June 29, tightly bound by ropes into platoons of eight. As one of the captives related it:

> In this way we were marched on foot to Providence sixteen miles; threatened and pricked by the bayonet if we lagged from fatigue, the rope severely chafing our arms; the skin was off mine. In two instances, when the soldiers were halted, we were refused the use of their cups to get water from the brook which passed the road, and had no water till we reached Greenville, about eight miles. It was a very hot day; I had no water or breakfast that morning, and I received no food until the next day in Providence. We were marched thus tied through the streets, and, after being exhibited, were put into the State prison.[8]

1824–1848: A Study of Liberal Movements in Politics (New Haven: Yale University Press, 1925), pp. 258, 286–289.

[6] Aaron White, Jr., to Dorr, September 5; William H. Smith to Dorr, September 3; W[alter] R. Danforth to Dorr, September 3, 1842, all in Dorr MSS.; [Frances H. (Whipple) McDougall], *Might and Right by a Rhode Islander,* 2nd. ed. (Providence: A. H. Stillwell, 1844), p. 257.

[7] The story was related by Almon D. Hodges, a lieutenant colonel in the Rhode Island Charter militia in 1842. See Almon D. Hodges, Jr., ed., *Almon Danforth Hodges and His Neighbors: An Autobiographical Sketch of a Typical Old Englander* (Boston: privately printed, 1909), p. 197.

[8] Deposition of Henry Lord, made under oath to B. F. Hallett, May 10, 1844, in *Burke's Report,* p. 317. Cf. other such depositions, *ibid., passim.,* Mowry, *Dorr War,* p. 227–232.

"If a band of *colored* men had been marched through the streets of Providence *under the same circumstances,*" remarked one bitter Dorrite pamphleteer, "all New England would have been ablaze." [9]

What became the most significant act of Algerine repression took place in the Bristol County town of Warren, near the Massachusetts border. Acting under martial law, an armed Charter militia band, including a sailor named Luther M. Borden, broke into the home of Dorrite militant Martin Luther [10] in the early morning hours of June 29. Unable to find their prey, who had fled into neighboring Massachusetts, the militiamen bullied and threatened his aged mother and the hired men.[11] Later that year Martin and Rachel Luther filed suits in federal court charging that Borden and the other militiamen had committed an illegal trespass on June 29, since the People's Constitution was right-

---

[9] [McDougall], *Might and Right*, p. 287.

[10] A farmer in 1842, Luther apparently had been a shoemaker and "trader" and may have had some pretentions to being a "gentleman." See the variety of occupational and status descriptions in the records of Luther's various court appearances. See his indictment for violation of the Algerine Law (September 1842), U.S. District Court papers, *Luther v. Borden* (November 1842) in *Burke's Report,* pp. 358, 800. A landholding freeman, Luther voted for the People's Constitution in December 1841. See voting lists for Warren, Bristol County, *ibid.,* p. 620. He had also been town moderator in Warren, receiving votes on April 18 for state and local officials under the People's Constitution. For Martin Luther's ideological apologia, see his long letter dated November 1 in *New Age,* November 11, 1842. Martin Luther was apparently unrelated to Seth Luther, the Providence carpenter.

[11] Martin Luther's deposition (April 3, 1844) in *Burke's Report,* pp. 322–324, gives a graphic account of the raid. Cf. plaintiff's declaration in *Luther v. Borden, ibid.,* pp. 358–359; Docket Record and Transcripts, National Archives, Record Group 267. Borden's name appears as chief defendant because of alphabetical order. The other militiamen were: Stephen Johnson, cooper; William L. Brown, carpenter; John H. Monroe, tailor; William B. Snell, custom house officer; James Gardner, merchant; Silas P. Martin and John Kelley, master mariners; and Hammond Sergeant, seaman. Writ of the Rhode Island District (U.S.) Court, October 6, 1842, in *Burke's Report,* p. 358; U.S. Supreme Court, Appellate Cases, *Luther v. Borden,* Docket Records and Transcripts, National Archives, Record Group 267. Monroe and Snell, both landholding freemen, had voted for the People's Constitution six months before. See voting lists for Warren, Bristol County, in *Burke's Report,* p. 620.

fully in force at the time. The ensuing *Luther v. Borden* cases, which eventually reached the U.S. Supreme Court on appeal, became the major judicial test of Dorrite political principles—the role they were intended to play.[12]

Continuing repression in Rhode Island caused some Law and Order partisans to worry lest the persecution of Dorrites raise up the Suffrage Party again. "Morally right or not," observed one wary Rhode Island conservative, such persecution was "certainly impolitic."

> [Too many] are apparently disposed to make use of the present excitement to direct it against some old political enemies to gratify private malice. . . . Those who are persecuted in this way may be silent for the present from motives of prudence, but if they have anything of human nature about them they will recall it against the present government & bye & bye the reaction against the RI [Law and Order] party will be terrible.[13]

---

[12] By claiming residence in Massachusetts, Martin Luther intended to secure a hearing in federal court and eventually to bring the case to the United States Supreme Court if necessary. Consenting to bring a test case, Luther was contending in behalf of Dorrite principles rather than merely for damages. Therefore he adopted a line of argument that included the most categorical assertion of Popular Constituent Sovereignty. Rachel Luther's parallel suit was linked with her sons' in federal court. These two suits (*Martin Luther v. Luther Borden, et al.; Rachel Luther v. Luther Borden, et al.*) must be distinguished from Martin Luther's trial and conviction under the Algerine Law. For the latter, see *Burke's Report*, pp. 800–804, which also contains (pp. 357 ff.) the papers filed by the plaintiffs in *Luther v. Borden.* Cf. Mowry, *Dorr War*, pp. 231–237; George Marshel Dennison, "The Constitutional Issues of the Dorr War: A Study in the Evolution of American Constitutionalism, 1776–1849" (Ph.D. Thesis, University of Washington, 1967), Chap. 7; C. Peter Magrath, "Optimistic Democrat: Thomas W. Dorr and the Case of *Luther v. Borden*," *Rhode Island History*, XXIX (August–November 1970), 97–98. For my own account of the judicial history of *Luther v. Borden*, see below, Chapter 7.

[13] E[lisha] R. P[otter, Jr.] to John Brown Francis, July 22, 1842, Francis Collection, RIHSL; P[otter] to John H. Clarke, July 3, 1842, Potter Collection, RIHSL. For Dorrite reactions to the persecutions, see H. Mills to Dorr, August 17, 1842; B[urrington] Anthony to Dorr, September 4, 1842, Dorr MSS.; Boston *Bay State Democrat*, July 2, 1842; *New Age*, October 28; December 16, 23, 1842.

In apparent response to such protests against Law and Order brutality, the Charter Government issued an order on July 5 halting arrests under martial law.[14] But the treatment of prisoners already arrested,[15] along with the bitter memory of military defeat, kept alive considerable sympathy for the rebels and their cause. The Dorrite persistence greatly perturbed Rhode Island conservatives and may have impelled them to carry through on their promises to draft a new, reformed constitution.

II

This new document, drafted in the fall of 1842 and promptly dubbed the "Algerine Constitution," [16] was no mere copy of the Landholders' Constitution. Conservatives had drawn a number of lessons from their March defeat.[17] Whig Senator James F. Simmons, one of the most powerful political figures in the state, came from Washington to play a leading role in the constitutional convention.[18] Simmons vehemently opposed any reference whatever to the supposed sovereignty of the people; to include that, he argued, would needlessly place "a powder magazine

---

[14] Broadside, *State of Rhode Island and Providence Plantations: Order No. 21 from Headquarters* (n.p., July 5, 1842), in Broadside Collection, John Hay Library, Brown University.

[15] For a graphic account of Dorrite prison experiences, see [McDougall], *Might and Right,* pp. 283–284. Frieze, author of the standard Law and Order account (*Concise History,* p. 122), observed that the prisoners were not incarcerated in the best hotels, to be "entertained in gentlemanly style, and treated daily to Madiera and Champaign [*sic*]." But, striving to be partial to the Charter Government, even Frieze had to admit "undue severity" in some cases.

[16] This was the term the Dorrites applied to the document. See *New Age,* November 25, 1842; Dorr to Philip B. Stinness, November 2, 1842, Dorr MSS.

[17] See pp. 59, 78–79.

[18] Two prominent Law and Order Democrats privately grumbled over the new document, calling it the *"Simmons* constitution." [Elisha R. Potter, Jr.] to John Brown Francis, November 27, 1842, Francis Collection, RIHSL. Earlier in the year Simmons had remained in Washington when the Landholders' Constitution was drafted and only sent a letter of advice to the February convention. See pp. 60–61.

beneath the fabric of civil society." [19] Instead of containing any invocation of potentially disruptive doctrines, the proposed constitution opened with George Washington's dictum that declared an existing constitution to be "sacredly obligatory on all" until "changed by an explicit and authentic act of the whole people." [20] Article XIII specified that any such change would have to be preceded by an act of the General Assembly,[21] as the radicals had long denied. Offsetting the conservative clause on constitutional change were provisions enlarging the suffrage and, as with both the People's and the Landholders' constitutions, permitting voting by the very enlarged electorate to be created under the new constitution. The Law and Order conservatives also fulfilled their earlier bargain with the black community, making it virtually certain that when ratification took place blacks would be refranchised.[22] Moreover, anticipating a Dorrite boycott of the balloting on the new constitution, they arranged for ratification by only a majority of votes cast instead of by the whole electorate.[23] By making a few well-chosen concessions, the Rhode Island conservatives intended to quiet the agitations.[24]

Although the Algerine Constitution contained provisions the Dorrites had long advocated, such as the invocation of God's blessing for the new enterprise,[25] radicals found the document

---

[19] Simmons in *Journal of the Convention Assembled to Frame a Constitution for the State of Rhode Island. . . . Sept. 1842* (Providence: Knowles, Anthony & Co., 1859), pp. 29–30.

[20] Rhode Island Constitution (November 1842), Article II, in Mowry, *Dorr War*, Appendix D, pp. [367]–368.

[21] *Ibid.*

[22] This was arranged by including on the ratification ballot a referendum on black voting, which placed the burden on those who wished to disfranchise blacks by requiring them to insert the word "white" into the suffrage clause of the new constitution. See *Journal of the Convention, Sept., 1842*, p. 60. Blacks, who were concentrated in Providence, voted on ratification of the new constitution as well as on the referendum for their own permanent enfranchisement.

[23] Mowry, *Dorr War*, p. 286.

[24] Boston *Daily Advertiser and Patriot*, November 22, 1842.

[25] Rhode Island Constitution (November 1842), Preamble, in Mowry, *Dorr War*, Appendix D, p. 367. For Dorrite opposition to the lack of such a statement in the Landholders' Constitution, see above, p. 62.

repugnant. The new constitution's apportionment provisions, while giving more power in the lower house to the northern towns, retained the old rural overrepresentation in the state Senate.[26] Most objectionable of all were the suffrage clauses. These granted the vote to most native Americans who could pay a newly instituted $1.00 poll tax [27] or who had property in land. The new constitution still discriminated against aliens and naturalized citizens; such people could vote only if they had lived in the state two years and owned the same amount—$134 in real estate—that had previously qualified all voters.[28] To the Dorrites, a few reformist concessions in the Algerine Constitution were small recompense for the loss of the great right of Popular Constituent Sovereignty for which they had contended.

The nativist issue raised by the partial retention of property qualifications was not new to the state. Old-time Rhode Island conservatives had long feared that extending the franchise to the foreign-born would be equivalent to handing over political power to an alien and sinister Catholic Church.[29] One Law and Order

---

[26] Rhode Island Constitution (November 1842), Articles V and VI, *ibid.,* pp. 376–377; Peter J. Coleman, *The Transformation of Rhode Island, 1790–1860* (Providence: Brown University Press, 1963), pp. 284–285. Although the lower house of 72 members was set at the ratio of one representative for every 1,530 inhabitants, subject to change after the 1850 census, every town was to have at least one representative, and no town or city could have more than one-sixth of the members. The Senate consisted of the Lieutenant Governor and one Senator from each town. See Appendix C.

[27] Rhode Island Constitution (November 1842), Article II, Section 2, in Mowry, *Dorr War,* Appendix D, p. 371; According to one Dorrite writer, the poll tax stirred "great indignation." See Catherine R. Williams, "Recollections of the Life and Conversation of Thomas W. Dorr, First Governor of Rhode Island Under the People's Constitution" (draft, n.d.), Dorr MSS., Vol. 2, p. 19.

[28] Rhode Island Constitution (November 1842), Article II, Section 1, in Mowry, *Dorr War,* Appendix D, pp. 370–371; Coleman, *Transformation of Rhode Island,* pp. 284–285; Chilton Williamson, "Rhode Island Suffrage Since the Dorr War," *New England Quarterly,* XXVIII (March 1955), 35–37.

[29] For earlier nativist opposition to suffrage extension, see Report of Benjamin Hazard against extension of suffrage to the Rhode Island General Assembly, 1829, in *Burke's Report,* pp. 384–386; [John Pitman], *To Members of the General Assembly of Rhode-Island* (Providence:

Democrat explained to ex-President Martin Van Buren that the prevalence of manufacturing in Rhode Island necessitated restrictions against the foreign workingmen who would soon inundate the little state and possibly dominate its political fortunes.[30] Other Democrats, however, would soon see political opportunity in championing the political rights of immigrants and continuing as well the struggle against Law and Order hegemony.

Ratification of the Algerine Constitution was a foregone conclusion. In drafting it Law and Order leaders had conceded just enough to wean most Rhode Islanders from Dorrism, ensuring that even a small voter turnout would result in ratification. Their radical opponents were in no position, five months after Chepachet, to call for armed defense of the People's Constitution. The most the exiled leader of the rebels could do was call for a boycott of the November elections, on the grounds that the Algerine Constitution was a completely illegal instrument deserving not even a negative vote.[31] Under the arrangements for ratification such a boycott would be futile except perhaps as a symbolic gesture. Law and Order members also wished to keep rebel sympathizers from the polls, and they used force and intimidation to do so.[32] Thus, although the total vote was far smaller than that cast for the Landholders' Constitution the previous March (only 25 percent of those eligible cast ballots), ratification was accomplished by a lopsided margin of 7,024 to 51.[33]

Knowles and Vose, 1842), pp. 21–23; *Charge of the Hon. Chief Justice Durfee, Delivered to the Grand Jury at the March Term of the Supreme Judicial Court, at Bristol, Rhode Island* . . . (n.p. [March 1842]), p. 10; Francis Wayland to Basil Manly, February 9, 1843, Wayland Papers, John Hay Library, Brown University. See also above, p. 9.

[30] E[lisha] R. Potter [Jr.] to Martin Van Buren, November 30, 1842, Van Buren Papers, LC.

[31] Dorr, Address to the People of Rhode Island, August 1843, in *Burke's Report*, p. 758; Catherine Williams, "Recollections of Dorr," p. 19; [McDougall], *Might and Right*, pp. 306–307.

[32] For Dorrite accounts of intimidation at the polls, see *New Age*, October 23; November 25, 1842; January 6, 1843. Independent verification is provided in the staunch Law and Order *Providence Journal* (January 3, 1843), which candidly admitted the truth of charges of voter intimidation. There was no secret ballot at this time in Rhode Island.

[33] See the voting frequencies in Appendix B.

The pattern of voter turnout in November 1842 cannot easily be correlated with previous Rhode Island constitutional referenda, but there are some similarities. The persistent split between the northern industrial towns and the agricultural districts in the southern part of the state [34] is again discernible; only 23 percent of the eligible voters came out in the former sections, compared with 33 percent in the latter. But the gap between these sections was closer than it had been in previous votes. Almost everywhere there was a falling off in the size of the previous ratifying vote.[35] An exception was Providence, where an increase of 200 votes seemed to indicate that the city's black population was eager to achieve permanent refranchisement. The ballot for ratification of the Algerine Constitution included a separate referendum on black suffrage, which passed, 3,157 to 1,004.[36] No sectional breakdown of the returns for this referendum appear to be available.

By late fall in 1842 the Rhode Island conservatives had consolidated their victory. Having cowed the Dorrites militarily, they had also silenced for the time being most political manifestations of radicalism. Timely concessions on suffrage extension had reduced the Dorrites to impotence. Sympathy for the radical cause still persisted, but it had not yet found its political outlet. Under the Law and Order domination the pacification of the state seemed complete. Not only had radicalism been crushed, but even ordinary political partisanship seemed muted now that a coalition of conservative Whigs and Democrats enjoyed a temporary political monoply in the state.

---

[34] See Table III, p. 55, and Table V, p. 88.

[35] Calculated from the voting frequencies shown in Appendix B.

[36] Boston *Daily Advertiser and Patriot,* November 23, 1842; *New Age,* December 2, 1842; Dennison, "Constitutional Issues of the Dorr War," p. 286. An increase of 200 votes in Providence over the balloting in March seemed to be due to the bloc vote of the city's blacks. See *New Age,* December 10, 1842. Cf. J. Stanley Lemons and Michael A. McKenna, "Re-enfranchisement of Rhode Island Negroes," *Rhode Island History,* XXX (February 1971), 3–13.

III

Undisputed Law and Order hegemony did not last long. Before the end of the year many Dorrites had become active in a movement to revive the moribund Rhode Island Democratic Party, which had never quite recovered from its defeat in 1840,[37] and which had subsequently been eclipsed by the Suffrage Party's radical crusade. The involvement of former radicals in such a partisan venture did not mark a sharp break for the Dorrite movement; its adherents had often vacillated between forcible measures and partisan political efforts.[38] Opposition to the Law and Order Party provided a way for them to reenter the arena of party politics without explicitly abandoning the principles of Dorrite radicalism. Lingering sympathy for the rebel cause, no longer potent enough to revive the People's Constitution, might yet be harnessed in the scramble for votes and patronage.

In December Democrats gathered in Providence to plan for the revival of their party, with two groups jockeying for power. Conservative Democrats, who had cooperated with the Law and Order coalition in suppressing Dorrism but who were uncomfortable associating with the Whigs, wished to use the meeting to repudiate radicalism and "put the party back on its old foundation" under "good and respectable men." [39] But the dominant group at the December Democratic convention refused to hold "political fellowship or communion" with renegades who had

---

[37] The victory in the Presidential election of 1840 was the culmination of Whig electoral successes in the preceding years, including the governorship wrested from the Democrats in 1838. See Edward Field, *State of Rhode Island at the End of the* [Nineteenth] *Century,* 3 vols. (Boston and Syracuse: Mason Publishing Co., 1902), I, 332 ff.

[38] For fuller discussion of this point, see the analysis of Dorrite ideology in Chapter 3.

[39] [Elisha R. Potter, Jr.] to John Brown Francis, November 27; December 22, 1842, Francis Collection; Philip Allen to Elisha R. Potter, Jr., December 2, 7, 1842, Potter Collection, both RIHSL. For the restlessness of conservative Democrats in the Whig-dominated Law and Order coalition, see E[lisha] R. P[otter, Jr.] to John Brown Francis, November 29, 1842, Francis Collection, RIHSL; Dexter Randall, *Democracy Vindicated and Dorrism Unveiled* (Providence: H. H. Brown, 1846), p. 41.

allied themselves with the "Federal party" and thus abandoned the sacred principles of American liberty.[40] The losing faction, defeated in floor battles and purged, glumly concluded: "[the] revolutionary party have now assumed to themselves the name of Democrats," [41] and "no decent man can continue with a party led by such Jacobites [sic]." [42] But the disgruntled conservatives who could not shake off their Law and Order identification misunderstood the motives of their opponents. Far from being Jacobin revolutionaries, the dominant group at the December convention actually consisted of men who had long been active in Democratic Party councils. Many had supported the Suffrage Party through the early spring, dissociating themselves only when Dorr advocated forcible measures.[43] Their partisan aims in December obliged them to declare fidelity to Dorrite principles, such as upholding "the original right of the people to make or alter their fundamental law at any time, without authority or a request of the existing government," and to express determination to establish "in fact, as well as in right," the Peo-

---

[40] Democratic Convention Address, December 20, 1842, in *New Age,* December 30, 1842.

[41] Elisha R. Potter, Jr., to the *Providence Evening Chronicle* (dated December 15; draft in Potter Collection, RISHL), published December 20, 1842. See *Burke's Report,* p. 241.

[42] John Brown Francis to Potter, December 20, 1842, Potter Collection, RIHSL.

[43] Available data suggests continuity in Democratic leadership over the watershed of the Dorr Rebellion. Delegates from at least half the thirty-one Rhode Island towns represented at a Democratic Party convention in 1839 (see roster of this Providence convention, January 25, 1839, broadside in WLHU) later were active in the Suffrage Party. While there is no complete roster of delegates to the Democratic Convention in December 1842, the partial list in *Burke's Report* (pp. 239–245) turns up many who were previously Dorrites, including at least twenty-five men who had been at the 1839 meeting. There was also a sectional aspect to this continuity of leadership, with the six agricultural towns of declining population in the southwestern part of the state exhibiting the least continuity. With the exception of the Blackstone River town of Smithfield in the north (where the leading local Democrat, Nathan B. Sprague, defected to Law and Order), most of the Dorrite centers in Providence County drew leaders from the local Democratic Party. Many of these men seemed to have returned to the Democracy after the close of the Rebellion.

ple's Constitution.[44] Such declarations were intended to tap the sympathy for Dorrism that remained after the suppression of the Rebellion and to exclude Law and Order members from the revived Democratic Party.

The major tasks of the Rhode Island Democrats in December and the months following, were practical party matters. Accordingly, many convention resolutions dealt with the partisan issues of the day—denouncing the "present Whig administration" of President John Tyler and pronouncing predictable partisan judgments on such national political questions as financial policy and the tariff. Turning to local Rhode Island affairs, the convention delegates denounced the Algerine Constitution, nevertheless urging "all democratic republicans" to swallow their distaste, register under its noxious provisions, and "be prepared, at the ballot-box, to assert and vindicate" sacred rights.[45] These resolutions gave notice that the Democrats had decided to contest the upcoming spring elections, a decision which was astounding to some of Dorr's supporters,[46] although it apparently had Dorr's own endorsement.[47] The December convention set up town committees and a State Central Committee [48] to prepare for what many believed would be a crucial canvass.

Both sides picked their candidates carefully. The Law and

[44] Resolutions of the Democratic State Convention, December 20, 1842, in *Burke's Report,* pp. 241–244; Democratic Convention *Address, New Age,* December 30, 1842.

[45] Resolutions of the Democratic State Convention, December 20, 1842, in *Burke's Report,* pp. 241–244.

[46] See the anguished puzzlement of "One of the common people," in *New Age,* December 16, 1842.

[47] Dorr to William Simons, in *New Age,* December 24, 1842.

[48] The State Central Committee included John S. Harris of Providence, formerly a leading Dorrite and clerk of the People's Legislature, and George T. Nichols, reputedly "head of the [Dorrite] insurgents" of North Kingston. See Proceedings of the Democratic State Convention, December 20, 1842, in *Burke's Report,* p. 244; [Law and Order] citizens of North Kingston to Governor S. W. King, February 16, 1843, Dorr MSS. Such former Dorrites as the Providence shoemaker-orator David Parmenter, the Chepachet innkeeper Jedediah Sprague, and the Providence grocer Benjamin Arnold, Jr., were active on the local level. See accounts of Democratic meetings in Providence and Glocester in *Burke's Report,* pp. 245–246.

Order Party chose as gubernatorial candidate James Fenner, the septuagenarian former Democratic governor, who had been among the most vehement anti-Dorrites on Samuel W. King's advisory council. The choice of a Democrat was calculated to win Democratic votes over to the conservative side.[49] In response, the reorganized Democrats ran an "Equal Rights" ticket headed by Thomas F. Carpenter, a leading Providence lawyer who had been the party's unsuccessful candidate for Governor in 1840 and 1842.[50] The Democratic electoral strategy was clear: Carpenter was a respected political figure in the state, who had run far ahead of Martin Van Buren in the Rhode Island balloting in 1840. Closely associated with the radicals as one of the Nine Lawyers of 1842, he could count on support from former Dorrites as well as traditional Democratic voters.[51] If the Democrats organized themselves energetically behind such an attractive candidate, they might defeat their Law and Order opponents in the spring canvass.

---

[49] Another former governor, William C. Gibbs, repeatedly appealed to Fenner to take the helm of the Law and Order coalition. See Gibbs to Fenner, March 26, 1842, XIII, 42, Peck MSS.; Gibbs to Fenner, January 19, 1843, Miller Collection, both RIHSL. Democrats learned of Fenner's plans by late November, and even some of those most sympathetic to the Law and Order cause were shocked by the choice of a man long out of touch with Democratic Party affairs in the state. See Philip Allen to Elisha R. Potter, Jr., November 28, December 7, 1842, Potter Collection, RIHSL. But these conservative Democrats soon assured themselves that the corpulent and crochety Fenner was "the only candidate who can ensure our success." William G. Goddard to Elisha R. Potter, Jr., December 24, 1842, Potter Collection, RIHSL. For Fenner's early career as U.S. Senator and Governor of Rhode Island, see [anon.], *Letters to James Fenner, Esq. in 1811 and 1831* (n.p. [1831]); Mowry, *Dorr War*, pp. 3, 45, 148, 272–273; *Representative Men and Old Families of Rhode Island*, 3 vols. (Chicago: Beers, 1908), I, 454; *Biographical Directory of the American Congress, 1774–1949*, Document No. 604, 81 Cong., 2 Sess., 1950, p. 881. James Fenner's political role and the careers of Elisha Potter, Jr., John Brown Francis, Tristam Burges, Duttee J. Pearce, and other Rhode Island politicians of this period badly need study.

[50] On Carpenter, see Abraham Payne, *Reminiscences of the Rhode Island Bar* (Providence: Tibbitts & Preston, 1885), Chap. 32; Mowry, *Dorr War*, pp. 49, 129, 134, 136, 272–273, 291.

[51] For these strategy calculations, see Dorr, Address to the People of Rhode Island, August 1843, in *Burke's Report*, p. 765.

Since the outcome of the balloting could not be safely predicted, conservatives took extreme measures to assure their victory. They warned Rhode Islanders that the election was "the most important that has ever agitated the State." The Whig *Providence Journal* grimly prophesied that if the Democrats won "property would melt away in taxes . . . , liberties would fall beneath the force of continued usurpation . . . [and] valuable rights would be at the mercy of demagougism [*sic*]." [52] Dorr's former legal mentor, John Whipple, rushed a heated pamphlet into print, attempting to prove that "The principles avowed by the [Carpenter party] . . . necessarily tend to annihilate all government, and to destroy the peace of all society." [53] Not willing to let the election results be determined even by these emotional appeals, the Law and Order Party also resorted to force and fraud. The campaign of 1843, wrote one recent student of American voting behavior, "was one of intimidation and corruption which exceeded any seen before in the State. . . ."

[M]ilitiamen were escorted to the polls. Employers threatened their employees with retaliation, and landlords their tenants, if they did not vote as they were told. Potential voters, illegal or otherwise, were held virtually incommunicado in factories and other buildings, to be produced under careful surveillance at the polls on election morning, having spent the night feasting and drinking.[54]

---

[52] *Providence Journal,* January 3, 1843. John Pitman viewed the spring electoral contest as being the Dorr Rebellion all over again in somewhat more respectable guise. See Pitman to Joseph Story, December 14, 1842, Pitman-Story Correspondence, William L. Clements Library, University of Michigan, Ann Arbor.

[53] *Address of John Whipple, to the People of Rhode-Island, on the Approaching Election* (Providence: Knowles and Vose, [March] 1843), p. 4. A Law and Order election broadside at the same time made equally dire predictions. See *"Dear Sir . . ."* (signed by John Brown Francis and others, March 23, 1843), Broadside Collection, John Hay Library, Brown University.

[54] Chilton Williamson, *American Suffrage: From Property to Democracy, 1760–1860* (Princeton, N.J.: Princeton University Press, 1960), p. 258. Cf. the only slightly more lurid contemporary Dorrite account [McDougall], *Might and Right,* p. 309. Ironically, one of the main arguments in John Whipple's Law and Order pamphlet was the danger to Rhode

In a voter turnout that rivaled the heavy balloting for and against the Landholders' Constitution a year before, the Law and Order Party took all major offices. Fenner defeated Carpenter for Governor by a vote of 8,990 to 7,427.[55] As in earlier canvasses, there was a strong sectional pattern evident in this election. Except for Providence and Warwick, the northern industrial towns voted roughly 3 to 2 against the Law and Order ticket, whereas the proportions were reversed for the southern agricultural districts.[56] Despite these mixed returns, the Law and Order Party exultantly claimed that the "finishing blow" had been dealt to Dorrism in Rhode Island.[57]

Even such a compulsive optimist as Dorr himself was depressed by the election outcome. "If our party will not fight or vote," he exclaimed in an uncharacteristic outburst written from New Hampshire, "in God's name what will they do!" Dorr lamented that his followers proved themselves "a set of slavish, abject, poor-spirited creatures who would do credit to the serfdom of Russia, and who ought to be attached to the soil, and sold and transferred with it. . . ." [58]

IV

Though defeated in the gubernatorial vote and in contests for all major statewide offices in 1843,[59] the Dorrite Democrats won more than two dozen seats in the General Assembly, from which they could continue to harass their Law and Order opponents. An opportunity to do so came in February 1844, when their contingent was augmented by a few members from the northern

---

Island of an ignorant Dorrite rabble herded to the polls by corrupt leaders. See *Address of Whipple,* p. 13.

[55] For voting returns, see Appendix B.

[56] See *ibid.*

[57] John Pitman to Joseph Story, April 8, 1843, Story Papers, LC; Christopher Allen to John Brown Francis, April 9, 1843, Francis Collection, RIHSL.

[58] Dorr to Aaron White, Jr., April 27, 1843, Dorr MSS.

[59] So weakened were the Democrats after the state elections of 1843 that they did not run a statewide ticket the following year, although they did pick up a few more votes in the General Assembly.

industrial towns. In all, twenty-six Democratic state legislators addressed a memorial to the United States House of Representatives calling for investigation of President Tyler's interference "in the internal affairs of a sovereign state." They demanded that the Federal Government intervene to guarantee Rhode Island's republican constitution *"which was rightfully and duly adopted in this State in December, 1841, and established and carried into effect by the organization of a government under it in May, 1842."* [60] In short, Congress should take over where Tom Dorr left off at Chepachet!

In Congress this memorial was introduced by Edmund Burke, a Representative from New Hampshire and long-time Dorrite sympathizer, and was referred to a select committee chaired by him. The committee included two Democrats besides Burke— George O. Rathbun of New York and John A. McClernand of Illinois. The two Whig members were Jacob A. Preston and John M. S. Causin, both of Maryland. [61] The Democratic majority of Burke's committee was likely to report in some favorable way on the memorial. [62]

This prospect alarmed Rhode Island conservatives. The Law and Order majority of the Rhode Island state legislature protested vehemently against the whole investigation in terms that sounded surprisingly like those of their Dorrite opponents, claiming unwarranted intervention in the state's internal affairs. [63] The same charge was echoed by the dissenting Whigs on Burke's

---

[60] Memorial of the Rhode Island Democratic Members of the General Assembly, February 1, 1844, in *Burke's Report*, pp. 1–4 (italics in the original).

[61] *Journal of the House of Representatives*, February 14, 1844, pp. 419–421. On the political affiliations of members of this select committee, see *Biographical Directory of American Congress*, pp. 675, 1285, 1480, 1499.

[62] For the strict party divisions on earlier Congressional considerations of the Rhode Island issues, see pp. 100–101.

[63] U.S. Congress, House, *Rhode Island. Protest of the Legislature of Rhode Island . . .* , Document No. 232, 28 Cong., 1 Sess., 1844. See also *Protest and Declaration of the Rhode Island General Assembly* (n.p., [29 March] 1844), Broadside Collection, John Hay Library, Brown University.

committee.[64] But the Dorrites, unembarrassed by the apparent violation of their states' rights principles, welcomed Congressional discussion and action. Dorr reported to Burke that the spirits of his local supporters had been revived by the prospect that the Rhode Island question would receive national exposure. Dorr added, significantly, that the likely Democratic Presidential contender would also benefit by a public airing of the issues.

> Nothing will do Mr. V[an] B[uren] more good, or the democracy more good, than the full, faithful, earnest discussion of this whole [Rhode Island] matter in Congress.

With the radical cause on the wane in Rhode Island, Dorr took pleasure in the knowledge that his movement was still able to harass the Whigs. By supporting the Algerines the Whigs "ally themselves at once with the Tories of the Revolution," he stated, "and they commend Clay to the People as an enemy of [popul]ar sovereignty." [65]

Edmund Burke, no less anxious to expose the Whigs as Tories in republican guise, presented his hefty *Report* to Congress in June. It included not only vigorous polemics against the Algerines, John Tyler, and opponents of the Dorrites generally, but also a thousand pages of appended documents on the Rhode Island struggle.[66] Occupying 150 of these pages were the printed lists of nearly fourteen thousand Rhode Islanders who had voted for the People's Constitution. The bulk of *Burke's Report* consisted of speeches, resolutions, legislative enactments, court

---

[64] U.S. Congress, House, *R. I. Memorial; Minority Report,* Report No. 581, 28 Cong., 1 Sess., 1844.

[65] Dorr to Edmund Burke, February 26, 1844, Burke Papers, LC. For discussion of the election of 1844, see below, pp. 165–166. Van Buren, defeated in his bid for reelection as President in 1840, was the leading Democratic candidate in 1844; he lost the nomination to "dark horse" James K. Polk.

[66] Dorr suggested the tone Burke should adopt in his *Report* and indicated some of the documents which should be reprinted, but Burke did not accept all these suggestions. Dorr to Burke, February 26, 1844; W[alter] S. Burges to Burke, January 6, 1845, both in Burke Papers, LC. See also H. H. Metcalf, "Hon. Edmund Burke," *The Granite Monthly,* III (March 1880), p. 202.

records and testimony of participants in the contest. Although Burke included many anti-Dorr items,[67] he selected and edited his material to uphold the radical cause. In his lengthy preface he contemptuously dismissed the argument that since all these events had taken place years before, no practical results could be attained "by agitating the matter at this day." The defeat suffered by the people of Rhode Island at the hands of the Charter authorities, Burke said, was of "the utmost importance [to] the people of the several States of this Union." If popular rights enshrined in the Declaration of Independence were trampled in Rhode Island, this "evil example" might "hereafter be regarded as a precedent" for similar outrages elsewhere. The least Congress could do in face of this assault on "the very foundation of free government" was to impress upon such "flagrant usurpation . . . the seal of its most decided and emphatic condemnation." [68]

In a minority report issued at the same time, the Whig dissenters on Burke's committee upheld the measures taken by the local authorities and by President Tyler to suppress the Dorr Rebellion. They also touched upon an issue that Burke had carefully avoided: slavery. The minority report accused the Dorrites of harboring principles that would tend to encourage servile insurrection and undermine the social order in the slaveholding states.[69] Although this charge may have had some remote theoretical plausibility, the fact was that the Dorrites (against Dorr's wishes) had spurned Negroes, driving Rhode Island blacks into the arms of the Law and Order Party. Southern Democrats in Congress were unimpressed by the Whig effort to portray Dorrism as a racial or sectional issue, and even the

---

[67] Burke reprinted the classic anti-Dorr statement, Judge Job Durfee's March 1842 charge to the Bristol Grand Jury (*Burke's Report*, pp. 706–717), and many other partisan statements of the "other side" in the struggle. No doubt Burke thought that merely to give these statements wide exposure was to damn them, and his selection and editing was biased in that sense. But Mowry exaggerated unfairly when he charged Burke with presenting not "a single document" on the Charter Government's side of the case. *Dorr War*, p. 277.

[68] *Burke's Report*, pp. 84–85.

[69] *Minority Report*, pp. 3–4.

Calhounites viewed the Rhode Island question primarily in terms of its likely impact on the Presidential race in 1844.[70]

Although both reports came before a Congress the Democrats controlled, the dominant party was at a loss as to how to proceed. Dorrites complained that inaction would be a "severe blow," [71] but they were unable to specify how even a sympathetic Congress at that late date could, as a practical matter, uphold the People's Constitution.[72] Burke's recommendations called for little more than verbal declarations in support of radical principles.[73] After weeks of inconclusive debate in the House of Representatives, they were finally submerged in the discussion on "the all absorbing Texas question." [74] By early 1845 the Dorr Rebellion was a dead issue in Congress. In Rhode Island, however, there was important, unfinished business on the local level.

V

Dorr, in unrepentant exile, was still an unsettling factor in Rhode Island politics. Just before the critical spring elections of 1843, he left New Hampshire and moved to Massachusetts, apparently in anticipation of his triumphal reentry into Rhode

---

[70] For the evolution of Calhoun's ideas on the Dorr Rebellion, see Calhoun to William Smith, July 3, 1843, in R. K. Crallé, ed., *The Works of John C. Calhoun,* 6 vols. (New York: P. Smith Co., 1853–1855), VI, 209 [–239]; Calhoun to Robert M. T. Hunter, September 30, October 24, 1843, Hunter Papers, University of Virginia Library; Hunter to Calhoun, in Chauncey S. Boucher and Robert P. Brooks, eds., *Correspondence Addressed to John C. Calhoun, 1837–1849* [*Annual Report of the American Historical Association for 1929*] (Washington, D.C.: U.S. Government Printing Office, 1930), pp. 186–187.

[71] W[alter] S. Burges to Edmund Burke, January 13, 1845, Burke Papers, LC.

[72] This same difficulty was to plague Dorrite attempts to gain retributive justice in the courts. See Chapter 7.

[73] *Burke's Report,* p. 86.

[74] W[alter] R. Danforth to Edmund Burke, January 18, 1845, Burke Papers, LC. See also Charles O. Lerche, Jr., "The Dorr Rebellion and the Federal Constitution," *Rhode Island History,* IX (January 1950), 4–8; Mowry, *Dorr War,* pp. 274–280.

Island after the expected Law and Order defeat. Conservatives were deeply worried about his presence right across the state line,[75] although none of them seem to have been aware of his one surreptitious visit to Rhode Island.[76] When the Law and Order Party won the election, he had to rethink his position.

A major result of this reconsideration was Dorr's apologetic Address of August 1843, in which he reviewed the events of the previous years. He refused to repudiate the suffrage cause, now "made sacred by defeat." Although he blamed this outcome mainly on weak-kneed supporters who had failed to respond to their Governor's call for aid at Chepachet, his hope of eventual victory was almost unshakeable. "In our political faith," he stated, "there is no despair." Dorr claimed to be struggling not merely for party hegemony in one state, but in behalf of universal principles of liberty which had to be sustained in America or not at all. The very fact that the Algerines used force and intimidation to win the election suggested to him weakness rather than strength:

> The conclusion is, that the present [Law and Order] party ascendancy is unnatural and factitious; not self-sustained, but propped up for an uncertain period by external applicances, and destined to fall away when the pressure shall be withdrawn, and the public mind shall revert to its ordinary state.

He hinted vaguely at some future action by Congress or the courts but declined to discuss these remote possibilities. For the present, he explained, the Law and Order electoral triumph had annulled whatever reasons he had to remain in exile.[77] "At an

---

[75] Aza Arnold to Thomas Arnold, March 2, 1843, in John P. Roche, ed., "Convicts, Bartenders and New York Radicals: A Quaker View of Dorr's Rebellion," *Bulletin of the Friends Historical Association*, XLII (Spring 1953), 41–44; Elizabeth C. Taylor to Capt. Edward C. Taylor, April 4, 1843, Dorr War Folder, Newport Historical Society.

[76] Dorr to Aaron White, Jr., April 27, 1843, Dorr MSS.; Newton, "Rebellion in Rhode Island," p. 172.

[77] Dorr's logic was somewhat obscure here. Apparently he meant that until the April 1843 elections, he served the people's cause better (in some unnamed way) by remaining outside Rhode Island. Many contemporaries, however (and not just Algerines) suspected that fear or cowardice kept him away from Rhode Island. He took pains to refute this imputa-

early day," he dramatically proclaimed, "I shall return to Rhode Island." [78]

Dorr must have known that a return to Rhode Island would mean arrest and trial for treason, an ordeal that some of his followers had endured.[79] As he had promised, he reentered

---

tion of cowardice in his Address to the People of Rhode Island, April 1843, *Burke's Report*, p. 762.

[78] *Ibid.*, pp. 731–766 (quotations from pp. 764, 766). This lengthy Address, an eloquent apologia, is dated Boston, August 10. It contains Dorr's most extensive reflections on the rebellion that goes by his name. It also describes in greater detail than any other contemporary source the philosophic and strategic assumptions of the Rhode Island radical movement, especially its commitment to the elusive notion of the Invisible Hand. Hence I have made extensive use of this document throughout this study, especially in the examination of Dorrite ideology in Chapter 3.

[79] See the trial records of Martin Luther, Benjamin Bosworth and Wilmarth Heath, *Burke's Report,* pp. 800–813. However, the leading Algerine Law prosecution for treason had been the case of Franklin Cooley, the Providence stonecutter and long-time free suffrage agitator who was tried in December 1842. The prosecution contended that Cooley had violated the Algerine Law by serving as representative from Providence in the People's Legislature. The defense responded that the alleged acts of treason were not criminal at all, since they were committed under legitimate authority. The People's Constitution, Cooley's counsel argued, had been drafted in accordance with the most sacred principles of American liberty. The defense offered evidence on its ratification, only to have the prosecution object on the grounds that such evidence was irrelevant to the issue of the case—whether or not Cooley had violated the Algerine Law. Sustaining the prosecution, the Rhode Island Supreme Judicial Court ruled that the legitimacy of the People's Constitution could not be argued from the bar or submitted to a jury; such questions of "law" were exclusively for the magistrates to decide. The judges denied the other major defense contentions and charged the jury to presume the validity of the Algerine Law. Despite these rulings, five members of the jury refused to convict Cooley, and the state declined to press the case further, permitting this one Dorrite militant to go free. For Cooley's early involvement in the suffrage struggles, see above, pp. 18 ff., Marvin E. Gettleman and Noel P. Conlon, eds., "Responses to the Rhode Island Workingmen's Reform Agitation of 1833," *Rhode Island History,* XXVIII (August 1969), 88. By 1842 Cooley, no longer a humble workingman, owned a prosperous store in Providence selling monuments, tombstones, sills and hearths. See his advertisement in Providence *Daily Express,* March 29, 1842. The fullest account of the Cooley trial is in *New Age,* December 2, 9, 16, 23, 1842. See also [McDougall], *Might and Right,* pp. 309–310. Arguing for the State of Rhode Island were Attorney Gen-

Rhode Island in October 1843, and was promptly arrested on the streets of Providence.[80] Confined to jail in that city until arraignment on charges of treason,[81] Dorr was finally brought to trial in the spring of 1844. Over the strenuous opposition of the defendant and his counsel,[82] the trial was held in Newport County, where the conservatives were sure of obtaining a jury

---

eral Albert C. Greene and Samuel Ames, Dorr's brother-in-law. Samuel Y. Atwell, one of the "Nine Lawyers," defended Cooley, with the assistance of the Boston reform advocate Robert Rantoul. The judges in Cooley's case were the same three who had issued the *ex cathedra* opinion against the People's Constitution earlier that year. On the verdict in Cooley's case, some conservatives believed that the jury members, although chosen from a panel in which all swore allegiance to the Charter Government, included a few Dorrite sympathizers who pledged falsely. See Boston *Daily Advertiser and Patriot,* December 15, 1842. But another explanation can be found in one of the subordinate arguments of defense counsel Atwell, who in addition to maintaining that Cooley committed no treason, insisted that any conviction of treason must be based on extremely rigid constitutional rules of evidence (two witnesses to the overt act). He then was able to cast doubt on the testimony of prosecution witnesses by getting them to admit that they acually could not clearly remember Cooley's presence at the session of the People's Legislature in early May. See *New Age,* December 16, 1842. Apparently neither Atwell nor Rantoul argued that treason, a crime against the supreme sovereignty, could only be a federal offense, a point that would come up in Dorr's own case.

[80] Details of the arrest are from *Providence Journal,* November 1, 1843; George Turner, *The Case of Thomas W. Dorr, Explained* (n.p. [May 1845]), p. 2, copy in WLHU dated in the hand of Walter S. Burges; Mowry, *Dorr War,* p. 241.

[81] It was not precisely clear to contemporaries just what Rhode Island treason act Dorr was alleged to have violated, the Algerine Law of 1842 or the criminal code of 1838. The trial record on both the local and national levels shows that both laws were invoked. See report of the 1844 trial in *Burke's Report,* pp. 865–1048, *passim;* transcript of *Thomas W. Dorr v. Rhode Island* (n.d.), pp. 24–25, Supreme Court Records, National Archives, Washington, D.C. But this does not seem to have been an important matter.

[82] Samuel Y. Atwell, one of the Nine Lawyers and a former state legislator from Glocester who had served as Cooley's counsel, was also prepared to serve as Dorr's defense attorney. Atwell was ill at the time of the trial and joined the argument only at the very close. Dorr assumed the task of defending himself with the assistance of George Turner, a Democratic attorney from Newport.

that would convict.[83] Defense demands for change of venue were framed in such a way as to associate Dorr's case with the American Revolutionary patriots who protested King George III's policy of trying colonists in distant jurisdictions, far from their homes.[84]

The rest of the defense argument also rested on the tenets of the Declaration of Independence. Championing not only himself, but the "doctrines of '76," which he saw at stake, Dorr challenged the court to "try the principles of American Government and the rights of the American people." [85] Dorr could hardly have believed that Rhode Island magistrates, some of whom had played an active role opposing the rebels in 1842,[86] would judicially uphold the radical ideology two years later. But he did hope that despite the selection process, the members of the jury would not sit as mere "ciphers" in his case. He urged them, as heirs of the sacred traditions of American liberty, to "hear, judge and determine for themselves" not only questions of fact, but issues of law as well.[87] At the very least, Dorr hoped to use the trial as a vehicle to air again the principles of suffrage ideology, in particular the legitimate right of the people to make constitutions.

The court allowed little leeway for these Dorrite strategies. Judges were ready with precedents from previous cases [88] when

---

[83] For argument on the question of the legality of the Newport trial, see Report of Treason Trial of Dorr, *Burke's Report,* pp. 1023–1024, 1038–1040. Defense attorneys appealed to ancient common law authority and to American usage on this point, contending that their unfamiliarity with the local population in Newport County caused them to use up peremptory challenges to jurors who might easily have been dismissed "for cause." But the jury panel had been carefully pruned before the trial began. For an amusing discussion of the circumstances under which the panel of 108 prospective jurors included 107 Whigs, see *ibid.,* p. 975.

[84] *Ibid.,* pp. 1023–1024, 1038–1040.

[85] Dorr's arguments, *ibid.,* pp. 969, 1045.

[86] Three of the four judges had also tried Franklin Cooley (see note 78, pp. 160–161) and had issued the *ex cathedra* judgment against the Dorrites in the spring of 1842 (pp. 62–63).

[87] Defense counsel Turner's argument, *Burke's Report,* p. 1018.

[88] Most frequently used were precedents from Franklin Cooley's treason trial a year and a half earlier. See, for example, *ibid.,* p. 999.

the defense sought to introduce evidence on the legitimacy of the rebel movement or tried to argue that the Algerine Law was unconstitutional. The court consistently ruled such "political questions" out of order in a court of law. To such rulings Dorr and his attorneys replied with a variety of arguments. First, they urged the judges not to be bound by the rulings in previous cases, since a new constitution had gone into force in the interim, putting the Rhode Island Supreme Judicial Court on a new footing.[89] Second, observing that the court's personnel had changed,[90] the defense called for fresh argument on the points that only three of the magistrates had passed on previously.[91] Despite these defense arguments, the judges refused to depart from precedent and charged the jury to consider only the facts of the case (those overt acts that Dorr made no attempt to deny) and to accept the law as set down by the magistrates.[92]

The court relented slightly on one procedural point—the defense contention that treason could be committed only against the United States and not against an individual state such as Rhode Island. Declaring this to be a question that had not been raised in any previous case, the judges permitted argument.[93] Defense counsel, ready with voluminous authorities on the theory of unitary sovereignty, were eager to discuss the novel question of treason against a state. They sought to prove that since treason was by definition a crime against the highest power in a community, it could not apply to a mere division of that community.[94] This argument implicated the Dorrite advocates

---

[89] See the interchange between the judges and defense, *ibid.*, pp. 918–920.

[90] Under the Charter, Rhode Island's Supreme Judicial Court had been a three-member panel, whereas under the new constitution that was in force, the number was four. The personnel of the old court was retained, while George A. Brayton had become the fourth judge.

[91] See the arguments of Dorr, Atwell and Turner, *ibid.*, pp. 919, 923, 1020.

[92] See the sharp exchange between the judges and counsel Turner on this matter, *ibid.*, pp. 1018–1019. Cf. Durfee's charge to the jury, *ibid.*, pp. 991–992, and the entire trial record, *passim*.

[93] Unanimous declaration of the four-judge panel, *ibid.*, p. 926.

[94] See the arguments of Turner and Dorr, *ibid.*, pp. 926 ff.; *The Conspiracy to Defeat the Liberation of Gov. Dorr; Or, the Hunkers and*

in a maze of inconsistencies [95] and completely failed to convince the judges, who decided that "wherever allegiance is due, there treason may be committed. Allegiance is due to a State, and [therefore] treason may be committed against a State of this Union." [96] The court solemnly instructed the jurors to discount contrary defense arguments; the jury would not have to consider any question of "mere constitutional law" to find Dorr guilty of treason.[97] The Newport jurors, in no mood to defy judicial instructions, found Dorr guilty of treason. One of them mentioned after the trial: "There was nothing for us to do—the Court had made everything plain for us." [98]

Dorr's widely publicized courtroom speech, delivered before his sentencing, dramatized what he considered his judicial martyrdom. He declared "the plain truth" that he had not received at the hands of the Rhode Island magistrates "the fair trial by an impartial jury, to which, by law and justice," he was entitled. He had faced a panel he believed to have been unfairly chosen, and he had not been permitted to lay before even these biased jurors the only defense he had—argument on the legitimacy of his allegedly criminal acts. In his view the trial, though

---

Algerines Identified, and their Policy Unveiled; To which is Added, A Report on the Case Ex Parte Dorr . . . (New York: John Windt, 1845), *passim.*

[95] It was hard to reconcile states' rights (a Dorrite rallying cry in 1842, when the Tyler Administration in Washington threatened to intervene in Rhode Island) with notions of federal supremacy in the treason trial of 1844. The two ideas could conceivably have been reconciled on a theoretical plane, but there is evidence that the inconsistency disturbed the Dorrites and probably contributed to their dissatisfaction with *Dorr v. Rhode Island* as a good judicial test of their principles. See Dorr to [Walter S. Burges], n.d. [1845], Dorr MSS., Vol. 20. For Dorrite states' rights beliefs, see Dorr's proclamation of May 16, 1842, in Boston *Bay State Democrat,* May 17, 1842; Dorr's Address to the People of Rhode Island, August 1843, in *Burke's Report,* pp. 746–749.

[96] For Chief Justice Job Durfee's charge to the jury in Dorr's treason trial (which must be distinguished from Durfee's charge to the Bristol grand jury in March 1842—see above, pp. 74 ff.), see *ibid.,* pp. 991–999, (the quotation on treason is from p. 993). Daniel Webster later quoted this passage in the U.S. Supreme Court argument of *Luther v. Borden* (see p. 193).

[97] Report of Dorr's treason trial, *Burke's Report,* pp. 991–992.

[98] *Ibid.,* p. 999.

carried out "through the forms of law . . . was destitute of the reality of justice, and was but a ceremony preceding conviction." The judges had conducted themselves in a spirit of partisan revenge, the defendant declared, and had even tried to annul "the great principles which sustain and give vitality to our democratic republic, and which are regarded by the great body of our fellow-citizens as a portion of the birthright of a free people." [99]

Unmoved by either Dorr's eloquence or counsel's request for a stay of sentence pending appeal, the court denied that it had been swayed by political motives and handed down its savage judgment: "the said Thomas W. Dorr be imprisoned in the State prison at Providence in the county of Providence, for the term of his natural life, and there kept at hard labor in separate confinement." [100]

VI

Dorr's conviction in June had obvious partisan potential for the Presidential election of 1844. The Democrats strove to associate their Whig opponents with the suppression of republican institutions and the repudiation of democratic principles.[101] The Whig candidate, Henry Clay, was on record as believing the Rhode Island upheaval to have been "wanton defiance of established authority," [102] and other major Whig spokesmen had sim-

---

[99] Dorr's final speech of June 25, 1844, *ibid.,* pp. 1043–1046. See also broadside editions in RIHSL, John Hay Library, Brown University, and WLHU, where Dorr's speech appears over an electoral appeal for Polk and Dallas.

[100] Report of Dorr's treason trial, *Burke's Report,* p. 1046. This treason conviction deprived Dorr of all political rights, a fact which would soon cause the Rhode Island conservatives considerable political embarrassment. See pp. 169–170.

[101] For Democratic strategies in 1844, see George Bancroft to his wife, September 1844, M. A. DeWolfe Howe, ed., *The Life and Letters of George Bancroft,* 2 vols. (New York: Charles Scribner's Sons, 1908), II, 257. Cf. [George Ticknor Curtis], *Merits of Thomas W. Dorr and George Bancroft as They Are Politically Connected, by a Citizen of Massachusetts* (Boston: John H. Eastburn, [1844]), *passim.*

[102] See Clay's "retirement speech," June 9, 1842, Daniel Mallory, ed., *The Life and Speeches of the Hon. Henry Clay . . . ,* 2 vols. (New York: VanAmringe & Bixby, 1857), II, 590–594.

ilar views.[103] The imprisoned Dorr himself, since the collapse of the Rhode Island suffrage movement all the more ardently devoted to the Democratic Party, heartily endorsed the partisan exploitation of his case.[104]

When James K. Polk narrowly won the Presidential election in 1844, some claimed that the Rhode Island issue gave him the margin of victory.[105] It is hard to defend this proposition, since the Whigs carried every county in the state, but conceivably Dorr's sympathizers elsewhere may have favored the Democratic candidate. At any rate, once Polk was in the White House, he liberally rewarded the Dorrite Democrats with federal patronage in Rhode Island,[106] much to the disgust of Law and Order Democrats.[107]

---

[103] See the discussion of Senate roll call votes, pp. 100–101; Horace Greeley's New York *Tribune* editorials, June 27, 28, 1844; and June 30, 1845, in Glyndon G. Van Deusen, *Horace Greeley: Nineteenth Century Crusader* (Philadelphia: University of Pennsylvania Press, 1953), p. 75; *Niles' National Register,* September 14, 1844. Frederick W. Seward, ed., *Autobiography of William H. Seward,* 3 vols. (New York: D. Appleton Co., 1877–1891), I, 601–603; Harriet A. Weed, ed., *Life of Thurlow Weed, Including his Autobiography. . . ,* 2 vols. (Boston: Houghton Mifflin and Co., 1883–1884), I, 530 ff.

[104] Dorr to W[alter] S. Burges, November 12, 1844, Dorr MSS. Electoral broadsides in 1844 printed excerpts from Dorr's final speech before sentencing with appeals to vote for Polk and Dallas.

[105] Such a claim was made in Turner, *Case of Dorr,* p. 6. In Rhode Island Clay carried every county, winning 7,322 to Polk's 4,867. See Walter Dean Burnham, ed., *Presidential Ballots, 1836–1892* (Baltimore: The Johns Hopkins Press, 1955), pp. 720–723.

[106] On Rhode Island patronage under Polk, see D[exter] Randall to Wilmarth Heath, January 3, 1845, Peck MSS., RIHSL; Edmund Burke to George Bancroft, March 10, 24, 1845, Bancroft Papers, Massachusetts Historical Society; Aaron White to Walter S. Burges, May 15, 1845, and Dorr to Burges, August 16, 1845, both in Dorr MSS.; Williams, "Recollections of Dorr," p. 51; Dexter Randall, *Democracy Vindicated and Dorrism Unveiled* (Providence: H. H. Brown, 1846), pp. 66–71. The President's main channel of information on Rhode Island appointments was: Dorr to Burges to Edmund Burke to Secretary of the Navy George Bancroft.

[107] E. J. Mallett to George Bancroft, March 12, 1845, Bancroft Papers, Massachusetts Historical Society; J. Howe to James F. Simmons, November 13, 1845, Simmons Papers, LC; Olney Ballou to Dorr, January 26, 1846, Dorr MSS.

Whether or not Dorr's imprisonment had a noticeable effect on national politics, it certainly had great impact on subsequent political developments within Rhode Island. His maltreatment in prison generated much politically charged sympathy. The sentence of solitary confinement was enforced against him "with great strictness, not to say severity." [108] He was forbidden to communicate in writing, or by visits, with anyone outside except his legal counsel, Walter S. Burges. Even Dorr's parents had a difficult time gaining access to him. His requests for permission to take a daily stroll in the prison corridors and for use of books other than the few devotional tracts in the warden's office were brutally refused. State officials claimed that such extreme precautions were necessary lest the convicted rebel stir up further trouble among his followers, but Dorrites suspected that the government was really attempting to break Dorr's will.[109] The prisoner amused himself for over a year by painting fans or writing in a minuscule hand, surreptitious notes to be smuggled to the outside.[110] As ever, he took great interest in political developments and eagerly sought every scrap of information that he could get on the Dorrite-Democratic memorial to Congress and on the appeals to the federal courts.

---

[108] [Anon.], *Jails and Prisons of Rhode Island, 1638–1877* (Providence: Angell, Burlingame and Co., 1877), p. 29, copy in RIHSL.

[109] *Ibid.;* Williams, "Recollections of Dorr," p. 53; Turner, *Case of Dorr,* pp. 9–10; [Treadwell], *Conspiracy to Defeat the Liberation of Dorr,* p. 18. In these charges and defenses of 1844–1845 is reflected Rhode Island's small contribution to one of America's antebellum social and intellectual controversies—the debate over two different "systems" of prison discipline, the separate and the congregate. For discussion of this antebellum debate, see Blake McKelvey, *American Prisons: A Study in American Social History Prior to 1915* (Chicago: University of Chicago Press, 1936), Chaps. 1, 2. Still useful is the contemporary account of Gustave de Beaumont and Alexis de Tocqueville, *Du Système pénitentiaire aux États-Unis et de son application en France* (Paris, 1833), pp. 37–50 and *passim.*

[110] Dorr's prison correspondence with his mother, with Catherine Williams (a childhood friend) and with his legal advisers may be found in the Dorr MSS., Vols. 19, 20. Rhode Island officials probably knew about this illegal correspondence but winked at it so long as none of Dorr's letters were published or used for political purposes. On the difficulties of communicating with Dorr in prison, see W[alter] S. Burges to Edmund Burke, January 6, 1845, Burke Papers, LC.

In response to this imprisonment and cruel punishment a Dorr Liberation Society emerged in Rhode Island. Organized by an obscure New York lawyer named Francis C. Treadwell, who came to Rhode Island soon after Dorr's trial, this new group included many members of the former Suffrage Party. Women played a prominent role in it.[111] The Society carried out extensive propagandizing throughout Rhode Island and even sold "stock" to raise money for appeal to a higher court. Dorr himself, as well as his parents, refused to have anything to do with Treadwell's schemes. In a private letter Dorr denounced the meddling of "federal lawyers" and found the "stock" sales particularly distasteful.[112] Despite this lack of encouragement,

---

[111] For the founding of the Society, see [Treadwell], *Conspiracy to Defeat the Liberation of Dorr*, pp. 10, 16. Women played a subtle but important role in the deradicalization of Dorrism. Not only did they participate in the Dorr Liberation Society (itself a step away from radical action), but earlier, after the failure of armed adventures in May and June of 1842, women staged political rallies, organized clambakes, drafted petitions and otherwise publicized the Dorrite cause. They did this in defiance of martial law, suspecting that the Law and Order authorities would not apply the Algerine Law to them. With women moving into the limelight Suffrage men were able to ease out of their radical commitments more smoothly and imperceptibly. Dorrite women never raised the demand that suffrage be extended to them, a fact which reenforced their deradicalizing role in the Rhode Island struggle. By taking over part of the radical agitation in 1842, the Dorrite women stamped the suffrage movement with the aura of a "lost cause." For the role of women in the Dorr Rebellion, see Williams, "Recollections of Dorr," pp. 38–50; [Treadwell], *Conspiracy to Defeat the Liberation of Dorr*, p. 16; Boston *Bay State Democrat,* September 15, 1842; Nicholas Power to Dorr, June 12, 1842; Nehemiah Thurber to Dorr, August 31, 1842, Dorr MSS.; and two broadsides: *Young Women's Suffrage Fair* (n.p. [1842]); *Rhode Island Algerines Appeal* (n.p. [1842]), both in Broadside Collection, John Hay Library, Brown University.

[112] Dorr to [Catherine Williams], January 18, 1845, Dorr MSS. Dorr may have been mistaken in his belief that Treadwell was a ("federal") Whig. Though by 1861 Treadwell was an active Republican, earlier he had vehemently opposed the Whigs and their gubernatorial candidate in New York, William H. Seward. See [Treadwell], *Copy of Application to the Governor and Senate of New-York* . . . (n.p. [March 1839]), copy in New York Public Library. In a later pamphlet, *Secession an Absurdity,* . . . (New York: Torrey Bros., 1861), copy in New York Historical Society. Treadwell explained that he had been sent to Rhode Island in 1844 by the Society of Land Reformers in New York, a group dedi-

Treadwell went ahead with the local agitation for "liberation" and on his own authority brought appeal of Dorr's conviction to the Supreme Court in 1845. The high tribunal rejected this plea,[113] but the agitation that accompanied the liberation movement had a deeply corrosive effect on the conservative political coalition that had defeated Dorrism in Rhode Island.

VII

By 1845 the Law and Order coalition, which had dominated the state since 1842, was beginning to show signs of weakness. Conservative Whigs and Democrats who had come together in the coalition hoped to make its dominance permanent.[114] But the resurgence of the Dorrite wing of the Democratic Party startled them, and they had to fight hard to put down even the deradicalized movement that contested the state elections in 1843. In the spring of 1844 there was no opposition to the Law and Order state ticket, but the national Democratic victory that fall and the subsequent channeling of federal patronage to former Dorrites upset conservative hopes of perpetual hegemony in Rhode Island. Most disconcerting of all was the continuing widespread sympathy for Dorr's plight. The martyred People's Governor was the symbol of past conservative hostility to reform, of Algerine repression and judicial tyranny. The longer he suffered in prison, the more precarious was the Law and Order coalition.

Registering its own weakened position, the conservative gov-

---

cated to opening public lands to actual settlers. On this organization, see Helene Sara Zahler, *Eastern Workingmen and National Land Policy, 1829–1862* (New York: Columbia University Press, 1941). Although Zahler mentions Treadwell's work in Rhode Island (*ibid.*, p. 49), she does not clarify the connection between land reform and Dorrism, nor does she adequately explain Treadwell's extraordinary behavior in 1844. Treadwell, son of a Brooklyn baker, was active for decades in New York politics. See Henry Wilson, ed., *The Directory of the City of New-York for 1852–1853* (New York: John F. Trow, [1852]), p. 661. See Plate 11.

[113] For discussion of *Ex Parte Dorr,* 3 Howard (1845) 103, see Chapter 7.

[114] On the origins of the Law and Order coalition and its early pretentions, see Chapters 3 and 4.

ernment offered early in 1845 to release Dorr, but only if he pledged to "bear true faith and allegiance to the State of Rhode Island and Providence Plantations; and . . . support the constitution and laws of this State and of the United States." [115] Law and Order authorities overlooked the point that under the terms of Dorr's treason conviction he had been stripped of all political rights, including the right to swear oaths.[116] Despite official willingness to waive this technical point of law, and despite an urgent appeal from his mother,[117] Dorr insisted he could not comply with the governmental request. He would accept nothing but unconditional liberation.[118]

Although this proud and petulant stand undoubtedly stemmed from Dorr's innermost convictions, it also conformed to the ironic political realities in Rhode Island: only as a martyr in prison, commanding wide sympathy, could Dorr wield power over his opponents. Freed, he would be little more than the discredited leader of a defeated rebellion. Law and Order members perceived this perhaps more clearly than Dorr himself. Ascribing only cynicism to Dorr's actions, they accused him of obstinately making political capital out of his extended prison term.[119] In vain they fulminated against misplaced solicitude for the former rebel:

> [I]f there is to be any sympathy . . . in relation to the troubles in Rhode Island, [we hope it will] . . . be a sympathy for violated law, and a suffering community, and not for those who

---

[115] Rhode Island Acts and Resolves (January 1845), p. 59, quoted in Mowry, *Dorr War,* p. 255.

[116] See note 100, p. 165.

[117] Extract of a letter from Dorr to his mother, February 2, 1844 (i.e., 1845), Dorr MSS. In this letter Dorr expressed surprise that his mother, with her sense of pride and honor, would urge him to admit wrongdoing by seeking General Assembly pardon. He begged her not to repeat such advice. Confident that his cause was just, Dorr only regretted that he had not served it to better effect.

[118] Turner, *Case of Dorr,* pp. 3–6; Williams, "Recollections of Dorr," p. 40; Mowry, *Dorr War,* p. 256.

[119] *Providence Journal,* August 26, 1844; Newport *Herald of the Times,* August 29, 1844; S. F. Man to James F. Simmons, February 14, 1845, Simmons Papers, LC.

are receiving the punishment which the law has provided for their offences.[120]

But politically charged sympathy for the martyr they had created continued to embarrass and undermine the Law and Order coalition.

In the early spring of 1845 a group of former Whig adherents of Law and Order saw political advantage in breaking party ranks to embrace the cause of Dorr's liberation. Led by Charles Jackson, a General Assembly representative from Providence, and with the active support of Senator James Fowler Simmons, this group of defectors formed a temporary alliance with the Dorrite Democrats to support a "liberation" ticket in the April elections.[121] Both parties to this bargain were

---

[120] N. R. Knight and others, *Address to the People of the United States* (Providence, 1844), p. 12, copy in RIHSL. This Address, issued in October, represented the Law and Order coalition's agonized protest against persistent Dorrism in Rhode Island and against what they saw as the misplaced sympathies of Dorrite supporters elsewhere. It was signed by a bipartisan group of twenty-one prominent Rhode Island conservatives, including Senator James F. Simmons and state legislator Charles Jackson, both of whom would soon break with Law and Order on the question of Dorr's liberation.

[121] This abbreviated account of Rhode Island political intricacies in 1845 is based upon newspaper sources and a wide variety of other primary materials. Dorr's dim prison perception of events is reflected in his correspondence with Catherine Williams, January–April 1845, Dorr MSS., Vol. 19. Democratic strategy is clearly shown in Walter S. Burges' letters to Edmund Burke, Burke Papers, LC. The complementary Whig-Liberationist outlook is reflected in the correspondence of James Fowler Simmons, Simmons Papers, LC. Other manuscript materials, particularly the John Brown Francis and Elisha R. Potter, Jr., collections, RIHSL, also illustrate the complex political interplay in 1844–1845. Among the more important broadsides of the period, all to be found in the John Hay Library, Brown University, are: *To the Whigs of Rhode Island* (Providence, March 20, 1845), by Charles Jackson; Open letter of James F. Simmons to Henry B. Anthony ([March] 1845); *Sir* (February 1845); *Important Resolutions Suppressed!!* (Providence, March 29, 1845); *The Great Political Car and Last Load of Patriots* (March 1845). Political cartoons also flourished, of which *The Four Traitors* is a good example. See Plate 12. See also [Treadwell], *Conspiracy to Defeat the Liberation of Dorr*, pp. 17–18; Turner, *Case of Dorr*, pp. 1–2; [William G. Goddard], *Letter to the Hon. James F. Simmons* (Providence, April 1845), copy in WLHU; Randall, *Democracy Vindicated and Dorrism Unveiled*, pp. 67–78.

heavily motivated by political considerations. The Democrats, out of power in Rhode Island for over half a decade, hoped to regain strength by allying themselves with a segment of the dominant Whigs. Reenforcing these political aims was the personal obligation to Dorr felt by many Democrats who had been close to him.[122] For some ambitious Whigs the Law and Order Party, tied as it was to past local achievements in suppressing Dorrism, had become a political dead end. With the exception of widespread sympathy for Dorr, mass interest in issues stemming from the Rebellion had waned.[123] This evaporation of radicalism in the state made it possible for Rhode Island politicians to make deals with their former political enemies.

Though hidebound Law and Order members denounced the "Liberation Whigs" as opportunists and even traitors,[124] this new electoral coalition was successful in 1845. Charles Jackson defeated James Fenner, the Law and Order candidate for Governor, winning support not only in the formerly Dorrite towns in the northern industrial regions of Rhode Island, but also in some of the rural agricultural towns that had been centers of opposition to Dorrism in 1842 and 1843.[125] This campaign initiated the fragmentation of the Rhode Island Whig Party, which in conjunction with national political developments led to the emergence of a new state Republican Party in the next decade.[126] For the Democrats 1845 was also a turning

---

[122] As Dorr wrote from prison to Catherine Williams: "The democrats owe it to me to open these doors. . . ." Dorr to Williams, March 7, 1845, Dorr MSS. Many Rhode Island Democrats who had been Dorrites knew that the party's modest political comeback had been facilitated by Dorr's incarceration. Also, many of these men were technically as guilty of treason (as it was defined in Rhode Island at the time) as Dorr himself.

[123] On the lapse into relative political apathy after the electoral outpourings of 1841–1843, see Williamson, "Rhode Island Suffrage Since the Dorr War," pp. 35–37; Williamson, *American Suffrage,* p. 259.

[124] In addition to the sources already cited in note 121, see James B. Angell to Arthur Lippitt, April 6, 1845, John Hay Library, Brown University, where the future president of the University of Michigan denounced the base treachery of Jackson, Simmons and other liberationists as the actions not of men but of "lower mammalia."

[125] See the electoral data in Appendix B.

[126] There is no adequate account of Rhode Island political development in the antebellum period. The papers of James F. Simmons, whose

point. Although they would not be able to win political victories on their own for some years, their temporary coalition with the Liberation Whigs put them on the road to an eventual comeback in the state. The immediate result of the Liberation victory was the quaintly worded "Act to pardon certain offences against the sovereign power of this State and to quiet the minds of the good people thereof," which passed the General Assembly on June 27, 1845.[127]

It was indeed a quiet liberation when Dorr, his health ruined by twenty months of imprisonment, climbed into the carriage that came for him at the Gaspée Street jail the same day the act of liberation was passed.[128] Dorr's liberation marked the end of an era in Rhode Island politics. His freedom had been secured through concerted efforts by some of his most ardent opponents as well as by men and women who professed to follow his ideals. Clearly, Dorrism had become transformed from a fighting creed to a bargaining token among calculating politicians. This was no surprising development; elements of opportunism and ambivalence had weakened the radical movement from its inception, and they were crucial in bringing about its final defeat. Ironically, the very opportunism that helped undermine the Rebellion also kept alive sympathy for its imprisoned leader. But after Dorr's liberation in 1845 there remained only the slender hope that the federal judiciary, which had not yet deliberated on a number of Dorr Rebellion cases, would somehow vindicate the radical cause.

---

career symbolized the transformation of Whiggery into Republicanism, will be a major source for any future study.

[127] Rhode Island Acts and Resolves (June 1845), p. 11, quoted in Mowry, *Dorr War,* pp. 256–257.

[128] Dorr himself had specified that there be no "fanfare or parade" at the time of his liberation. See Dorr to [Catherine Williams], April 25 [1845], Dorr MSS., Vol. 19; Field, *State of Rhode Island and Providence Plantations,* I, 352. By not counting the time Dorr spent in prison after his arrest in the fall of 1843, Mowry (*Dorr War,* p. 256) arrived at the erroneous date of twelve months for the term of incarceration.

7

The Judiciary
vs. the Rebels
1842 to 1849

I

The political efforts that culminated in Thomas Dorr's liberation, and in the subsidence of the suffrage movement, occurred
simultaneously with legal contests over the radical principles
of Dorrism. Appeals to the courts to uphold the right of
Popular Constituent Sovereignty were partly a reflection of
Dorrite inability to achieve victory by armed struggle; they also
expressed the faith of many Rhode Island rebels that official
America could not repudiate the revolutionary significance of
1776. Defeat on the battlefield and in the political arena only
reenforced hopes that vindication could be achieved in the
courts.[1]

These hopes somehow survived many unmistakable expres-

---

[1] The eventual Dorrite willingness to submit the question of disputed
sovereignty in Rhode Island to court test came only after defeat had
undermined the radicals' initial reluctance to do so. On this change, see
George M. Dennison, "Thomas Wilson Dorr: Counsel of Record in
Luther v. Borden," *St. Louis University Law Journal,* XV (Spring 1971),
404. Dennison's explanation of the change as some momentous intellectual transformation from a Jeffersonian perspective to an outlook in
the tradition allegedly founded by James Wilson is unnecessarily complicated; the switch in Dorrite strategy can be explained far more
economically in light of expediency.

sions of judicial hostility. As has been noted, state and federal jurists took every opportunity to declare unfavorably on the rebel movement, often when no specific case was before them. As early as March 1842, during the struggle over the Land-holders' Constitution, the three judges of Rhode Island's Su-preme Court issued an *ex cathedra* advisory opinion declaring the Dorrite movement treasonable. A few weeks later one of this judicial trio delivered a scathing attack on the Dorrites in the guise of a general charge to a Bristol grand jury.[2]

No less hostile to the People's Constitution was Federal District Judge John Pitman in his January 1842 pamphlet *To the Members of the General Assembly*.[3] Urging Joseph Story to give copies of this pamphlet to other members of the United States Supreme Court, Pitman fleetingly wondered if it would brand him as a "political judge." Story reassured him, revealing his own conservative bias:

> If ever there was a case that called upon a judge to write and speak openly and publicly, it was the very case [4] then before you. The Constitution of Rhode Island was to be overturned by a self-created body, and I know no duty more sacred in every citizen than upon such an emergency to come forth and resist, by all the just and moral means in his power, such pro-ceedings. I do not well see how your reasoning is to be met or censured. . . . What is a Republican government worth if an unauthorized body may thus make, promulgate, and compel obedience to a Constitution at its own mere will and plea-sure? [5]

---

[2] *Citizens of Rhode Island! Read! Mark! Learn!* (n.p. [March 1842]), Broadside Collection, WLHU. See also *Charge of the Hon. Chief Justice Durfee, Delivered to the Grand Jury at the March Term of the Supreme Judicial Court, at Bristol, Rhode-Island* . . . (n.p., [March 1842]), copy in New York Public Library. See pp. 74 ff.

[3] [Pitman], *To the Members of the General Assembly of Rhode-Island* (Providence: Knowles and Vose, [January] 1842). For discussion of this pamphlet, see above, pp. 73–74.

[4] By "case" Story meant "issue," for no legal case had yet arisen from the Dorr Rebellion, and Pitman's pamphlet contained no judicial argu-ment.

[5] Pitman to Story, January 24, 1842, Pitman-Story Correspondence, Wil-liam L. Clements Library, University of Michigan, Ann Arbor; Story to Pitman, February 10, 1842, in W. W. Story, ed., *Life and Letters of*

Justice Story himself was also an active—if cautious—partisan in the Rhode Island struggle. As early as April 1842 he wrote to Secretary of State Daniel Webster to alert the Washington authorities to the proceedings of the Suffrage Party, which he said were "without law and against law." There was no need to wait for actual insurrection to break out, he claimed; in his opinion President Tyler had the power and the responsibility to take forceful anticipatory action against the Dorrites. At the very least, the President should issue a strong proclamation. "Of course I do not wish to be known in this matter," Story added; "my sole object is peace." [6] Story had good reason to be circumspect. As federal judge for the Rhode Island Circuit, he might eventually try any suit arising from the insurrection. He had no intention to disqualify himself by a premature public disclosure of his views.[7] In June 1842 he did, however, deliver an oblique attack on the Dorrites in the form of an address, "On the Law of Treason," which included extrajudicial observations upon the "alarming crisis of the public affairs in Rhode-Island," and paid "just tribute to the excellent institutions and past history of the State." [8]

Joseph Story, 2 vols. (Boston: Little, Brown, 1851), II, 416. Another important anonymous Dorr Rebellion pamphlet by Pitman was *A Reply to the Letter of the Hon. Marcus Morton, Late Governor of Massachusetts, on the Rhode-Island Question, by one of the Rhode Island People* (Providence: Knowles & Vose, 1842). Cf. above, Chapter 6. Pitman did not limit his extrajudicial activity merely to pamphleteering. He lectured publicly against the People's Constitution in March 1842. He may have been among the framers of the Algerine Law, and even have shouldered arms in the Charter militia in May. John Pitman to Elisha R. Potter, Jr., March 5, 1842, Potter Collection, RIHSL; *New Age,* April 9, 1842; [Charles C. Jewett], *The Close of the Late Rebellion in Rhode Island: An Extract from a Letter by a Massachusetts Man Resident in Providence* (Providence: B. Cranston, [May?] 1842), p. 7.

[6] Story to Webster, April 26, 1842 (copy), Daniel Webster Papers, New Hampshire Historical Society. Story wrote to Webster apparently on the suggestion of Judge John Pitman. See Pitman to Story, March 30, 1842, Pitman-Story Correspondence, Clements Library. This began Webster's intimate connection with the Rhode Island struggle, a connection that made him, in Dorr's eyes at least, the major ideological antagonist.

[7] [Elisha R. Potter, Jr.] to Joseph Story (copy), March 10, 1842; Story to Potter, April 7, 1842, both in Potter Collection, RIHSL.

[8] *Charge of Mr. Justice Story on the Law of Treason, Delivered to the Grand Jury of the Circuit Court of the United States, Holden at New-*

The conservative inclinations of judges revealed themselves not only in extrajudicial utterances but in courtroom behavior as well. The Algerine Law prosecutions and convictions in 1842 were hardly conducted as models of judicial impartiality. Dorr's own treason trial also showed conservative partisanship on the part of the presiding magistrates. The *Luther v. Borden* cases, to be discussed later, were argued before unfriendly judges, especially in the lower federal courts.

Judicial hostility toward the doctrines and actions of the Rhode Island rebels reflected more than the animus of a few particular judges; it was implicit in the changing nature of American jurisprudence at the time. In the early nineteenth century American law took on a conservative coloration as judges fought egalitarian political tendencies and took responsibility for counteracting the alleged excesses of democracy. This upsurge of judicial conservatism involved efforts to elevate magisterial authority, attempts to decrease the power of juries, and a campaign to enhance the majesty of established institutions.[9] Such forces, at work in Rhode Island [10] and throughout

---

port . . . June 15, 1842, Published at the Request of the Grand Jury, and the Rhode-Island Bar (Providence: H. H. Brown, 1842), p. [5], copy in RIHSL.

[9] Perry Miller, *The Life of the Mind in America: From the Revolution to the Civil War* (New York: Harcourt, Brace and World, 1965), Book Two, *passim*. Some contributors to the "new legal history" read another story in the evolution of early-nineteenth-century American law—the creative elaboration of a sturdy legal structure for the development of American enterprise. See, for example, James Willard Hurst, *Law and Social Process in United States History: Five Lectures Delivered at the University of Michigan* . . . (Ann Arbor: University of Michigan Law School, 1960); Leonard W. Levy, *The Law of the Commonwealth and Chief Justice Shaw: The Evolution of American Law, 1830–1860* (New York: Harper Torchbooks, 1967). Without discussing here some of the particular formulations in these important works (see, however, the discussion of Hurst's view of the Dorr Rebellion, in my bibliographical essay, p. 249), I wish to state that the creative responsibility that Hurst and Levy discern in legal doctrines on business and industrial development may have gone along with the political conservatism that Miller describes. For a perceptive treatment of simultaneous though apparently contradictory trends in judicial interpretation, see Robert J. Harris, "Chief Justice Taney: Prophet of Reform and Reaction," *Vanderbilt Law Review*, X (February 1957), 227–257. For some of the limitations of the

the federal and state judiciaries, made it highly unlikely that Dorrite claims would receive a favorable hearing.

II

Martin Luther's trespass suit against Luther Borden and eight other Law and Order militiamen began its long journey to the United States Supreme Court in the fall of 1842.[11] The case was argued in the Federal Circuit Court for Rhode Island in 1843. Since Luther had fled Rhode Island after the revolutionary days in June 1842 and had taken up temporary residence in Massachusetts, he was entitled to bring his suit directly into federal court. Dorrites hoped that the case, since it was not confined to the local courts, would speedily reach the nation's highest judicial tribunal.[12]

As presiding judge in the circuit court where Luther's case was first argued in November 1843, Joseph Story did little to dispel the impression that he was a bitter opponent of the Dorrite rebels.[13] He gave very little time to Luther's suit, explaining that he had "an important hearing" pending in Boston.[14] When defense counsel rose to make his closing argument,

---

new legal history, see Harry N. Scheiber, "At the Borderland of Law and Economic History: the Contributions of Willard Hurst," *American Historical Review*, LXXV (February 1970), 744–756.

[10] Miller's evidence for the conservative upsurge included references to the opinions of Rhode Island jurist Job Durfee. See *Life of the Mind in America*, p. 180.

[11] For the origin of this case, see pp. 142–143.

[12] For an insightful account of the political and legal strategies of this case, see C. Peter Magrath, "Optimistic Democrat: Thomas W. Dorr and the case of Luther v. Borden," *Rhode Island History*, XXIX (August–November 1970), 99–104.

[13] For Dorrite opinion of Story's biases, see *New Age*, April 1, 1842; David Parmenter to Dorr, June 14, 1842, Dorr MSS. Law and Order men knew Story was on their side. See John Brown Francis to Elisha R. Potter, Jr., April 28, 1842, Potter Collection, RIHSL. Although John Pitman was one of the two judges of record hearing this case in circuit court, he does not appear to have played any active role.

[14] Story's charge to the jury, in U.S. Congress, House, *R.I. Memorial; Minority Report*, Report No. 581, 28 Cong., 1 Sess., 1844, p. 164. This

Story called the lawyer to the bench and advised him to be brief. The hapless attorney explained to the jury: "I had intended to present to you my view of this case but the judge tells me he wants to leave by the next train, and that he will take care of the cause of the State." [15] Story did indeed act more like an additional lawyer against Luther [16] than an impartial judge. He dismissed, without permitting argument, the main contention of the plaintiff—that the People's Government and not the Charter regime was the legitimate power in Rhode Island in 1842.[17] Calling Luther a "notorious" sympathizer with the rebels, Story justified the rough treatment of aged Rachel Luther as necessary and even allowed himself to express feelings of humiliation as a "Massachusetts man" that "any man could be found among her citizens so abandoned as to aid a movement to suppress the government of a neighboring State." [18]

Story's charge to the jurors virtually directed them to find the defendants, who had acted under martial law, innocent of

---

report, a dissent from the pro-Dorr *Burke's Report* (see above, pp. 155–158) contains the *Providence Journal's* version of the Circuit Court proceeding in *Luther v. Borden.*

[15] See Abraham Payne, *Reminiscences of the Rhode Island Bar* (Providence: Tibbitts & Preston, 1885), p. 37. The attorney was John Whipple.

[16] Defense attorneys for the Law and Order militia included Samuel Greene, Alfred Bosworth, and John Whipple. Whipple was the main counsel in the circuit court. He also argued in the Supreme Court hearing of *Luther v. Borden* along with Daniel Webster in 1848 (see below, pp. 189–190). Before the case was argued in the lower court, Whipple was commended to Story as "a very zealous anti-dorrite." John Pitman to Story, May 6, 1843, Story Papers, LC. A leading Providence attorney, Whipple had trained young Thomas Dorr in the law. Cf. Payne, *Reminiscences of the Rhode Island Bar,* pp. 12–13, 33–37.

[17] *R. I. Memorial: Minority Report,* 1844, p. 165. In his article on "The Luther Cases in the Lower Courts" (*Rhode Island History,* XI [April 1952], 37–39), Mahlon W. Hellerich made a serious error. Assuming that the material in *Burke's Report,* pp. 363–374, actually described the arguments in the Circuit Court, he mistakenly maintained that the main issues in the case were aired before Story. But that material merely represents the papers filed for appeal to the Supreme Court.

[18] Story's charge to the jury in *Minority Report,* pp. 163–167. Story was referring to Luther's residence of record in Massachusetts.

criminally trespassing against Luther.[19] Such law, he held, devolved sweeping powers. Every man, woman and child in a state under martial officers actually administered martial law, he went on to observe, and the defendants, too, had a wide latitude "to act according to the exigency of the case." Of course, the judge added, abuses of martial law could not be condoned. But he made clear his own opinion that the militia band arresting Martin Luther had acted well within permissible limits.[20]

A verdict of not guilty [21] was a foregone conclusion, but the Dorrites had long been prepared to carry an appeal to the Supreme Court. Judges Story and Pitman cooperated in facilitating appeal.[22] Dorrites hoped for a fairer hearing in Washington, where they had much support and where the high court included a number of potential sympathizers. Vindication of the

---

[19] Plaintiff's counsel, Benjamin F. Hallett (see below, pp. 184–185), sought to exclude the peaceful town of Warren, where the alleged trespass took place, from the territory covered by martial law on the grounds that such extraordinary law applied only to the actual localities in which fighting occurred. Hallett also challenged the power of the legislature to declare martial law, and argued that when applied rightly it covers those persons actually bearing arms. See *Minority Report*, p. 160; Hellerich, "Luther Cases in the Lower Courts," pp. 39–40.

[20] *Minority Report*, pp. 160–162; Hellerich, "Luther Cases in the Lower Courts," pp. 40–42.

[21] See *Burke's Report*, p. 375, for the report of the jury's verdict. Hellerich's statement ("Luther Cases in the Lower Courts," p. 42) that "the jury could not agree on a verdict" is a misinterpretation of the garbled *Providence Journal* account of the case in *Minority Report*. Hellerich confused the two Luther cases. A verdict *was* rendered in Martin Luther's case, but the jury could not agree in the parallel Rachel Luther case. See *Providence Journal*, April 19, 1844. In order to facilitate simultaneous appeal of both cases to the Supreme Court, Story and Pitman agreed to an artificial division of judicial opinion, a procedure not to Chief Justice Taney's liking. See his caustic comments in *Luther v. Borden*, 7 Howard 1 (1849), 47. For an expert discussion of the mechanics of the case, see George Marshel Dennison, "The Constitutional Issues of the Dorr War: A Study in the Evolution of American Constitutionalism, 1776–1849" (Ph.D. thesis, University of Washington, 1967), p. 379.

[22] *Burke's Report*, p. 375. This cooperation consisted of their artificial division of opinion (described in the preceding note) as well their aid in the preparation of the trial record for appeal.

People's Constitution and the doctrine of Popular Constituent Sovereignty might yet be obtained.[23]

III

While *Luther v. Borden* was awaiting consideration by the Supreme Court, fresh judicial appeals were aimed at reversing Dorr's treason conviction. At his 1844 trial Dorr had contended that there was no such crime as treason against a state, a plea which the local court had rejected. He hoped for a more favorable decision from a higher tribunal, and to that end sought advice from prominent Democrats in Washington. New York Senator Silas Wright conferred with colleague Thomas Hart Benton of Missouri and replied to Dorr at length. Although both Senators agreed with Dorr's position that treason could only be committed against the "supreme sovereignty" of the nation and not against one of its mere territorial subdivisions, they doubted that the Supreme Court, which usually leaned "so strongly to sustain" state court decisions, would adopt such reasoning. Wright also predicted that the Supreme Court would find the Rhode Island Charter regime to be a "republican form" of government within the meaning of the Federal Constitution and would probably hand down an adverse decision against insurrectionary groups or individuals. He therefore advised Dorr against placing any great reliance on appeal of his treason conviction.[24] Perhaps discouraged by this advice, Dorr hesitated more than a year before appealing his case.

Meanwhile the Dorr Liberation Society, working against the imprisoned rebel's wishes, had taken legal action.[25] Francis C. Treadwell, counsel for the Society, appealed to the Supreme Court for a writ of *habeas corpus* on the grounds that the court convicting Dorr had refused to admit argument on what was the key issue in the case—whether treason could be committed against a state. Treadwell also explained that since "personal

---

[23] For analysis of this naïve expectation, see Magrath, "Optimistic Democrat," *passim*.

[24] Wright to Dorr, February 13, 1844, Dorr MSS.

[25] On Dorr's estrangement from and hostility to the movement dedicated to his liberation, see above, pp. 168–169.

access to Dorr" had been denied by the Rhode Island authorities, the appeal had to go up to the high tribunal on counsel's authority alone.[26] The Supreme Court rejected Treadwell's appeal without reaching the substantive issues. Citing the Judiciary Act of 1789, Justice John McLean found that the Court lacked the power to issue writs of *habeas corpus* against decisions of state tribunals. It was therefore "unnecessary to decide whether the counsel [had] stated a case. . . ." [27] Thus the Rhode Island radicals got little satisfaction from the first Supreme Court test of Dorrism.

Within weeks of the adverse decision in *Ex Parte Dorr* another appeal, this time for a writ of error, was on its way to the Supreme Court.[28] The new action, brought by attorneys George Turner and Walter S. Burges on Dorr's behalf, rested on the same grounds as the *Luther v. Borden* appeal—that the People's Constitution had been the legitimate and supreme law in Rhode Island during the conflict in 1842 and that Dorr had been legally Governor. This case, *Thomas W. Dorr v. Rhode Island,* never reached a decision by the Supreme Court, although the

---

[26] [Francis C. Treadwell], *The Conspiracy to Defeat the Liberation of Gov. Dorr; Or, The Hunkers and Algerines Identified, and Their Policy Unveiled; To which is Added, A Report on the Case Ex Parte Dorr . . .* (New York: John Windt, 1845), p. 21; *Ex Parte Dorr* 3 Howard 103 (1845), 103–104.

[27] *Ibid.;* Francis P. Weisenburger, *The Life of John McLean: A Politician on the United States Supreme Court* [Ohio State University, *Studies . . . in History and Political Science,* No. 15] (Columbus, Ohio: Ohio State University Press, 1937), p. 164. A number of writers on the legal issues emerging from the Dorr Rebellion have overlooked this case or misunderstood its significance. Willard Hurst's account (*Law and Social Process in United States History,* pp. 258–259) is marred by the overlooking of *Ex Parte Dorr* (1845). In an insightful essay on *Luther v. Borden* ("Law, Politics and Chief Justice Taney: A Reconsideration of the Luther v. Borden Decision," *American Journal of Legal History,* XI [October 1967], 385), Michael A. Conron mistakenly wrote that the Supreme Court refused a writ of error in *Ex Parte Dorr* (1845). It was instead a writ of *habeas corpus* that McLean denied, explicitly leaving the way open for later appeal on a writ of error. (*Ex Parte Dorr* 3 Howard 103 [1845], 106.)

[28] The appeal was filed on February 7, 1845. See transcript of *Thomas W. Dorr v. Rhode Island,* Supreme Court Records, National Archives, Washington, D.C.

contending attorneys assembled materials for argument.[29] Postponed from term to term, the case was finally withdrawn in 1849 after the decision in *Luther v. Borden* had been rendered. Dorr explained then that his case had been "virtually disposed of" by the high court's decision in the *Luther* cases.[30]

IV

Almost four years elapsed between the initial appeal to the Supreme Court and the argument of the *Luther* cases in January 1848. Absences and vacancies on the bench, including the death of Joseph Story, were responsible for the repeated delays.[31] Though Dorrites lamented the "masterly inactivity" of the law,[32] they had the satisfaction of knowing that as time was passing the composition of the court was shifting in their favor. Story's successor was Dorrite sympathizer Levi Woodbury of New Hampshire, and by 1848 Democratic appointees were in a majority on the high tribunal.[33] But it was doubtful that the Dorrite cause

---

[29] *Dorr v. Rhode Island* was a parallel case to *Luther v. Borden.* Both cases went up to the Supreme Court together; they had the same attorneys listed for argument (though *Dorr v. Rhode Island* never reached the stage of argument), and much the same documentary material was assembled for both cases. Magrath's shrewd study of Dorrite legal strategies ("Optimistic Democrat") is weakened by the author's misunderstanding of the relation between these cases.

[30] Dorr to Benjamin F. Hallett, November 27, 1849, Correspondence of Supreme Court appellate cases [case No. 2532], National Archives, Washington, D.C.

[31] Docket Record of *Luther v. Borden,* appellate case No. 2419, Supreme Court Records, National Archives, Washington, D.C., Record Group No. 267; Maurice G. Baxter, *Daniel Webster and the Supreme Court* ([Amherst, Mass.]: University of Massachusetts Press, 1966), p. 60.

[32] George Turner to Dorr, February 25, 1846, Dorr MSS.

[33] See Charles Warren, *The Supreme Court in United States History,* rev. ed., 2 vols. (Boston: Little, Brown, 1926), II, 185–195. Some Dorrites were ecstatic when President Polk appointed Woodbury, who had openly sympathized with the Rhode Island rebels. B. F. Hallett exclaimed on hearing the news that "it would be glory to try that case [*Luther v. Borden*]" before Woodbury. Hallett to Walter S. Burges, September 25, 1845, Dorr MSS.; Charles G. Sellers, *James K. Polk: Continentalist, 1843–1846* (Princeton, N.J.: Princeton University Press, 1966), p. 298. Woodbury's opinion in this case gave the Dorrites little pleasure.

was any nearer judicial vindication than it had been in 1844 or 1842.

Formidable legal talent had been assembled for the case. Benjamin F. Hallett, a leading Massachusetts Democrat who had represented Luther in the circuit court trial, again argued the Dorrite position. A former resident of Providence, Hallett took a deep interest in the plight of Rhode Island's disfranchised citizens, aiding the Dorrite cause whenever possible.[34] He was to be joined by George Turner, the attorney from Newport who had helped defend Dorr at the rebel leader's treason trial. Although Turner worked hard on the preparation of the case, traveling frequently to Washington, illness prevented him from participating in argument before the Supreme Court.[35] Dorrites hoped to obtain assistance from other attorneys in the nation's capital.[36] Finally they did succeed in getting the Attorney General of the United States, Nathan Clifford, to serve in his private capacity.[37]

---

[34] See Benjamin F. Hallett to his father-in-law, Samuel Larned, June 14, 23, 1842, Green Papers, RIHSL; P[aul] H. B[uck], "Hallett, Benjamin Franklin," in Alvin Johnson and Dumas Malone, eds., *The Dictionary of American Biography,* 22 vols. (New York: Charles Scribner's Sons, 1928–1958), VIII, 154–155.

[35] See many letters from Dorr to Turner, 1846–1848, in Newport Historical Society, Newport, Rhode Island; Dorr to Edmund Burke, January 10, 1846, Burke Papers, LC; Olney Ballou to Dorr, January 26, 1846, Dorr MSS.

[36] Among the names that Dorrites mentioned as possible counsel in *Luther v. Borden* were James Buchanan, Silas Wright, Thomas Hart Benton, and other Congressional luminaries. Dorr to Walter S. Burges, March 18, 1844, Dorr MSS. There was even a possibility that Dorr himself might serve as Luther's attorney. See Martin Luther to Dorr, December 22, 30, 1845, and March 1, 1847, Dorr MSS.; Dorr to Wilmarth Heath, January 12, 1846, Peck MSS., RIHSL; Dennison, "Dorr: Counsel of Record," pp. 410 ff. (See above, note 1, p. 174). Finally, Robert J. Walker of Mississippi, a leading Democratic lawyer, agreed to aid in the preparation of the case, but he did not argue before the Supreme Court. See Edmund Burke to Walker, January 17, 1846, Newport Historical Society; Docket Record of *Luther v. Borden,* Appellate Case No. 2419, Supreme Court Records, National Archives, Washington, D.C., Record Group No. 267.

[37] Despite the claim that he was not an official spokesman of the Polk Administration, Clifford's service in this case was consistent with Polk's policy (mainly expressed through distribution of patronage) of support

Defense counsel was even more distinguished. John Whipple, a leading Providence lawyer and active Law and Order partisan in Rhode Island who had opposed Hallett in the lower court, again argued the case for Borden and the militiamen. Along with Whipple was Daniel Webster, the most celebrated courtroom lawyer of the day, whose oratorical prowess was becoming legendary.[38] When Hallett heard that Webster would appear, he became frightened and briefly thought of withdrawing from the case.[39]

Even if they had confronted lesser legal opponents, Luther's attorneys would have faced a difficult task. Counsel Hallett admitted how hard it would be to argue that the People's Government had been legal in 1842 and that the Charter authorities had represented an illegal, usurping regime. He conceded that the maxim "the judicial power, in its decisions, must follow the political power" was one that "no lawyer would deny." [40] Plaintiff's lawyers also had to demonstrate that a decision retroactively favoring the People's Government would not upset the orderly functions of government in Rhode Island. They had to see to it that the efforts of their client's party to initiate a new government were distinguished from a forceful but unsuccessful insurrection that no court would condone. They also had to challenge the invocation of martial law in Rhode Island in the summer of 1842 as well as dissuade the Supreme Court from dismissing the case—on a technicality or on the grounds of want of jurisdiction—without deciding on the philosophical and constitutional questions.

Hallett's argument on these points "lasted for three days, and extended over a great variety of matter." He used irony, logic and eloquence, spiced with historical allusion and learned citations. The court reporter admitted being "at a loss to give even

---

for the former rebels in Rhode Island. A New York *Tribune* editorial commented that Clifford's appearance in this case was "pretty work for the law adviser of the president." Quoted in Warren, *Supreme Court in United States History*, II, 190.

[38] Baxter, *Webster and the Supreme Court*, p. 63.

[39] Hallett to Walter S. Burges, January 19, 1847, Dorr MSS.

[40] *The Right of the People to Establish Forms of Government. Mr. Hallett's Argument in the Rhode Island Causes Before the Supreme Court of the United States . . .* (Boston: Beals & Greene, 1848), p. 31.

a skeleton" of Hallett's argument.[41] Attorney General Clifford's part in the case was apparently limited to the matter of martial law.

Hallett's impassioned argument was the last major restatement of Dorrite ideology. In pamphlet form it was entitled *The Right of the People to Establish Forms of Government*.[42] Its major point was that disputes about the precise procedure of constitutional change were of a lower order than the great, settled matter of where ultimate political power lay. "[A] mere matter of form" in revising constitutions, said Hallett, "should never override substance in a great right." The overwhelming popular ratification of the People's Constitution provided precisely that substantial act of popular sovereignty on which Hallett rested his client's claims. He argued that in American political communities the higher power to make and amend constitutions was unquestionably lodged with the people [43] and could never be subordinate to the secondary, derived power of the legislature. Hallett ridiculed the contention that only with previous legislative authorization could the people of a state amend or change their constitution. If the American people were so limited, then their "boasted sovereignty" was "but a mockery, a delusion and a snare." Hallett asked:

Will this Court say to the people of each State in this Union, that true it is they are the source of all political power, but if

---

[41] *Luther v. Borden,* 7 Howard 1 (1849), 21; cf. Supreme Court's minutes for the case, National Archives (Vol. "L," pp. 5683, 5690).

[42] A drastically abridged version appears in Joseph L. Blau, ed., *Social Theories of Jacksonian Democracy: Representative Writings of the Period, 1825–1850* (New York: Liberal Arts Press, 1954), pp. 100–128. Except for a few legal touches for the Supreme Court argument, Hallett's statement was vintage Dorrite doctrine *circa* 1842 or even 1834.

[43] Hallett cited an "array of authorities and unbroken precedents" to prove this doctrine of Popular Constituent Sovereignty, including Joseph Story's authoritative *Commentaries on the Constitution of the United States,* 3 vols. (Boston: Hilliard and Gray, 1845), I, 198. This and other citations of Story's authority (Hallett, *Right of the People,* pp. 5, 25, 39) were apparently aimed at counterbalancing his previous decision in this very case. For an exhaustive review of the sources and precedents of Hallett's argument, see Dennison, "Constitutional Issues of the Dorr War," pp. 383–403. Cf. my critical discussion of Dennison in the bibliographical essay, below, p. 247.

they presume to exercise their sovereignty in establishing or
changing constitutions of government, without consent of the
Legislature, they shall be followed with pains and penalties,
enforced by the lawless despotism of Martial Law, and backed
by the whole military power of the United States, called out
by the President to suppress insurrection and domestic violence! . . . [A]ll American precedents . . . demonstrate that the
assumption that . . . reforms and changes in government . . .
must emanate from the established government, and not from
the people, is the dogma of despotism! . . .

[It] were as absurd to concede entire freedom to the individual and deny his right to move a hand without the leave
of a master, as to affirm a sovereignty of the people incapable
of taking the first step to make or remodel their frame of government. . . . [Our opponents] make the mode [of constitutional change] an ins[u]perable barrier to the exercise of the
right, the form superior to the substance.

Such a sacrifice of substance to form was, he claimed, incom-
patible with American democracy.[44]

No less at variance with American traditions, as the Dorrites
viewed them, was the contention that their peaceful attempt to
change the organic law of Rhode Island was the same as revolution by force.

[T]here was no *rebellion,* because a new fundamental law was
established, and new duties created between the people and
their agent, the government. There was no *treason,* for a new
oath and a new allegiance grew out of this fundamental change
of law. . . . Under the American system, it was the exercise of
an inherent, inalienable, fundamental right.

The real act of rebellion was committed by the Charter Government, Hallett asserted, turning his opponents' arguments against
them; its resistance to the Dorrite Constitution and to the
measures taken in accordance with it amounted to an illegal war
against the people of Rhode Island.[45]

In order to counter arguments that a favorable verdict for
the plaintiff would disturb settled conditions in Rhode Island,
Hallett argued that the major practical effect of such a judgment

---

[44] *Right of the People,* p. 40.

[45] *Ibid.,* pp. 7, 10, 24, 31 (italics in the original).

would merely be to grant Luther the $5,000 to which he was entitled.[46] He was not contending that the Supreme Court should retroactively install the People's Constitution, which in Dorrite eyes had been the legitimate one in 1842. The usurping Charter Government had only come to an end in the spring of 1843 when the people of Rhode Island "permitted" the new constitution to come into force. Luther was not requesting from the court any decision against this new regime, merely a vindication of the principles the Dorrites had struggled for in 1842.[47]

Hallett devoted much of his argument to the question of martial law, under which the defendants justified their nocturnal foray against the Luther homestead. Restating and refining the points he had made before the lower court, he argued that the legislature had no power to institute "this anomalous system of lawless military violence, known as Martial Law," and that even if it did, the power "was defective and inoperative, and gave no such summary power as that set up by the defendants." The statewide establishment of martial law by the Rhode Island General Assembly in June 1842 had contravened not only the Federal Constitution and Rhode Island's own Bill of Rights, he said, but the Charter of 1663 as well. With an impressive array of precedents, Hallett urged the Court to reject "the monstrous absurdity that a legislature, by two words, may place itself and all the people of a State under a military despotism." [48]

Hallett was apprehensive that the Court might dispose of the case without passing on the great question of Popular Constituent Sovereignty. He repeatedly urged the Court not to evade its obligation to reach the merits of the dispute. "[U]pon the pleading and record of this case," he argued, "the Court cannot determine the issue [of] whether a trespass was nor was not committed, without first deciding what were the constitution and frame of government in force in Rhode Island at the time." [49]

---

[46] Dennison, "Constitutional Issues of the Dorr War," p. 361.

[47] *Right of the People,* pp. 26, 31.

[48] *Ibid.,* pp. [64]–70. The two words he was referring to were "martial law."

[49] *Right of the People,* pp. 5, 7, 9. Hallett even invoked Joseph Story's posthumous authority by referring to the opinion of "the learned Judge since deceased" that the main issue in the case "must be met, and must

The entire philsophical structure and political significance of Dorrism depended on the Court's answer.[50]

V

The defendants had far less at stake. Their side had already won the struggle in Rhode Island years before, and the Dorrites had not been a viable political force in the state since 1845. Even if a verdict were handed down against Luther Borden and the other militiaman, they would probably not have to pay damages.[51] Moreover, the defendants' attorneys, having won the case in the lower courts, were no doubt confident that the Supreme Court would affirm Joseph Story's judgment and finally lay to rest the radical Dorrite claims.

John Whipple led off [52] with a passionate attack on the

---

be passed upon in the indispensable exercise of the ordinary judicial functions of this high tribunal." *Ibid.*, p. 5. Story probably did wish to see *Luther v. Borden* decided on its merits, since he helped facilitate simultaneous appeal of both *Luther* cases to the Supreme Court. But the fact that the Court did not reach the major issues, and found instead that it lacked jurisdiction, flatly contradicts Hellerich's superficial conclusion ("Luther Cases in the Lower Courts," p. 45) that "had Judge Story lived until 1849, he would have known the satisfaction of reading a majority decision of the Supreme Court which confirmed the position he had taken when he had heard the Luther Cases in the lower courts." Hellerich's lame qualification of this judgment (*ibid.*, p. 44) hardly distracts from its inaccuracy.

50 Dorrites rested their theory on the assumption that the American political system would have to respond to appeals based on the Declaration of Independence. Hence their political failure necessarily invalidated their political arguments. They were not aware that the revolutionary principles of 1776 had already been ejected from the mainstream of American political conviction. See Gordon S. Wood, *The Creation of the American Republic, 1776–1787* (Chapel Hill: University of North Carolina Press, 1969), pp. 519–524, and my discussion of Dorrite ideology, above, pp. 63–73.

51 The State of Rhode Island had assumed the costs of defense in the *Luther v. Borden* cases, as well as in *Dorr v. Rhode Island*. See Newport *Herald of the Times*, November 6, 1845; Hallett, *Right of the People*, p. 28; Levi Woodbury's dissent in *Luther v. Borden*, 7 Howard 1 (1849), 87.

52 His argument, unlike Hallett's, took only one day to deliver. See Supreme Court minutes, National Archives (Vol. "L," pp. 5092–5093, January 28, 1848).

Dorrites, substantiating Hallett's fears that "one of the distinguished [opposing] counsel" would allow his "local feelings" of
political partisanship to shape his legal argument.[53] Whipple
haughtily dismissed Dorrite claims to legitimacy as the mad
fantasies of ambitious "office-hunters and fifth rate politicians"
who, having been justly suppressed in Rhode Island, now dared
to press their case before the Supreme Court. He urged the
judges to repudiate the alleged "right of peaceful revolution"
and the doctrine of Popular Constituent Sovereignty. "The
[Federal] Constitution," Whipple flatly stated, had "annihilated
the right of revolution" by setting up a republican government
which in its excellence removed all possible causes of serious
political discontent in America. The visionary theory that popular majorities could frame fresh constitutions and create new
governments would destroy government by law and substitute
mob rule. To counter such threats of domestic rebellion, state
governments were bound to employ military force, even if
"every one of the rebels" might be shot down. No militia officer "would be guilty of any crime should a thousand lives be
destroyed," Whipple claimed. How then could Borden and the
other defendants be criminally liable for a mere night raid on
the Luther farmhouse? The Supreme Court, he concluded, had
to refute the challenge that Dorrism posed to orderly, republican
government.[54]

Daniel Webster took a more ironic, light-hearted tone in his
argument.[55] He admitted that the case was novel. It seemed, he
said, that the plaintiff sought to bring a case of mistaken identity
from the lower court. "Mr. Dorr, instead of being a traitor or

---

[53] *Right of the People*, p. 10.

[54] Whipple's argument appears in Daniel Webster and John Whipple,
The Rhode-Island Question (Providence: Charles Burnett, 1848), pp. 4,
14–15, 20–23, 30–33. Whipple exempted Dorr from his general excoria-
tion of the Rhode Island insurrectionists of 1842, many of whom "forsook
their own standard" when armed hostilities broke out. "Dorr was made of
much better stuff," Whipple conceded. "Though a fanciful, visionary and
very obstinate zealot, he was true to his own dogmas, and to his own
party" (*ibid.*, p. 29).

[55] Webster appeared on January 27, 1848. See Supreme Court minutes,
National Archives (Vol. "L," p. 5694); Baxter, *Webster and the Supreme
Court*, pp. 61–63.

an insurrectionist, was the real Governor of the State at the time; . . . the force used by him was exercised in defence of the constitution and laws, and not against them; . . . he who opposed the constituted authorities was not Mr. Dorr, but Gov. King; . . . it was *he* who should have been indicted, and tried, and sentenced." Such an unconventional and diverting case, Webster stated,

> . . . may perhaps give vivacity and variety to judicial investigations. It may relieve the drudgery of perusing briefs, demurrers, and pleas in bar, bills in equity and answers; and introduce topics which give sprightliness, freshness, and something of an uncommon public interest, to proceedings in courts of law.

Although Webster doubted that the Supreme Court could "take judicial cognizance" of the issues in the case, since they were political, he welcomed the opportunity to debate on "the true character of our American system of popular liberty" with "learned counsel" Hallett. "[H]arm can never come from" such discussion, he said, when "addressed to reason and not to passion" and when conducted "before magistrates and lawyers, and not before excited masses out of doors." [56]

When Webster began his political debate with Hallett he conceded, as Whipple had the day before,[57] that the people were indeed sovereign.[58] But he argued that such sovereignty had to be exercised "through the prescribed forms of law." Otherwise, he said, "we shall wander as widely from the American track as the pole is from the track of the sun." In the American political system prior legislative authorization was necessary before a new constitution could be framed. The Founding Fathers had

---

[56] Webster's argument in Webster and Whipple, *Rhode-Island Question,* pp. 35–36.

[57] Whipple's argument, *ibid.,* p. 23.

[58] Webster saw no "particular merit in asserting a doctrine like this . . . in the midst of twenty millions of people, when nineteen millions, nine hundred and ninety-nine thousand, nine hundred and ninety-nine of them, hold it, as well as himself. . . . He who would argue against this must argue without an adversary." *Ibid.,* p. 38. Cf. Taney's similar statement of formal adherence to the principles of majority rule in *Luther v. Borden,* 7 Howard 1 (1849), 47.

proceeded in this way in 1786, and all the new state constitutions had been drafted "by conventions called by the Legislature, as an ordinary exercise of legislative power," Webster argued. "Now what state," he asked, "ever altered its Constitution in any other mode?" [59] He found no justification for gauging popular will in "tumultuous assemblies, by which the timid are terrified, the prudent are alarmed, and by which society is disturbed." He asked:

> In what State has an assembly, calling itself the people, been held without law, without authority, without qualifications, without certain officers, with no oaths, securities, or sanctions of any kind, met and made a constitution, and called it the Constitution of the STATE? [60]

Having dismissed the Dorrite movement as a tumultuous upsurge of "anarchy," [61] he argued that however much the Supreme Court might be amused by his debate with Hallett, it could not "try the matters which the plaintiff . . . offered to prove." In the eyes of the law, he declared, there was no People's Constitution, no other Governor of Rhode Island in 1842 than Samuel Ward King, and no legitimate authority other than the Charter Government,[62] which had representatives in both houses of Congress and which had every right to appeal to the Federal

---

[59] Hallett and other Dorrites had attempted to use the precedent of the admission to the Union of Michigan in 1836 on the request of an unauthorized assemblage. See *New Age*, April 19, 1842; Hallett, *Right of the People*, pp. 58–60. Also, in 1836 Maryland experienced what one scholar called a "preface to the Dorr Rebellion." See A. Clarke Hagensick, "Revolution or Reform in 1836: Maryland's Preface to the Dorr Rebellion," *Maryland Historical Magazine*, LVII (December 1962), 346–366. Dennison ("Constitutional Issues of the Dorr War," pp. 61–65, 89–126) discusses the precedents for Dorrite measures, confusing what was seized upon in desperate argument with a genuine tradition.

[60] Webster's argument, in *Rhode-Island Question*, pp. 40–43.

[61] *Ibid.*, pp. 42, 43, 55.

[62] Webster allowed himself two sentences of criticism of the Charter Government, which, he said, might "have discreetly taken measures at an earlier period for revising the constitution." But it was an "error into which prudent and cautious men would fall." *Ibid.*, p. 54. His colleague Whipple had been closely associated with the Charter Government.

Government and invoke martial law [63] in its own defense. No judicial scrutiny of the sovereignty of such a government was possible, he maintained, nor could the courts judge the claims of another government pretending to succeed it.

Said Webster, quoting Job Durfee, Rhode Island Chief Justice:

> Courts and juries, gentlemen, do not count votes to determine whether a constitution has been adopted or a governor elected, or not. Courts [merely] take notice without proof offered from the bar, what the constitution is or was, and who is or was the governor of their own State.

Otherwise, he argued, a defendant who had tried to overthrow an existing regime could "come into court and say, 'I thought that I was but exercising a constitutional right and I claim an acquittal on the grounds of mistake.' "

> Were it so, there would be an end to all law and all government. Courts and juries would have nothing to do but sit in judgment upon indictments, in order to acquit or excuse. The accused has only to prove that he has been systematic in committing a crime, and that he thought that he had a right to commit it; and, according to this doctrine, you must acquit.

For a court to enter any judgment in the case would therefore be to transform it from a judicial to a political tribunal, dealing out patents of sovereignty to litigants "according to rules of our own making, and heretofore unknown in courts." [64]

Webster concluded that the People's Government whose legitimacy was at the heart of Luther's case had as little existence in fact as in law:

---

[63] Martial law, Webster stated, places "the land" under the law of the camp. Citing Joseph Story, he justified resort to military authority "in cases where the civil law is not sufficient." Martial law, he said, "confers summary power, not to be used arbitrarily or for the gratification of personal feelings of hatred or revenge, but for the preservation of order and of the public peace." *Ibid.*, p. 54.

[64] Webster's argument (quoting Durfee throughout), *ibid.*, pp. 49–50.

It never performed one single act of government. It never did a thing in the world! All was patriotism and all was paper; and with patriotism and paper it went out on the 4th of May [1842], admitting itself to be, as all must regard it, a contemptible *sham!*

The feeble efforts of the Rhode Island rebels to challenge established authority, he happily observed, had been unavailing in the face of the "sober wisdom" of the people who remained committed to regular and orderly government.[65] Surely the nation's highest court, being equally solicitous of American liberty, would, as the people and magistrates of Rhode Island had done, wisely reject Dorrism and all its pretensions.

VI

Webster's confidence in the Supreme Court's sobriety was well founded. The decisions in *Luther v. Borden,* handed down a year after argument,[66] were a resounding defeat for the Dorrites. The sole dissenter, former Dorrite sympathizer Levi Woodbury, disagreed with the majority only on the issue of martial law. The Court's decision, written by Chief Justice Roger Brooke Taney with four other justices concurring,[67] firmly repudiated Dorrism.

To Taney, this was a case of great consequence. The plaintiff was seeking to determine legally whether the People's Constitution had annulled the Charter Government in Rhode Island between May 1842 and May 1843, before the new constitution had gone into force. If this was the case, then not only was Borden's assault an illegal trespass, but also

---

[65] Webster's argument in *Rhode-Island Question,* p. 54. Like many other conservative critics of Dorrism, Webster both excoriated the rebels for their revolutionary aims and ridiculed them for having done such a bad job of carrying them out.

[66] The Court's decisions were handed down on January 3, 1849. Supreme Court minutes, National Archives (Vol. "L," pp. 5840–5841).

[67] Taney was joined by Justices John McLean, Samuel Nelson, Robert C. Grier (all of whom Dorr thought could be relied on to be favorable to the Suffrage Party. See Dorr to Hallett and Turner, February 2, 1847, Dorr MSS.) and James M. Wayne. Justices John Catron, Peter V. Daniel (who Dorr also thought was sympathetic) and John McKinley did not participate in the decision because of illness.

the laws passed by [the Charter] . . . legislature during that time were nullities; its taxes were wrongfully collected; its salaries and compensations to its officers illegally paid; its public accounts improperly settled; and the judgments and sentences of its courts in civil and criminal cases null and void, and the officers who carried their decisions into operation answerable as . . . criminals.

Vehemently denying counsel Hallett's contention that a decision for the plaintiff would have no unsettling effect on Rhode Island's political and social fabric, Taney raised the specter of endless litigation. Juries might disagree in such cases.

[A]nd, as a verdict is not evidence in a suit between different parties . . . , the question [of] whether acts done under the charter government during the period in contest are valid or not must always remain unsettled and open to dispute.

"When the decision of this court might lead to such results," Taney warned, "it becomes its duty to examine very carefully its own powers before it undertakes to exercise jurisdiction." [68]

The major question in the Court's decision was whether its own jurisdiction extended to "political questions." Taney, who less than a decade later in *Dred Scott v. Sandford* would help thrust the Court precipitously into thorny national political issues,[69] stressed in 1849 the judiciary's obligation "not to pass beyond its appropriate sphere of action, and to take care not to involve itself in discussions which properly belong to other forums." Such issues as the locus of sovereignty in a community, the mode by which that sovereignty might be exercised, and disputes over competing constitutions are political by nature and not resolvable in any court, said Taney. State courts could not deal with such questions, since they derived their legitimacy from "established government[s] capable of enacting

---

[68] *Luther v. Borden,* 7 Howard 1 (1849), 38–39, 41–42.

[69] *Dred Scott v. Sandford,* 19 Howard 393 (1857). Among the vast literature on the *Dred Scott* case, see Wallace Mendelson, "Dred Scott's Case—Reconsidered," *Minnesota Law Review,* XXXVIII (December 1953), 16–28; Arthur Bestor, Jr., "State Sovereignty and Slavery: A Reinterpretation of Proslavery Constitutional Doctrine, 1846–1860," *Journal of the Illinois State Historical Society,* LIV (Summer 1961), 148–174.

laws, and of appointing judges to expound and administer them." It was necessary that such courts affirm "the existence and authority" of the governments under which they exercised judicial power. The Rhode Island judiciary in cases such as Thomas Dorr's treason trial had already pronounced the Charter Government as the legal one in the state between 1842 and 1843. Federal courts were also powerless to decide such questions. Taney observed the "well settled rule" that "the courts of the United States adopt and follow the decisions of the State courts in questions which concern merely the constitution and laws of the State." He even reprimanded the lower court for admitting evidence to prove that the Charter regime was legitimate, contending that such legitimacy should have been assumed from the outset. His conclusion was that the Supreme Court could not express its opinion "upon political rights and political questions" as urged to do by the plaintiff. "The judgment of the Circuit Court must therefore be affirmed," he said.[70]

Although disclaiming any judicial authority to decide on the substantive issues in *Luther v. Borden,* Taney conveyed his belief that the Dorrite movement in Rhode Island had been an "unlawful opposition" deservedly suppressed by local and federal authorities. Responsibility to deal with disputed sovereignty was not vested in the courts, he said, but in the "political" branches of government—the state legislature and the Governor as well as Congress and the President. Local jurisdictions, accord-

---

[70] *Luther v. Borden,* 7 Howard 1 (1849), 42–44, 46–47. Without citing precedents, Taney decided this case consistently with an earlier series of property disputes arising out of Latin American independence movements, in which the Supreme Court had avoided giving decisions on the grounds that "political questions" had been involved. Cases dealing with Indian treaties sometimes fell into a like category. Also, a boundary dispute that was argued before the Supreme Court by Daniel Webster in 1846 was treated by Taney as a "political question." See Oliver P. Field, "The Doctrine of Political Questions in the Federal Courts," *Minnesota Law Review,* VIII (May 1924), 485–513; Charles G. Post, *The Supreme Court and Political Questions* (Baltimore: Johns Hopkins Press, 1936); Baxter, *Webster and the Supreme Court,* pp. 52–58, 63–65; Martin Shapiro, *Law and Politics in the Supreme Court* (New York: The Free Press, 1964) Chap. 5; Dennison, "Constitutional Issues of the Dorr War," Chap. 9; Conron, "Law, Politics and Chief Justice Taney," pp. 377–388; Magrath, "Optimistic Democrat," pp. 94–112.

ing to Taney, not only enjoyed the authority to invoke martial law, but in this particular instance had used the power wisely and with appropriate restraint.[71] He expressed similar satisfaction with the Federal Government's handling of the Rebellion: President Tyler, acting by authority of Congress,[72] had correctly backed the Charter regime in 1842 as the legitimate government of Rhode Island. Taney's hearty approval of wide Presidential latitude in *Luther v. Borden* struck a strong note of Jacksonian nationalism.[73]

> It is said that this power in the President is dangerous to liberty, and may be abused. All power may be abused if placed in unworthy hands. But it would be difficult, we think, to point out any other hands in which this power would be more safe, and at the same time equally effectual. When citizens of the same State are in arms against each other, and the constituted authorities unable to execute the laws, the interposition of the United States must be prompt, or it is of little value. . . . [T]he elevated office of the President, chosen as he is by the people of the United States, and the high responsibility he could not fail to feel when acting in a case of so much moment, appear to furnish as strong safeguards against a wilful abuse of power as human prudence and foresight could well provide.[74]

---

[71] *Luther v. Borden,* 7 Howard 1 (1849), 45–46. Justice Woodbury strongly dissented from the majority opinion on this point.

[72] Taney stated that Congress had primary authority to deal with contested state sovereignty by deciding which rival delegation to seat. "It is true," he said, "that the contest in this case did not last long enough to bring the matter to this issue; and as no senators or representatives were elected under the authority of the government of which Mr. Dorr was the head, Congress was not called upon to decide the controversy. Yet the right to decide is placed there, and not in the courts." *Luther v. Borden,* 7 Howard 1 (1849), 45–46.

[73] In 1842 the ailing Andrew Jackson himself had endorsed the Dorrite principles of Popular Constituent Sovereignty. See p. 66 n.

[74] *Luther v. Borden,* 7 Howard 1 (1849), 43–45. After noting that Congress had not acted in this case, Taney also mentioned that, although empowered to intervene militarily in Rhode Island, President Tyler had not done so. But "by announcing his determination, [he] was as effectual as if the militia had been assembled" under Presidential order. *Ibid.,* 44. Ironically, the power of the Invisible Hand (exercised through the nation's Chief Executive) was used against the Dorrites. For their own theoretical attempt to enlist such power, see above, pp. 69–70.

For a decision purporting to prove that the Supreme Court lacked jurisdiction in this case, Taney's opinion contained a clear endorsement of the conservative viewpoint on the Dorr Rebellion, including support for federal intervention in the dispute.

Giving a more restrained version of the "political questions" doctrine was the lone dissenter in the case. Justice Levi Woodbury admitted that before his appointment to the bench he had "frequently and publicly avowed" his support of the Dorrite rebels, but that as a member of the Supreme Court he was not entitled simply to translate his political convictions into judicial pronouncements. The Court's role, he said, was at once too modest and too sensitive for such blatant political lawmaking. Woodbury believed that the courts might become corrupted if they undertook to decide fundamental "political" questions. Judges were too far removed from the community; their decisions had an air of finality, whereas "a wrong decision by a political forum can often be peacefully corrected by new elections or instructions in a single month." Judicial bodies, if charged with responsibilities beyond their capacities, would tend to become "a new sovereign power in the republic, in most respects irresponsible and unchangeable for life, and one more dangerous, in theory at least, than the worst elective oligarchy in the worst of times." [75]

Though Woodbury agreed with Taney and the majority that no court could pass on the issues of disputed sovereignty in *Luther v. Borden,* he said he did believe that a judgment in favor of the plaintiff could be made on the narrower issue of the abuse of martial law. Filling the bulk of his dissenting opinion with a learned inquiry into English and American precedents, Woodbury found strict limits on martial law. He also found that the Rhode Island General Assembly and the Charter Government had greatly exceeded those limits in 1842. Borden and the other Charter militiamen had violated the Luthers' "sanctity of domestic life" and had used unnecessary force on an aged, unarmed woman "without good cause." The Supreme Court could and should, Woodbury urged, award damages to the plaintiffs in this case without presuming to decide weighty political ques-

---

[75] *Luther v. Borden,* 7 Howard 1 (1849), 51–53.

tions and without disturbing the tranquillity of Rhode Island's political system. But Taney and the majority refused to follow Woodbury into the ancient history of martial law, considering such inquiry irrelevant to the "construction of the Rhode Island law" and useless to test "the lawfulness of the authority exercised by the [Charter] government." [76]

The Supreme Court's decision in 1849 concluded the Dorrites' efforts to uphold the principles of Popular Constituent Sovereignty. In *Luther v. Borden* their defeat became indelibly registered in American constitutional law and their radicalism even further removed from the mainstream of American political life.

---

[76] *Ibid.*, pp. 59–88, 46.

Conclusion

Despite a prison term that ruined his health, Dorr did not completely end his political career upon regaining freedom in 1845. In the years that followed he closely monitored the progress of the *Luther v. Borden* cases. He received the news of the Supreme Court's adverse decision with his characteristic optimism, hoping that Justice Taney's disclaimer of judicial power somehow left the way open for the eventual triumph of the People's Constitution.[1] But there was no practical way to realize this goal, and from the late forties to the early fifties Dorr's political activity was mainly confined to drafting legislation and resolutions for the Rhode Island Democratic Party [2] and advising on patronage.[3] In 1848 certain Free Soil leaders solicited his support,[4] but he refused to repudiate his traditional party allegiance. To Dorr the Democratic Party represented a "broad & high standard of principle, which rebukes all selfish or sordid aims, all defects, shortcomings & inconsistencies in those who profess to follow it, and [which] guides them on to

---

[1] C. Peter Magrath, "Optimistic Democrat: Thomas W. Dorr and the case of *Luther v. Borden*," *Rhode Island History*, XXIX (August–November 1970), 111.

[2] See Dorr MSS., correspondence, 1845–1853.

[3] *Ibid.* Dorr was himself mentioned for an appointive diplomatic post, but his health was too poor. See J[ohn] L. O'Sullivan to George Bancroft, August 4, 1845, Bancroft Papers, Massachusetts Historical Society.

[4] See *Free Soil Ticket* (n.d. [1848]), in Dorr MSS., which listed William H. Seward as candidate for President, Joshua R. Giddings for Vice President, and which named Dorr prospective Postmaster General.

progressive attainments." [5] When the Democrats came back to power in Rhode Island they rewarded him by restoring his civil and political rights in 1851 and then, four years later, by legislatively annulling his treason conviction.[6] But Dorr did not long outlive this vindication; he died on December 27, 1854, at the age of forty-nine.

Dorr's partisan devotion to the Democratic Party obscured for him the profound failure of the radical movement he had led. Unable to uphold the People's Constitution or the principles of Popular Constituent Sovereignty, many Suffragists also found an outlet for their political energies in the party, which emerged strengthened from the Dorr Rebellion.[7] In bitter contests for office and patronage it became possible to overlook and then forget that they had once sought different and perhaps nobler goals.

The defeat of Dorr's movement resulted from a combination of "internal" and "external" factors. Radicals stressed the latter. They blamed John Tyler's threat of intervention and the sinister role of Daniel Webster, who supposedly encouraged the President to suppress popular rights in Rhode Island.[8] They also

---

[5] Dorr to John G[reenleaf] Whittier, November 6, 1848, Peck MSS., RIHSL, XIII, 66.

[6] Arthur May Mowry, *The Dorr War: Or, The Constitutional Struggle in Rhode Island* (Providence: Preston & Rounds, 1901), pp. 257–259. Mowry and other antiradical writers delight in pointing out that Dorr was vindicated by action of precisely that legislative authority over the judiciary he had once opposed.

[7] See Chapter 6. For years after the Rebellion former Dorrites were active in Democratic Party affairs on both the local and national levels. See list of delegates to the 1844 Democratic National Convention (*Baltimore Sun,* May 28, 1844) and the *Proceedings of the Democratic National Convention . . . in Baltimore, May 22, 1848* (n.p., n.d.) in which Duttee J. Pearce, Walter S. Burges, Olney Ballou, Hezekiah Willard, and other former Dorrites represented Rhode Island.

[8] Not only as Tyler's Secretary of State in 1842, but later as anti-Dorr counsel in *Luther v. Borden* and as eminent propagator of what seemed to be an "aristocratic" doctrine of the sovereignty of corporate bodies over the people, Webster appeared as the secret hand to many Dorrites. See *New Age,* April 19, 1842; Edmund Burke to Dorr, May 8, 1842; Dorr's notes on a meeting with Webster, May 10, 1842 (see above, p. 109); Dorr to Aaron White, Jr., May 12, 1842, the last three items in Dorr

held local authorities, who actually did mount armed resistance against the rebels, responsible for their defeat. Dorrites never developed any clear understanding of how they themselves had contributed to this defeat or why they had succumbed to mere threats of federal force and to belated repressive acts by their Rhode Island opponents.[9] The ease with which former rebels could switch their political activity to conventional party channels stimulated no great introspection. Their own "internal" shortcomings—an ambiguous ideology that fostered paralyzing and debilitating optimism,[10] lack of social solidarity among various strata in the radical movement, inept leadership and racial prejudice—remained largely hidden from them. The Dorrites suffered gravely from not subjecting their own movement and doctrines to the critical scrutiny reserved for their opponents.

Despite the unique factors that brought an unself-conscious radical upheaval to the nation's tiniest state in the 1840s, the Dorr Rebellion was an event of more than local significance. Nowhere else had a colonial Charter continued in force so long and local elites been in a better position to block reform. In response to these conservative forces, rebels in Rhode Island drew a radical ideology directly from the American political tradition, testing more fully than ever before—or since—the meaning of the revolutionary principles of 1776 in a society where those principles had presumably triumphed. Agitating

---

MSS.; Dorr, *Address to the People of Rhode Island,* August 1843, in *Burke's Report,* pp. 740–742.

[9] The Charter authorities, as I have shown in Chapters 3 to 5, were at first at a loss to deal with the Suffrage Party and its initial measures and hence did nothing. This inaction permitted the Dorrites, who enjoyed initiative, to come as close to victory as they did. Along with giving them time to maneuver relatively unhindered for so long, official inaction also deprived the Dorrites of the opportunity to build support on the basis of any brutal or repressive acts of their opponents. By the time these acts were committed, it was too late to seek support. Thus the rebels themselves, in attacking the Providence arsenal, performed the first dramatic acts of political violence in the Rhode Island contest. There is no evidence that conservatives consciously tried to maneuver the radicals into "firing the first shot"; that it worked out this way seems to have been the unintended consequence of official lethargy.

[10] Aileen Kraditor, "American Radical Historians on Their Heritage," *Past & Present,* No. 56 (August 1972), pp. 136–153.

Congress and neighboring states, involving the national executive, and giving rise to a major Supreme Court decision, the Dorr Rebellion was not confined to Rhode Island; its relevance to political concerns elsewhere and its importance as a radical movement invite the wider exploration attempted here.

Although the Dorrites came close to winning the contest in Rhode Island,[11] they had their greatest significance as defeated rebels. Defeat seems to be the usual fate for radical movements in America, especially those that assay armed insurrection against established governments.[12] Not only are radicals invariably thwarted in their immediate aims,[13] but they rarely convey any revolutionary legacy to successors.[14] In this respect

---

[11] A possible scenario might have been: endorsement of force by a significant body of Suffragists in early May 1842, when it seemed possible to seize power in Rhode Island; appointment by the People's Legislature of a Dorrite candidate to fill the unexpired term of recently-deceased United States Senator Nathan Dixon; willingness of Congress to seat such a candidate in place of Charter appointee William Sprague; strict neutrality toward the contesting Rhode Island groups by the President. None of these possibilities was inconceivable at the time. Had they taken place, the outcome of the Dorr Rebellion might have been opposite from what actually occurred. Historians have recently been reminded by David Hackett Fischer (*Historians' Fallacies: Toward a Logic of Historical Thought* [New York: Harper Torchbooks, 1970], pp. 15–21) that concern with such hypothetical issues leads them into the "fallacy of fictional questions." While Fischer is undoubtedly right that historians' main concern is with what happened rather than with what might have happened, the understanding of actual reality may be enriched by consideration of the manifold possibilities in historical situations.

[12] I have reviewed some of the relevant literature in "American Radicalism: A Bibliographical Survey [Part I]," *Stacks: Publication of the Libraries of the Polytechnic Institute of Brooklyn,* No. 24 (March 1970), and shall not offer any extensive bibliographical listing here.

[13] Merton L. Dillon has persuasively argued that even the abolitionists, who alone of antebellum radicals might be thought of as exceptions to this rule of general failure, also had their deepest aims blasted. See his "The Failure of the American Abolitionists," *Journal of Southern History,* XXV (May 1959), 159–177.

[14] James M. McPherson has suggested one important thread of continuity in "The Antislavery Legacy: From Reconstruction to the NAACP," in Barton J. Bernstein, ed., *Towards a New Past: Dissenting Essays in American History* (New York: Pantheon Books, 1968), pp. 126–157. With this possible exception, there is little continuity in American radical

America differs markedly from Europe, where even defeated radical movements in the eighteenth and nineteenth centuries fed an underground tradition out of which socialism eventually sprang.[15] One of the consequences of the absence of a mature radical movement in the present-day United States has been inadequate exploration of early American radicalism,[16] a complementary shortcoming of both scholarship and society that I would hope can soon be remedied.

---

movements before the twentieth century. Successive movements do develop repeatedly in which each, with little knowledge of or interest in predecessors, goes ahead in the struggle against the evils of its own age. For a suggestive exploration of the paradoxical frequency of the reappearance of radicalism (and reform) in an America that habitually rejects movements for fundamental change, see Warren I. Susman, "The Persistence of American Reform," in Daniel Walden, ed., *American Reform: The Ambiguous Legacy* (Yellow Springs, Ohio: The Ampersand Press, 1967), Chap. 8.

[15] While avoiding the danger of making the history of radical ideas "into a genealogical system," K. D. Tönnesson ("The Babouvists: From Utopian to Practical Socialism," *Past & Present*, No. 22 [July 1962], 60–76) had suggested strong threads linking the French Revolution with later socialist movements. See also Isaac Deutscher, *The Prophet Armed: Trotsky, 1879–1921* (New York: Vintage Books, 1965), pp. 91–97, 134, 390–391.

[16] See the bibliography cited above, note 12. One study that deserves to be singled out as an example of the way in which a radical historical outlook can illuminate the past in new and unexpected ways is Aileen S. Kraditor's *Means and Ends in American Abolitionism: Garrison and His Critics on Strategy and Tactics, 1834–1850* (New York: Pantheon Books, 1969).

Appendix A

The People's Constitution*

Proposed Constitution of the State of Rhode Island and Providence Plantations as finally adopted by the People's Convention Assembled at Providence on the 18th Day of November, 1841 (Providence: Office of the *New Age*, 1841), copy in RIHSL.

We, the people of the State of Rhode Island and Providence Plantations, grateful to Almighty God for his blessing vouchsafed to the "lively experiment" of religious and political freedom here "held forth" by our venerated ancestors, and earnestly imploring the favor of his gracious providence towards this our attempt to secure upon a permanent foundation the advantages of well-ordered and rational liberty, and to enlarge and transmit to our successors the inheritance that we have received, do ordain and establish the following constitution of government for this state.

Article I   Declaration of Principles and Rights

1. In the spirit and in the words of Roger Williams, the illustrious founder of this state, and of his venerated associates, we declare "that this government shall be a democracy," or government of the people, "by the major consent" of the same, "only in civil things." The will of the people shall be expressed by representatives freely chosen, and returning at fixed periods to their constituents. This state shall be, and forever remain, as

in the design of its founder, sacred to "soul liberty," to the rights of conscience, to freedom of thought, of expression, and of action, as hereinafter set forth and secured.

2. All men are created free and equal, and are endowed by their Creator with certain natural, inherent, and inalienable rights, among which are life, liberty, the acquisition of property, and the pursuit of happiness. Government cannot create or bestow these rights, which are the gift of God; but it is instituted for the stronger and sure defence of the same, that men may safely enjoy the rights of life and liberty, securely possess and transmit property, and, so far as laws avail, may be successful in the pursuit of happiness.

3. All political power and sovereignty are originally vested in, and of right belong to, the people. All free governments are founded in their authority, and are established for the greatest good of the whole number. The people have, therefore, an unalienable and indefeasible right, in their original, sovereign, and unlimited capacity, to ordain and institute government, and in the same capacity to alter, reform, or totally change the same, whenever their safety or happiness requires.

4. No favor or disfavor ought to be shown, in legislation, toward any man, or party, or society, or religious denomination. The laws should be made not for the good of the few, but of the many; and the burdens of the state ought to be fairly distributed among its citizens.

5. The diffusion of useful knowledge, and the cultivation of a sound morality in the fear of God, being of the first importance in a republican state, and indispensable to the maintenance of its liberty, it shall be an imperative duty of the legislature to promote the establishment of free schools, and to assist in the support of public education.

6. Every person in this state ought to find a certain remedy, by having recourse to the laws, for all injuries or wrongs which may be done to his rights of person, property, or character. He ought to obtain right and justice freely and without purchase, completely and without denial, promptly and without delay, conformably to the laws.

7. The right of the people to be secure in their persons, houses, papers, and possessions, against unreasonable searches and seizures, shall not be violated; and no warrant shall issue

but on complaint in writing upon probable cause, supported by oath or affirmation, and describing as nearly as may be the place to be searched, and the person or things to be seized.

8. No person shall be held to answer to a capital or other infamous charge, unless on indictment by a grand jury, except in cases arising in the land or naval forces, or in the militia, when in actual service, in time of war or public danger. No person shall be tried, after an acquittal, for the same crime or offence.

9.[1] Every man being presumed to be innocent until pronounced guilty by the law, all acts of severity, that are not necessary to secure an accused person, ought to be repressed.

10. Excessive bail shall not be required, nor excessive fines imposed, nor cruel or unusual punishments inflicted; and all punishments ought to be proportioned to the offence.

11. All prisoners shall be bailable upon sufficient surety, unless for capital offences, when the proof is evident or the presumption great. The privilege of the writ of habeas corpus shall not be suspended, unless when, in cases of rebellion or invasion, the public safety shall require it.

12. In all criminal prosecutions, the accused shall have the privilege of a speedy and public trial, by an impartial jury; be informed of the nature and cause of the accusation; be confronted with the witnesses against him; have compulsory process to obtain them in his favor, and at the public expense, when necessary;[2] have the assistance of counsel in his defence, and be at liberty to speak for himself. Nor shall he be deprived of his life, liberty, or property, unless by the judgment of his peers, or the law[3] of the land.

13.[4] The right of trial by jury shall remain inviolate, and in

---

[1] This paragraph did not appear in the *Articles of a Constitution Adopted by the People's Convention, Held October 4, 1841* . . . (Providence: Office of the *New Age*, 1841), hereafter cited as: *October Draft.*

[2] The passage "and at the public expense, when necessary" did not appear in the *October Draft.*

[3] "Laws" in *October Draft.*

[4] This section, in a slightly different form, appeared in the list of "Propositions not acted upon" in the *October Draft.*

all criminal cases the jury shall judge both of the law and of the facts.

14. Any person in this state, who may be claimed to be held to labor or service, under the laws of any other state, territory, or district, shall be entitled to a jury trial, to ascertain the validity of such claim.

15. No man in a court of common law shall be required to criminate himself.

16. Retrospective laws, civil and criminal, are unjust and oppressive, and shall not be made.

17. The people have a right to assemble in a peaceable manner, without molestation or restraint, to consult upon the public welfare; a right to give instructions to their senators and representatives; and a right to apply to those invested with the powers of government for redress of grievances, for the repeal of injurious laws, for the correction of faults of administration, and for all other purposes.

18. The liberty of the press being essential to the security of freedom in a state, any citizen may publish his sentiments on any subject, being responsible for the abuse of that liberty; and in all trials for libel, both civil and criminal, the truth, spoken from good motives, and for justifiable ends, shall be a sufficient defence to the person charged.

19. Private property shall not be taken for public uses without just compensation, nor unless the public good require it; nor under any circumstances until compensation shall have been made, if required.

20. The military [5] shall always be held in strict subordination to the civil authority.

21. No soldier shall, in time of peace, be quartered in any house, without the consent of the owner; nor in time of war, but in manner to be prescribed by law.

22. Whereas Almighty God hath created the mind free, and all attempts to influence it by temporal punishments, or burdens, or by civil incapacitations, tend to beget habits of hypocrisy and meanness; and whereas a principal object of our venerated ancestors in their migration to the country, and their settlement of this state, was, as they expressed it, to hold forth a lively experi-

---

[5] "Military power" in the *October Draft.*

ment, that a flourishing civil state may stand, and be best maintained, with full liberty in religious concernments: We therefore declare that no man shall be compelled to frequent or support any religious worship, place, or ministry whatsoever, nor be enforced, restrained, molested, or burdened in his body or goods, nor disqualified from holding any office, nor otherwise suffer, on account of his religious belief; and that all men shall be free to profess, and by argument to maintain, their opinions in matters of religion; and that the same shall in no wise diminish, enlarge, or affect their civil capacities; and that of all other religious rights and privileges of the people of this state, as now enjoyed, shall remain inviolate and inviolable.

23. No witness shall be called in question before the legislature, nor in any court of this state, nor before any magistrate or other person authorized to administer an oath or affirmation, for his or her religious belief, or opinions, or any part thereof; and no objection to a witness, on the ground of his or her religious opinions, shall be entertained or received.

24. The citizens shall continue to enjoy, and freely exercise, all the rights of fishery, and privileges of the shore, to which they have been heretofore entitled under the charter and usages of this state.

25. The enumeration of the foregoing rights shall not be construed to impair nor deny others retained by the people.

Article II   Of Electors and the Right of Suffrage

1. Every white male citizen of the United States, of the age of twenty-one years, who has resided in this state for one year, and in any town, city, or district of the same for six months [6] next preceding the election at which he offers to vote, shall be an elector of all officers who are elected, or may hereafter be made eligible, by the people. But persons in the military, naval, or marine service of the United States, shall not be considered as having such established residence, by being stationed in any garrison, barrack, or military place in any town or city in this state.

2. Paupers and persons under guardianship, insane, or luna-

---

[6] Three months in *October Draft*.

tic, are excluded from the electoral right; and the same shall be forfeited on conviction of bribery, forgery, perjury, theft, or other infamous crime, and shall not be restored unless by an act of the General Assembly.

3. No person who is excluded from voting, for want of the qualification first named in section first of this article, shall be taxed, or be liable to do military duty; provided that nothing in said first article shall be so construed as to exempt from taxation any property or persons now liable to be taxed.

4. No elector who is not possessed of, and assessed for, ratable property in his own right, to the amount of one hundred and fifty dollars, or who shall have neglected or refused to pay any tax assessed upon him, in any town, city, or district, for one year preceding the town, city, ward, or district meeting at which he shall offer to vote, shall be entitled to vote on any question of taxation, or the expenditure of any public moneys in such town, city, or district, until the same be paid.

5. In the city of Providence, and other cities, no person shall be eligible to the office of mayor, alderman, or common councilman, who is not taxed, or who shall have neglected or refused to pay tax, as provided in the preceding section.

6. The voting for all officers chosen by the people, except town or city officers, shall be by ballot; that is to say, by depositing a written or printed ticket in the ballot box, without the name of the voter written thereon. Town or city officers shall be chosen by ballot, on the demand of any two persons entitled to vote for the same.

7. There shall be a strict registration of all qualified voters in the towns and cities of the state; and no person shall be permitted to vote, whose name has not been entered upon the list of voters before the polls are opened.

8. The General Assembly shall pass all necessary laws for the prevention of fraudulent voting by persons not having an actual, permanent residence, or home, in the state, or otherwise disqualified according to this constitution; for the careful registration of all voters, previously to the time of voting; for the prevention of frauds upon the ballot box; for the preservation of the purity of elections; and for the safekeeping and accurate counting of the votes; to the end that the will of the people may be freely and fully expressed, truly ascertained, and effectually

exerted, without intimidation, suppression, or unnecessary delay.

9. The electors shall be exempted from arrest on days of election, and one day before, and one day after the same, except in cases of treason, felony, or breach of the peace.

10. No person shall be eligible to any office by the votes of the people, who does not possess the qualifications of an elector.

Article III   Of the Distribution of Powers

1. The powers of the government shall be distributed into three departments—the legislative, the executive, and the judicial.

2. No person or persons connected with one of these departments shall exercise any of the powers belonging to either of the others, except in cases herein directed or permitted.

Article IV   Of the Legislative Department

1. The legislative power shall be vested in two distinct Houses: the one to be called the House of Representatives, the other the Senate, and both together the General Assembly. The concurrent votes of the two Houses shall be necessary to the enactment of laws; and the style of their laws shall be: "Be it enacted by the General Assembly, as follows."

2. No member of the General Assembly shall be eligible to any civil office under the authority of the state, during the term for which he shall have been elected.

3. If any representative, or senator, in the General Assembly of this state, shall be appointed to any office under the government of the United States, and shall accept the same, after his election as such senator or representative, his seat shall thereby become vacant.

4. Any person who holds an office under the government of the United States may be elected a member of the General Assembly, and may hold his seat therein, if, at the time of his taking his seat, he shall have resigned said office, and shall declare the same on oath, or affirmation, if required.

5. No member of the General Assembly shall take any fees,

be of counsel or act as advocate in any case pending before either branch of the General Assembly, under penalty of forfeiting his seat, upon due proof thereof.

6. Each House shall judge of the election and qualifications of its members; and a majority of all the members of each House, whom the towns and senatorial districts are entitled to elect, shall constitute a quorum to do business; but a smaller number may adjourn from day to day, and may compel the attendance of absent members, in such manner, and under such penalties, as each House may have previously prescribed.

7. Each House may determine the rules of its proceedings, punish its members for disorderly behavior, and, with the concurrence of two thirds of the members elected, expel a member; but not a second time for the same cause.

8. Each House shall keep a journal of its proceedings, and publish the same when required by one fifth of its members. The yeas and nays of the members of either House shall, at the desire of any five members present, be entered on the journal.

9.[7] Neither House shall, without the consent of the other, adjourn for more than two days, nor to any other place than that at which the General Assembly is holding its session.

10. The senators and representatives shall, in all cases of civil process, be privileged from arrest during the session of the General Assembly, and for two days before the commencement, and two days after the termination, of any session thereof. For any speech in debate in either House, no member shall be called in question in any other place.

11. The civil and military officers, heretofore elected in grand committee, shall hereafter be elected annually by the General Assembly, in joint committee, composed of the two Houses of the General Assembly, excepting as is otherwise provided in this constitution; and excepting the captains and subalterns of the militia, who shall be elected by the ballots of the members composing their respective companies, in such manner as the General Assembly may prescribe; and such officers, so elected, shall be approved of and commissioned by the governor, who shall determine their rank; and, if said companies shall neglect or refuse to make such elections, after being duly notified, then

---

[7] This paragraph did not appear in the *October Draft*.

the governor shall appoint suitable persons to fill such offices.

12. Every bill and every resolution requiring the concurrence of the two Houses, (votes of adjournment excepted), which shall have passed both Houses of the General Assembly, shall be presented to the governor for his revision. If he approve of it, he shall sign and transmit the same to the secretary of state; but if not, he shall return it to the House in which it shall have originated, with his objections thereto, which shall be entered at large on their journal. The House shall then proceed to reconsider the bill; and if, after such reconsideration, that House shall pass it by a majority of all the members elected, it shall be sent, with the objections, to the other House, which shall also reconsider it; and, if approved by that House, by a majority of all the members elected, it shall become law. If the bill shall not be returned by the governor within forty-eight hours (Sundays excepted) after it shall have been presented to him, the same shall become a law, in like manner as if he had signed it, unless the General Assembly, by their adjournment, prevent its return; in which case, it shall not be a law.

13. There shall be two sessions of the General Assembly in every year; one session to be held at Newport, on the first Tuesday of June, for the organization of the government, the election of officers, and for other business; and one other session on the first Tuesday of January, to be held at Providence, in the first year after the adoption of this constitution and in every second year thereafter. In the intermediate years, the January session shall be forever hereafter held in the counties of Washington, Kent, or Bristol, as the General Assembly may determine before their adjournment in June.

Article V   Of the House of Representatives

1. The House of Representatives shall consist of members chosen by the electors in the several towns and cities, in their respective towns and ward meetings,[8] annually.

2. The towns and cities shall severally be entitled to elect

---

[8] At this point the *October Draft* has the phrase "on the third Wednesday of April."

members according to the apportionment which follows, viz.: Newport to elect five; Warwick, four; Smithfield, five; Cumberland, North Providence, and Scituate, three; Portsmouth, Westerly, New Shoreham, North Kingstown, South Kingstown, East Greenwich, Glocester, West Greenwich, Coventry, Exeter, Bristol, Tiverton, Little Compton, Warren, Richmond, Cranston, Charlestown, Hopkinton, Johnston, Foster, and Burrillville, to elect two, and Jamestown, Middletown, and Barrington, to elect one.

3. In the city of Providence, there shall be six representative districts, which shall be the six wards of said city; and the electors resident in said districts, for the term of three months next preceeding the election at which they offer to vote,[9] shall be entitled to elect two representatives for each district.

4. The General Assembly, in case of great inequality in the population of the wards of the city of Providence, may cause the boundaries of the six representative districts therein to be so altered as to include in each district, as nearly as may be, an equal number of inhabitants.

5. The House of Representatives shall have authority to elect their own speaker, clerks, and other officers. The oath of office shall be administered to the speaker by the secretary of state, or, in his absence, by the attorney general.

6. Whenever the seat of a member of the House of Representatives shall be vacated by death, resignation, or otherwise, the vacancy may be filled by a new election.

Article VI   Of the Senate

1. The state shall be divided into twelve senatorial districts; and each district shall be entitled to one senator, who shall be annually chosen by the electors in his district.

2. The first, second, and third representative districts in the city of Providence, shall constitute the first senatorial district; the fourth, fifth, and sixth representative districts in said city, the second district; the town of Smithfield, the third district; the

---

[9] The phrase "at which they offer to vote" did not appear in the *October Draft.*

towns of North Providence and Cumberland, the fourth district; the towns of Scituate, Glocester, Burrillville, and Johnston, the fifth district; the towns of Warwick and Cranston, the sixth district; the towns of East Greenwich, West Greenwich, Coventry, and Foster, the seventh district; the towns of Newport, Jamestown, and New Shoreham, the eighth district; the towns of Portsmouth, Middletown, Tiverton, and Little Compton, the ninth district; the towns of North Kingstown and South Kingstown, the tenth district; the towns of Westerly, Charlestown, Exeter, Richmond, and Hopkinton, the eleventh district; the towns of Bristol, Warren, and Barrington, the twelfth district.

3. The lieutenant governor shall be, by virtue of his office, president of the Senate; and shall have a right, in case of an equal division, to vote in the same; and also to vote in joint committee of the two Houses.

4. When the government shall be administered by the lieutenant governor, or he shall be unable to attend as president of the Senate, the Senate shall elect one of their own members president of the same.

5. Vacancies in the Senate, occasioned by death, resignation, or otherwise, may be filled by a new election.

6. The secretary of state shall be, by virtue of his office, secretary of the Senate.

Article VII   Of Impeachments

1. The House of Representatives shall have the sole power of impeachment.

2. All impeachments shall be tried by the Senate; and when sitting for that purpose, they shall be on oath or affirmation. No person shall be convicted, except by a vote of two thirds of the members elected. When the governor is impeached, the chief justice of the Supreme Court shall preside, with a casting vote in all preliminary questions.[10]

3. The governor, and all other executive and judicial officers, shall be liable to impeachment, but judgment, in such cases, shall

---

[10] The phrase "in all preliminary questions" did not appear in the *October Draft.*

not extend further than to removal from office. The party convicted shall, nevertheless, be liable to indictment, trial, and punishment, according to law.

Article VIII   On the Executive Department

1. The chief executive power of this state shall be vested in a governor, who shall be chosen by the electors,[11] and shall hold his office for one year, and until his successor be duly qualified.

2. No person holding any office or place under the United States, this state, any other of the United States,[12] or any foreign [13] power, shall exercise the office of governor.

3. He shall take care that the laws are faithfully executed.

4. He shall be commander-in-chief of the military and naval forces of the state, except when called into the actual service of the United States; but he shall not march nor convey any of the citizens out of the state, without their consent, or that of the General Assembly, unless it shall become necessary in order to march or transport them from one part of the state to another, for the defence thereof.

5. He shall appoint all civil and military officers whose appointment is not by this constitution, or shall not by law be otherwise provided for.

6. He shall, from time to time, inform the General Assembly of the condition of the state, and recommend to their consideration such measures as he may deem expedient.

7. He may require from any military officer, or any officer in the executive department, information upon any subject relating to the duties of his office.

8. He shall have power to remit forfeitures and penalties, and to grant reprieves, commutation of punishments, and pardons after conviction, except in cases of impeachment.

9. The governor shall, at stated times, receive for his services a compensation which shall not be increased nor diminished during his continuance in office.

---

[11] In the *October Draft* this reads: ". . . by the qualified electors."

[12] The phrase "any other of the United States" did not appear in the *October Draft.*

[13] The word "foreign" did not appear in the *October Draft.*

10. There shall be elected, in the same manner as is provided for the election of governor, a lieutenant governor, who shall continue in office for the same term of time. Whenever the office of governor shall become vacant by death, resignation, removal from office, or otherwise, the lieutenant governor shall exercise the office of governor until another governor shall be duly qualified.

11. Whenever the offices of governor and lieutenant governor shall both become vacant, by death, resignation, removal from office, or otherwise, the president of the Senate shall exercise the office of governor until a governor be duly qualified; and should such vacancies occur during a recess of the General Assembly, and there be no president of the Senate, the secretary of state shall, by proclamation, convene the Senate, that a president may be chosen to exercise the office of governor.

12. Whenever the lieutenant governor or president of the Senate shall exercise the office of governor, he shall receive the compensation of governor only; and his duties as president of the Senate shall cease while he shall continue to act as governor; and the Senate shall fill the vacancy by an election from their own body.

13. In case of a disagreement between the two Houses of the General Assembly respecting the time or place of adjournment, the person exercising the office of governor may adjourn them to such time or place as he shall think proper; provided that the time of adjournment shall not be extended beyond the first [14] day of the next stated session.

14. The person exercising the office of governor may, in cases of special necessity, convene the General Assembly at any town or city in this state at any other time than hereinbefore provided. And, in case of danger from the prevalence of epidemic or contagious diseases, or from other circumstances, in the place in which the General Assembly are next to meet, he may, by proclamation, convene the Assembly at any other place within the state.

15. A secretary of state, a general treasurer, and an attorney general, shall also be chosen annually, in the same manner, and

---

[14] The word "first" was omitted, apparently inadvertently, from the *October Draft.*

for the same time, as is herein provided respecting the governor. The duties of these officers shall be the same as are now, or may hereafter be, prescribed by law. Should there be a failure to choose either of them, or should a vacancy occur in either of their offices, the General Assembly shall fill the place by an election in joint committee.

16. The electors in each county shall, at the annual elections, vote for an inhabitant of the county to be sheriff of said county for one year, and until a successor be duly qualified. In case no person shall have a majority of the electoral votes of his county for sheriff, the General Assembly, in joint committee, shall elect a sheriff from the two candidates who shall have the greatest number of votes in such county.

17. All commissions shall be in the name of the State of Rhode Island and Providence Plantations, sealed with the seal of the state, and attested by the secretary.

Article IX   General Provisions

1.[15] This constitution shall be the supreme law of the state; and all laws contrary to or inconsistent with the same, which may be passed by the General Assembly, shall be null and void.

2. The General Assembly shall pass all necessary laws for carrying this constitution into effect.

3. The judges of all the courts, and all other officers, both civil and military, shall be bound by oath or affirmation to the due observance of this constitution, and of the constitution of the United States.

4. No jurisdiction shall, hereafter, be entertained by the General Assembly in cases of insolvency, divorce, sale of real estate of minors, or appeal from judicial decisions, nor in any other matters appertaining to the jurisdiction of judges and courts of law. But the General Assembly shall confer upon the courts of the state all necessary powers for affording relief in the cases

---

[15] In the *October Draft* this article began with sections describing the circumstances of how the new regime would come into force and what features of the previous government would be retained. These went into Article XIV, Sections 5, 6, 20.

herein named; and the General Assembly shall exercise all other jurisdiction and authority which they have heretofore entertained, and which is not prohibited by, nor repugnant to, this constitution.

5. The General Assemby shall from time to time cause estimates to be made of the ratable property of the state, in order to [establish] the equitable apportionment of state taxes.

6. Whenever a direct tax is laid by the state, one sixth part thereof shall be assessed on the polls of the qualified electors: provided that the tax on a poll shall never exceed the sum of fifty cents; and that all persons who actually perform military duty, or duty in the fire department, shall be exempted from said poll tax.

7. The General Assembly shall have no power hereafter to incur state debts to an amount exceeding the sum of fifty thousand dollars, except in time of war, or in case of invasion, without the express consent of the people. Every proposition for such increase shall be submitted to the electors at the next annual election, or on some day to be set apart for that purpose; and shall not be further entertained by the General Assembly, unless it receive the votes of a majority of all the persons voting. This section shall not be construed to refer to any money that now is, or hereafter may be, deposited with this state by the general government.

8. The assent of two thirds of the members elected to each House of the General Assembly shall be requisite to every bill appropriating the public moneys, or property, for local or private purposes; or for creating, continuing, altering, or renewing any body politic or corporate, banking corporations excepted.

9. Hereafter, when any bill creating, continuing, altering, or renewing any banking corporation, authorized to issue its promissory notes for circulation, shall pass the two Houses of the General Assembly, instead of being sent to the governor, it shall be referred to the electors for their consideration, at the next annual election, or on some day to be set apart for that purpose, with printed tickets containing the question, "Shall said bill" (with a brief description thereof) "be approved, or not?" and if a majority of the electors voting shall vote to approve said bill, it shall become a law; otherwise not.

10. All grants of incorporation shall be subject to future acts

of the General Assembly, in amendment or repeal thereof, or in any wise affecting the same; and this provision shall be inserted in all acts of incorporation hereafter granted.

11. The General Assembly shall exercise, as heretofore, a visitatorial power over corporations. Three bank commissioners shall be chosen at the June session for one year, to carry out the powers of the General Assembly in this respect. And commissioners for the visitation of other corporations, as the General Assembly may deem expedient, shall be chosen at the June session, for the same term of office.

12.[16] No city council, or other government, in any city, shall have power to vote any tax upon the inhabitants thereof, excepting the amount necessary to meet the ordinary public expenses in the same, without first submitting the question of an additional tax, or taxes, to the electors of said city; and a majority of all who vote shall determine the question. But no elector shall be entitled to vote, in any city, upon any question of taxation thus submitted, unless he shall be qualified by the possession, in his own right, of ratable property to the amount of one hundred and fifty dollars, and shall have been assessed thereon to pay a city tax, and shall have paid the same, as provided in section fourth of Article II. Nothing in that article shall be so construed as to prevent any elector from voting for town officers, and, in the city of Providence, and other cities, for mayor, aldermen, and members of the common council.

13. The General Assembly shall not pass any law, nor cause any act or thing to be done, in any way to disturb any of the owners or occupants of land in any territory now under the jurisdiction of any other state or states, the jurisdiction whereof may be ceded to, or decreed to belong to, this state, and the inhabitants of such territory shall continue in the full, quiet, and undisturbed enjoyment of their titles to the same, without interference in any way on the part of this state.

---

[16] This section appeared, in a slightly different form, in the list of "propositions not acted upon" in the *October Draft*.

Article X   Of Elections

1. The election of the governor, lieutenant governor, secretary of state, general treasurer, attorney general, and also of senators and representatives to the General Assembly, and of sheriffs of the counties, shall be held on the third Wednesday of April annually.

2. The names of the persons voted for as governor, lieutenant governor, secretary of state, general treasurer, attorney general, and sheriffs of the respective counties, shall be put upon one ticket; and the tickets shall be deposited by the electors in a box by themselves. The names of the persons voted for as senators and as representatives shall be put upon separate tickets, and the tickets shall be deposited in separate boxes. The polls for all the officers' names in this section shall be opened at the same time.

3. All the votes given for governor, lieutenant governor, secretary of state, general treasurer, attorney general, sheriffs, and also for senators, shall remain in the ballot boxes till the polls be closed. These votes shall then, in open town and ward meetings, and in the presence of at least ten qualified voters, be taken out and sealed up, in separate envelopes, by the moderators and town clerks, and by the wardens and ward clerks, who shall certify the same, and forthwith deliver or send them to the secretary of state, whose duty it shall be securely to keep the same, and to deliver the votes for state officers and sheriffs to the speaker of the House of Representatives, after the House shall be organized, at the June session of the General Assembly. The votes last named shall, without delay, be opened, counted, and declared, in such manner as the House of Representatives shall direct; and the oath of office shall be administered to the persons who shall be declared to be elected, by the speaker of the House of Representatives, and in the presence of the House: provided that the sheriffs may take their engagement before a senator, judge, or justice of the peace.[17] The votes for senators shall be counted by the governor and secretary of state within seven days

---

[17] The phrase "provided that the sheriffs may take their engagement before a senator, judge, or justice of the peace" did not appear in the *October Draft.*

from the day of election; and the governor shall give certificates to the senators who are elected.

4.[18] The boxes containing the votes for representatives to the General Assembly in the several towns shall not be opened till the polls for representatives are declared to be closed. The votes shall then be counted by the moderator and clerk, who shall announce the result, and give certificates to the person selected. If there be no election, or not an election of the whole number of representatives to which the town is entitled, the polls for representatives may be reopened, and the like proceedings shall be had, until an election shall take place: provided, however, that an adjournment of the election may be made to a time not exceeding seven days from the first meeting.

5. In the city of Providence, and other cities, the polls for representatives shall be kept open during the whole time of voting for the day; and the votes in the several wards shall be sealed up, at the close of the meeting, by the wardens and ward clerks, in the presence of at least ten qualified electors, and delivered to the city clerks. The mayor and aldermen of said city or cities shall proceed to count said votes within two days from the day of election; and if no election, or an election of only a portion of the representatives whom the representative districts are entitled to elect, shall have taken place, the mayor and aldermen shall order a new election to be held, not more than ten days from the day of the first election; and so on, till the election of representatives shall be completed. Certificates of election shall be furnished to the persons chosen by the city clerks.

6. If there be no choice of a senator or senators at the annual election, the governor shall issue his warrant to the town and ward clerks of the several towns and cities in the senatorial district or districts that may have failed to elect, requiring them to open town or ward meetings for another election, on a day not more than fifteen days beyond the time of counting the votes for senators. If, on the second trial, there shall be no choice of a senator or senators, the governor shall certify the result to the House of Representatives, and as many senators as shall have been chosen, shall forthwith elect, in joint committee, a senator

---

[18] The version of this section in the *October Draft* had minor differences in phraseology.

or senators, from the two candidates who may receive the highest number of votes in each district.

7. If there be no choice of governor at the annual election, the speaker of the House of Representatives shall issue his warrant to the clerks of the several towns and cities, requiring them to notify town and ward meetings for another election, on a day to be named by him, not more than thirty nor less than twenty days beyond the time of receiving the report of the committee of the House of Representatives, who shall count the votes for governor. If on this second trial there shall be no choice of a governor, the two Houses of the General Assembly shall, at their next session, in joint committee, elect a governor from the two candidates having the highest number of votes, to hold his office for the remainder of the political year, and until his successor be duly qualified.[19]

8. If there be no choice of governor and lieutenant governor at the annual election, the same proceedings for the choice of a lieutenant governor shall be had as are directed in the preceding section: provided, that the second trial for the election of governor and lieutenant governor shall be on the same day: and also provided, that, if the governor shall be chosen at the annual election, and the lieutenant governor shall not be chosen, then the last-named officer shall be elected in joint committee of the two Houses, from the two candidates having the highest number of votes, without a further appeal to the electors. The lieutenant governor, elected as is provided in this section, shall hold his office as is provided in the preceding section respecting the governor.[20]

9. All town, city, and ward meetings for the choice of representatives, justices of the peace, sheriffs, senators, state officers, representatives to Congress, and electors of president and vicepresident, shall be notified by the town, city, and ward clerks, at least seven days before the same are held.

10. In all elections held by the people under this constitution, a majority of all the electors voting shall be necessary to the choice of the person or persons voted for.

11. The oath, or affirmation, to be taken by all the officers

---

[19] The term of office is not clearly specified in the *October Draft*.
[20] The last sentence of this section did not appear in the *October Draft*.

named in this article, shall be the following: You, being elected to the place (of governor, lieutenant governor, secretary of state, general treasurer, attorney general, or to the places of senators or representatives, or to the office of sheriff or justice of the peace,) do solemnly swear, or severally solemnly swear, or affirm, that you will be true and faithful to the State of Rhode Island and Providence Plantations, and that you will support the constitution thereof; that you will support the constitution of the United States; and that you will faithfully and impartially discharge the duties of your aforesaid office, to the best of your abilities and understanding: so help you God! or, this affirmation you make and give upon the peril of the penalty of perjury.

Article XI   Of the Judiciary

1. The judicial power of this state shall be vested in one Supreme Court, and in such other courts, inferior to the Supreme Court, as the legislature may, from time to time, ordain and establish; and the jurisdiction of the Supreme and of all other courts may, from time to time, be regulated by the General Assembly.

2. Chancery powers may be conferred on the Supreme Court; but no other court exercising chancery powers shall be established in this state, except as is now provided by law.

3. The justices of the Supreme Court shall be elected in joint committee of the two Houses, to hold their offices for one year, and until their places [21] be declared vacant by a resolution to that effect, which shall be voted for by a majority of all the members elected to the House in which it may originate, and be concurred in by the same vote of the other House, without revision by the governor. Such resolution shall not be entertained at any other than the annual session for the election of public officers; and in default of the passage thereof at the said session, the judge, or judges, shall hold his or their place or places for another year. But a judge of any court shall be remov-

---

[21] At this point the *October Draft* included the phrase "or the place of any one of them."

able from office, if, upon impeachment, he shall be found guilty of any official misdemeanor.

4. In case of vacancy by the death, resignation, refusal, or inability to serve, or removal from the state, of a judge of any court, his place may be filled by the joint committee, until the next annual election; when, if elected, he shall hold his office as herein provided.

5. The justices of the Supreme Court shall receive a compensation which shall not be diminished during their continuance in office.[22]

6. The judges of the courts inferior to the Supreme Court shall be annually elected in joint committee of the two Houses, except as herein provided.

7. There shall be annually elected by each town, and by the several wards in the city of Providence, a sufficient number of justices of the peace, or wardens resident therein, with such jurisdiction as the General Assembly may prescribe. And said justices or wardens (except in the towns of New Shoreham and Jamestown) shall be commissioned by the governor.

8.[23] The General Assembly may provide that justices of the peace, who are not reelected, may hold their offices for a time not exceeding ten days beyond the day of the annual election of these officers.

9. The courts of probate in this state, except the Supreme Court,[24] shall remain as at present established by law, until the General Assembly shall otherwise prescribe.

Article XII   Of Education

1. All moneys which now are, or may hereafter be, appropriated, by the authority of the state, to public education, shall be securely invested, and remain a perpetual fund for the main-

---

[22] The *October Draft* specified an "official term of one year," contradicting Article XI, Section 3, which allowed for longer terms.

[23] This section replaced the following in the *October Draft:* "The Judges of the Courts shall, in all trials, state the testimony and declare the law to the jury."

[24] The phrase "except the Supreme Court" did not appear in the *October Draft.*

tenance of free schools in this state; and the General Assembly are prohibited from diverting said moneys or fund from this use, and from borrowing, appropriating, or using the same, or any part thereof, for any other purpose, or under any pretence whatsoever. But the income derived from said moneys or fund shall be annually paid over, by the general treasurer, to the towns and cities of the state, for the support of said schools, in equitable proportions: [25] provided, however, that a portion of said income may, in the discretion of the General Assembly, be added to the principal of said fund.

2. The several towns and cities shall faithfully devote their portions of said annual distribution to the support of free schools; and, in default thereof, shall forfeit their shares of the same to the increase of the fund.[26]

3. All charitable donations for the support of free schools, and other purposes of public education, shall be received by the General Assembly, and invested and applied agreeable to the terms prescribed by the donors: provided the same be not inconsistent with the constitution, or with sound public policy; in which case the donation shall not be received.[27]

Article XIII   Amendments

The General Assembly may propose amendments to this constitution by the vote of a majority of all the members elected to each House. Such propositions shall be published in the newspapers of the state; and printed copies of said propositions shall be sent by the secretary of state, with the names of all the members who shall have voted thereon, with the yeas and nays, to all the town and city clerks in the state; and the said propositions

---

[25] The *October Draft* was more specific, directing that school monies be paid to the towns and cities "in equal proportions according to their population as ascertained by the census of the United States."

[26] This provision, worded slightly differently, appeared in Section I of the article (XI) "Of education" in the *October Draft*.

[27] This provision appeared in Section 2 of the article "Of education" in the *October Draft*. Another Section 3 there read: "The General Assembly shall make all the necessary provisions by law in carrying this article into effect."

shall be, by said clerks, inserted in the notices by them issued for warning the next annual town and ward meetings in April; and the town and ward clerks shall read said propositions to the electors, when thus assembled, with the names of all the representatives and senators who shall have voted thereon, with the yeas and nays, before the election of representatives and senators shall be had. If a majority of all the members elected at said annual meetings, present in each House, shall approve any proposition thus made, the same shall be published as before provided, and then sent to the electors in the mode provided in the act of approval; and if then approved by a majority of the electors who shall vote in town and ward meetings, to be specially convened for that purpose, it shall become a part of the constitution of the state.

Article **XIV** [28]   **Of the Adoption of the Constitution**

1. This constitution shall be submitted to the people, for their adoption or rejection, on Monday, the 27th day of December next, and on the two succeeding days; and all persons voting are requested to deposit in the ballot boxes printed or written tickets in the following form: I am an American citizen, of the age of twenty-one years, and have my permanent residence, or home, in this state. I am (or not) qualified to vote under the existing laws of this state. I vote for (or against) the constitution formed by the convention of the people, assembled at Providence, and which was proposed to the people by said convention on the 18th day of November, 1841.

2. Every voter is requested to write his name on the face of his ticket; and every person entitled to vote as aforesaid, who, from sickness or other causes, may be unable to attend and vote in the town or ward meetings assembled for voting upon said constitution, on the days aforesaid, is requested to write his name upon a ticket, and to obtain the signature, upon the back of the same, of a person who has given in his vote, as a witness

---

[28] This article did not appear in the *October Draft;* a few of its provisions (Sections 5, 6, 20) appeared in the article on "General Provisions" (XIII) in the *October Draft.*

thereto. And the moderator, or clerk, of any town or ward meeting convened for the purpose aforesaid, shall receive such vote, on either of the three days next succeeding the three days before named for voting on said constitution.

3. The citizens of the several towns in this state, and of the several wards in the city of Providence, are requested to hold town and ward meetings on the days appointed, and for the purpose aforesaid; and also to choose, in each town and ward, a moderator and clerk, to conduct said meetings and receive the votes.

4. The moderators and clerks are required to receive, and carefully to keep, the votes of all persons qualified to vote as aforesaid, and to make registers of all the persons voting; which, together with the tickets given in by the voters, shall be sealed up, and returned by said moderators and clerks, with certificates signed and sealed by them, to the clerks of the convention of the people, to be by them safely deposited and kept, and laid before said convention, to be counted and declared at their next adjourned meeting, on the 12th day of January, 1842.

5. This constitution, except so much thereof as relates to the election of the officers named in the sixth section of this article, shall, if adopted, go into operation on the first Tuesday of May, in the year one thousand eight hundred and forty-two.

6. So much of the constitution as relates to the election of the officers named in this section shall go into operation on the Monday before the third Wednesday of April next preceding. The first election, under this constitution, of governor, lieutenant governor, secretary of state, general treasurer, and attorney general, of senators and representatives, of sheriffs for the several counties, and of justices of the peace for the several towns, and the wards of the city of Providence, shall take place on the Monday aforesaid.

7. The electors of the several towns and wards are authorized to assemble on the day aforesaid, without being notified, as is provided in Section 9 of Article X, and without the registration required in Section 7 of Article II, and to choose moderators and clerks, and proceed in the election of the officers named in the preceding section.

8. The votes given in at the first election for representatives to the General Assembly, and for justices of the peace, shall be

counted by the moderators and clerks of the towns and wards chosen as aforesaid; and certificates of election shall be furnished by them to the representatives and justices of the peace elected.

9. Said moderators and clerks shall seal up, certify, and transmit to the House of Representatives all the votes that may be given in at said first election for governor and state officers, and for senators and sheriffs; and the votes shall be counted as the House of Representatives may direct.

10. The speaker of the House of Representatives shall, at the first session of the same, qualify himself to administer the oath of office to the members of the House, and to other officers, by taking and subscribing the same oath in the presence of the House.

11. The first session of the General Assembly shall be held in the city of Providence on the first Tuesday of May, in the year one thousand eight hundred and forty-two, with such adjournments as may be necessary; but all other sessions shall be held as is provided in Article IV of this constitution.

12. If any of the representatives, whom the towns or districts are entitled to choose at the first annual election aforesaid, shall not be then elected, or if their places shall become vacant during the year, the same proceedings may be had to complete the election, or to supply vacancies, as are directed concerning elections in the preceding sections of this article.

13. If there shall be no election of governor or lieutenant governor, or of both of these officers, or of a senator or senators, at the first annual election, the House of Representatives, and so many senators as are chosen, shall forthwith elect, in joint committee, a governor or lieutenant governor; or both, or a senator or senators, to hold their offices for the remainder of the political year; and, in the case of the two officers first named, until their successors shall be duly qualified.

14. If the number of justices of the peace determined by the several towns and wards on the day of the first annual election shall not be then chosen, or if vacancies shall occur, the same proceedings shall be had as are provided for in this article in the case of a non-election of representatives and senators, or of vacancies in their offices. The justices of the peace thus elected shall hold office for the remainder of the political year, or until the second annual election of justices of the peace, to be held on such day as may be prescribed by the General Assembly.

15. The justices of the peace elected in pursuance of the provisions of this article may be engaged by the persons acting as moderators of the town and ward meetings, as herein provided; and said justices, after obtaining their certificates of election, may discharge the duties of their office, for a time not exceeding twenty days, without a commission from the governor.

16. Nothing contained in this article, inconsistent with any of the provisions of other articles of the constitution, shall continue in force for a longer period than the first political year under the same.

17. The present government shall exercise all the powers with which it is now clothed, until the said first Tuesday of May, one thousand eight hundred and forty-two, and until their successors, under this constitution, shall be duly elected and qualified.

18. All civil, judicial, and military officers now elected, or who shall hereafter be elected by the General Assembly, or other competent authority, before the said first Tuesday of May, shall hold their offices, and may exercise their powers, until the time.

19. All laws and statutes, public and private, now in force, and not repugnant to this constitution, shall continue in force until they expire by their own limitation, or are repealed by the General Assembly. All contracts, judgments, actions, and rights of action shall be as valid as if this constitution had not been made. All debts contracted, and engagements entered into, before the adoption of this constitution, shall be as valid against the state as if this constitution had not been made.

20. The Supreme Court, established by this constitution, shall have the same jurisdiction as the Supreme Judicial Court at present established; and shall have jurisdiction of all causes which may be appealed to, or pending in the same; and shall be held at the same times and places in each county, as the present Supreme Judicial Court, until the General Assembly shall otherwise prescribe.

21. The citizens of the town of New Shoreham shall be hereafter exempted from military duty, and the duty of serving as jurors in the courts of this state. The citizens of the town of Jamestown shall be forever hereafter exempted from military field duty.

22. The General Assembly shall, at their first session after the adoption of this constitution, propose to the electors the question, whether the word "white," in the first line of the first section of Article II, of the constitution, shall be stricken out. The question shall be voted upon at the succeeding annual election; and if a majority of the electors voting shall vote to strike out the word aforesaid, it shall be stricken from the constitution; otherwise, not. If the word aforesaid shall be stricken out, Section 3 of Article II shall cease to be a part of the constitution.

23. The president, vice presidents, and secretaries shall certify and sign this constitution, and cause the same to be published.

Done in convention, at Providence, on the 18th day of November, in the year one thousand eight hundred and forty-one, and of American independence the sixty-sixth.

JOSEPH JOSLIN, *President of the Convention*
WAGER WEEDEN,   ⎫
SAMUEL H. WALES,   ⎬ *Vice Presidents*
Attest:
WILLIAM H. SMITH, ⎫ *Secretaries*
JOHN S. HARRIS,   ⎭

Appendix B

Rhode Island Voting Frequencies

SOURCES FOR APPENDIX B *

Column	Source
A	*Burke's Report,* p. 120.
B	*Ibid.*
C	*Ibid.*
D	Providence *Republican Herald,* November 4, 1840.
E	*Burke's Report,* p. 353.
F	Reports to the General Assembly, vol. 10, p. 96½. Providence State House.
G	*Burke's Report,* p. 453.
H	*Ibid.,* p. 119.
I	*Providence Journal,* April 6, 1843.
J	*Ibid.,* April 3, 1845.

* See note to Appendix C, p. 238.

	Rhode Island Senate Districts (People's Constitution)	Rhode Island Population, 1840	Adult White Males, c. 1841 (estimate)	Rhode Island Freemen, c. 1841 (estimate)	Gubernatorial Election, 1840	
					Whig	Dem.
		A	B	C	D	
Northern towns (with greatest concentration of industry)	1. Providence Wards 1, 2, 3 2. Providence Wards 4, 5, 6	23,172	5,579	1,610	1,036	236
	3. Smithfield	9,534	2,049	660	278	213
	4. Cumberland North Providence	9,431	2,133	675	305	181
	5. Scituate Glocester Burrillville Johnston	10,857	2,699	1,195	394	651
	6. Warwick Cranston	9,628	2,034	695	413	209
Southern towns (predominately agricultural)	7. East Greenwich West Greenwich Coventry Foster	8,539	2,084	990	474	488
	8. Newport Jamestown New Shoreham	9,767	2,313	823	473	263
	9. Portsmouth Middletown Tiverton Little Compton	7,107	1,769	720	375	246
	10. North Kingstown South Kingstown	6,627	1,486	680	315	324
	11. Westerly Charlestown Exeter Richmond Hopkinton	7,698	1,720	900	333	429
	12. Bristol Warren Barrington	6,477	1,718	650	402	150
	Totals	108,837	25,584	9,598	4,798	3,417

Ratification of People's Constitution, December 1841	Ratification of Landholders' Constitution, March 1842		Vote for People's Legislature, April 1842	Ratification of Algerine Constitution, November 1842	Gubernatorial Election, 1843		Gubernatorial Election, 1845	
	For	*Against*			*L & O*	*Dem.*	*L & O*	*Lib.*
E	F		G	H	I		J	
3,552	1,406	2,129	2,135	1,606	2,118	1,733	2,029	1,878
1,326	334	997	652	374	514	751	483	747
1,595	360	1,068	907	413	443	928	365	1,016
1,556	539	1,315	856	586	751	1,207	618	1,188
1,301	538	878	648	386	705	644	648	586
839	842	553	237	717	978	448	764	418
1,366	870	406	324	767	707	307	632	318
474	929	195	119	591	832	328	553	289
537	660	453	234	416	607	375	406	531
780	852	457	135	492	747	407	251	409
621	863	238	210	673	588	301	645	213
13,947	8,013	8,689	6,457	7,021	8,990	7,427	7,394	7,587

Appendix C

RHODE ISLAND APPORTIONMENT PLANS

Charter of 1663	lower house	4	2	4	8	6	24
	upper house	Ten Senators elected at-large					
People's Constitutional Convention October 1841		18	10	11	13	10	62
Landholders' Constitutional Convention November 1841		6	4	5	9	6	30
People's Constitution	lower house	12	5	6	10	6	39
	upper house	2	1	1	1	1	6
Landholders' Constitution	lower house	8	4	6	10	6	34
	upper house	2	1	1	3		7
Rhode Island Senate Districts (People's Constitution)		1 2	3	4	5	6	

[Numbers refer to Senatorial Districts under the People's Constitution, and are identical with those in Appendix B.]

Northern towns (with greatest concentration of industry)

RHODE ISLAND APPORTIONMENT PLANS (*Continued*)

7	8	9	10	11	12	Southern towns (predominately agricultural)	Rhode Island Totals
8	10	10	4	10	6	48	72
Ten Senators elected at-large							
11	12	9	6	9	8	55	117
9	7	9	5	10	6	46	76
8	8	7	4	8	5	40	79
1	1	1	1	1	1	6	12
8	8	8	4	8	6	42	76
2	4		4		2	12	19

SOURCES FOR APPENDIX C

Peter J. Coleman, *The Transformation of Rhode Island, 1790–1860* (Providence: Brown University Press, 1963), p. 280; People's Constitution, Article VI (in Appendix A); Landholders' Constitution, Article VI, in Arthur May Mowry, *The Dorr War; Or, The Constitutional Struggle in Rhode Island* (Providence: Preston & Rounds, 1901), pp. 355–356. [In this table, and the similarly constructed Appendix B, I make certain assumptions that should be explicitly admitted. Some of the northern towns listed above as being in People's Constitution Senatorial districts 1-6 were largely agricultural in their western areas. I have also included the maritime towns of Newport and Bristol, and the commercial centers of Warren and Barrington, under the "predominately agricultural" southern towns. It was necessary to commit these minor violations of consistency in order to present complete series of data, both in Appendices B and C.]

Bibliographical Essay

A. Primary Sources

The major sources for this study have been the rich manuscript collections in the John Hay Library, Brown University. Most of the material there relating to the Dorr Rebellion was collected by Providence publisher Sidney S. Rider (1833–1917). Hence it is presently catalogued and arranged in 46 volumes and bundles as the Rider Collection. There are many thousands of items in this collection, including Thomas Wilson Dorr's correspondence, 1820–1854; documents relating to Rhode Island's political affairs, 1833–1854; and correspondence of persons connected with the Dorr Rebellion, such as Governor James Fenner, William H. Smith, Walter S. Burges and others. Caricatures, cartoons and broadsides are also included in this collection.[1] It is cited throughout this study as the "Dorr MSS." [2]

Considerable additional material may be found in the Hay Library, including broadsides and pamphlets. One of the most important items is the manuscript "Records of the Commissioners Appointed by the General Assembly of the State of Rhode

---

[1] Philip M. Hamer's invaluable *Guide to Archives and Manuscripts in the United States* (New Haven: Yale University Press, 1961), p. 562, mistakenly lists 770 pieces relating to the Dorr Rebellion in the Brown Library. The librarians at Brown will soon recatalogue the Dorr MSS. A small portion of Rider's collection, consisting of 11 bundles of miscellaneous newspaper clippings along with some correspondence (only a little of it bearing on the Dorr Rebellion), found its way to the American History Division, New York Public Library.

[2] A few items from this collection have been presented in Marvin E. Gettleman and Noel P. Conlon, eds., "Responses to the Rhode Island Workingmen's Reform Agitation of 1833," *Rhode Island History*, XXVIII (August 1969), 75–94.

Island in June, 1842, to Examine the Prisoners Arrested During the Late Rebellion" (Providence, [June] 1842), which makes it possible now to move beyond impressionistic guesses about the social composition of the Dorrite movement.

The newly reorganized Rhode Island Historical Society Library (RIHSL) in Providence has rich collections of primary documentation. A small collection of Dorr MSS. there contains a few useful items. I have also used there the Carter-Danforth Papers, the Greene Papers and the Peck MSS. But most useful in the Society's collections are the John Brown Francis and Elisha R. Potter, Jr., collections (the latter relocated from the University of Rhode Island Library). These contain the candid interchanges between two important anti-Dorr Democrats and reveal a whole dimension of Rhode Island conservative political life from the 1830s to the 1850s.

For a Whig perspective, the storehouse of materials in the voluminous James Fowler Simmons Papers, Manuscripts Division, Library of Congress (LC), is indispensable. This collection contains reports coming to Simmons in Washington (where he was serving in the 1840s as United States Senator from Rhode Island) on the often day-to-day and even hour-to-hour events during the Dorr Rebellion, as well as discussions of conservative strategy. Simmons publicly detached himself from the Law and Order coalition in 1845, and his papers contain inside data on the Dorr liberation movement.

The John Pitman–Joseph Story Correspondence, which has recently become available to researchers in the William L. Clements Library, University of Michigan, Ann Arbor, contains the reactions of conservative jurists closely involved with developments in Rhode Island. It also sheds much new light on the background of the *Luther v. Borden* cases.

The Newport Historical Society has only a meager collection of materials on the Dorr Rebellion, despite the prominence of such Newport leaders as Duttee J. Pearce in the suffrage struggle.

Three series of manuscript sources in the Rhode Island State Archives (State House, Providence) record formal political developments: Reports to the General Assembly; Acts and Resolves of the General Assembly; and Records of the General Assembly. I have not been able to find roll call votes in these sources for key legislative enactments bearing on the Dorr Rebellion.

I have consulted many other manuscript collections but have found relevant material in only a few: the Edmund Burke Papers and the Levi Woodbury Papers (both in the Library of Congress [LC]), detail the activities of two New Hampshire residents who sympathized with the Dorr rebels, and the Joseph Story Papers in the same library have a few items on the anti-Dorr judiciary. The United States Supreme Court records in the National Archives, Washington, D.C., contain materials on the *Luther v. Borden* and *Dorr v. Rhode Island* cases. The William H. Seward Papers, Rush Rhees Library, University of Rochester, show how the Whig Governor of New York monitored events in nearby Rhode Island. The Daniel Webster Papers, New Hampshire Historical Society (copies made available through the courtesy of Professor Charles M. Wiltse) document the Tyler Administration's cautious involvement in 1842. The H. A. S. Dearborn Papers, Manuscript Division, New York Public Library, record Massachusetts Whig support for the Charter authorities. The George Bancroft Papers, Massachusetts Historical Society, contain some material on the Dorr Rebellion and its aftermath.

Newspaper sources include the *New Age and Constitutional Advocate,* the major Suffrage newspaper in Rhode Island, which merged in the spring of 1842 with the *Providence Express;* the Whig conservative *Providence Journal;* the *Providence Manufacturers and Farmers Journal;* the Newport *Herald of the Times* and the Newport *Mercury;* the Boston *Daily Advertiser and Patriot, Bay State Democrat,* and *The Liberator;* the New York *Daily Evening Post, Morning Courier and Enquirer, Tribune, Journal of Commerce* and *Subterranean.*

The major printed source is the frequently cited *Burke's Report,* or more formally, U.S. Congress, House, *Interference of the Executive in Affairs of Rhode Island,* Report No. 546, 28 Cong., 1 Sess., 1884, 1048 pp. This voluminous and partisan documentary history, containing many of Dorr's own speeches, the transcript of his treason trial, and vast quantities of additional material on the Dorr Rebellion, is not simply a source book; its framing and publication were events in the taming and subduing of radicalism in Rhode Island, as I have shown in Chapter 6.

Contemporary pamphlets, many of which delved deeply into the philosophical roots of American politics,[3] have provided an important source for this study. Among the major pro-Dorr materials are: Samuel Y. Atwell, Joseph K. Angell, Thomas F. Carpenter, David Daniels, Thomas W. Dorr, Levi C. Eaton, John P. Knowles, Duttee J. Pearce and Aaron White, Jr., "Right of the People to Form a Constitution; Statement of Reasons" (March 14, 1842), in *Rhode Island Historical Tracts,* no. 11 (Providence: S. S. Rider, 1880), the *Nine Lawyers' Opinion,* which set forth the theoretical assumptions of the Suffrage Party. Dorr was the major author of this important statement. The anonymous pamphlet *A Few Observations on the Government of the State of Rhode-Island &c. By A Citizen* (Providence: John Carter, 1807), copy in RIHSL, is an early anticipation of radical Dorrite ideology. Another anonymous pamphlet, *Facts Involved in the Rhode Island Controversy, With Some Views Upon the Rights of Both Parties* (Boston: B. B. Mussey, 1842), copy in New York Public Library, is a mildly pro-Dorr tract. William S. Balch, one of the few Rhode Island clergymen openly sympathetic to Dorrism, delivered a fiery sermon: *Popular Liberty and Equal Rights: An Oration Delivered before the Mass Convention of the RI Suffrage Association, Held on Dexter Training Ground, in Providence, July 5, 1841* (Providence: B. F. Moore, 1841), copy in New York Public Library. Dorrites considered *"The Affairs of Rhode Island," Being a Review of President Wayland's Discourse; A Vindication of the Sovereignty of the People and a Refutation of the Doctrines and Doctors of Despotism by a Member of the Boston Bar* (Boston: B. B. Mussey, 1842), copy in New York Public Library, written

---

[3] In an earlier version of his 1901 full-scale study of the Dorr Rebellion (see below, pp. 247–248), Mowry revealingly admitted that for him "perusal of these pamphlets [was] exceedingly monotonous." Arthur May Mowry, "The Constitutional Controversy in Rhode Island in 1841," in *Annual Report of the American Historical Association for the Year 1894* (Washington: Government Printing Office, 1895), p. 361. His boredom probably meant that he thought the radical Dorrite challenge to conventional political concepts was tedious and unimportant, an interpretative line he later followed.

(and published anonymously) by John A. Bolles, a "noble pamphlet." [4] *Letters of the Hon. C[hauncey] F[itch] Cleveland and Hon. Henry Hubbard, Governors of Connecticut and New Hampshire, to Samuel Ward King, the Charter Governor of Rhode Island, Refusing to Deliver Up Thomas Wilson Dorr, the Constitutional Governor of Said State, to the Usurping Authorities Thereof. Also, the Letters of Hon. Marcus Morton, And Others; to the Suffrage Clam-Bake at Medbury Grove, Seekonk, Mass. August 30, 1842* (Fall River, Mass.: Thomas Almy, September 1842), copy in WLHU, demonstrated out-of-state support for Dorr after the Chepachet debacle. Most of Dorr's published writing can be found in *Burke's Report,* but an exception is the anonymously published *Political Frauds Exposed; Or, a Narrative of the Proceedings of the "Junto in Providence" Concerning the Senatorial Question by Aristides* ([Providence: no publisher listed, 1838]), copy in New York Public Library, which suggests why he left the Whig Party. William Goodell's *The Rights and Wrongs of Rhode Island: Comprising Views of Liberty and Law, of Religion and Rights, as Exhibited in the Recent and Existing Difficulties in that State* [*Christian Investigator,* No. 8 (September 1842)] ([Whitesboro, N.Y.]: Press of the Oneida Institute, 1842), copy in New York Public Library, expressed a pro-Dorr abolitionist opinion, from which Goodell soon retreated.[5] The anonymous pamphlet by the (divorced) Mrs. Frances H. (Whipple) McDougall,[6] *Might and Right; by a Rhode Islander* (Providence: A. H. Stillwell, 1844), copy in New York Public Library, is the best and fullest contemporary Dorrite account of the Rebellion.

In a special category are two speeches by radical house carpenter Seth Luther, which predate the Dorr Rebellion by a decade but express a strain of working-class opinion which intruded somewhat embarrassingly into the middle-class free suffrage movement of the 1840s. See Luther, *An Address on the*

---

[4] Aaron White, Jr., to Dorr, June 18, 1842, Dorr MSS.

[5] See Goodell's retraction in response to William Lloyd Garrison's anti-Dorr statements, *Liberator,* October 14, 1842, p. 163.

[6] See Sidney S. Rider, "Bibliographical Memoirs of Three Rhode Island Authors," *Rhode Island Historical Tracts,* no. 11 (Providence: S. S. Rider, 1880).

Right of Free Suffrage, Delivered by the Request of Freeholders and Others of the City of Providence, Rhode-Island, in the Old Town House April 19 and Repeated April 26 at the Same Place, With an Appendix, Containing the Rhode Island Bill of Rights, and the Rejected Petition Presented in 1829 to the Legislature of Rhode-Island by Nearly 2000 Petitioners, Including 700 Freeholders who were all Denominated VAGABONDS and RENEGADES by Benjamin Hazard, who Reported on the Petition to the General Assembly (Providence: S. R. Weeden, 1833), and Luther, *An Address to the Working-Men of New-England, on the State of Education, the Condition of the Producing Classes in Europe and America. With Particular Reference to the Effects of Manufacturing (as Now Conducted) on the Health and Happiness of the Poor, and on the Safety of Our Republic* . . . (Boston: published by the author, 1832), copies of both in New York Public Library.

Legal materials and arguments constitute another body of contemporary pro-Dorr pamphlets. See especially George Turner, *The Case of Thomas W. Dorr Explained* (n.p. [May 1844]), copy in WLHU; Francis F. Treadwell's anonymous *Conspiracy to Defeat the Liberation of Gov. Dorr; Or, The Hunkers and Algerines Identified, and Their Policy Unveiled; To Which is Added, A Report on the Case of Ex Parte Dorr* . . . (New York: John Windt, 1845), copy in New York Public Library; and *The Right of the People to Establish Forms of Government: Mr. [Benjamin F.] Hallett's Argument in the Rhode Island Causes, Before the Supreme Court of the United States, January, . . . 1848.* . . . (Boston: Beales & Greene, 1848), copy in New York Public Library, the last major restatement of Dorrite ideology.

The extremely able corpus of contemporary conservative pamphlets includes Rev. S[ilas] A[xtell] Crane's sermon at the *Proceedings of the Citizens of East Greenwich and Vicinity on the Return of the Kentish Guards and Volunteers, Friday, July 1, 1842: After the Suppression of the Late Rebellion in this State; With an Address* (Providence: B. Moore, 1842), copy in New York Public Library, which illustrates clerical opposition to the Rebellion. The anonymous pamphlet by George Ticknor Curtis, *Merits of Thomas W. Dorr and George Bancroft as They Are Politically Connected, By a Citizen of Massachusetts* (Boston: John H. Eastburn [1844]), copy in New York Public Library, expresses hostile Whig opinion of the Dorrite-Democratic alliance. The *Charge of the Hon. Chief Justice* [Job] *Durfee, Delivered to the Grand Jury at the March Term of the Supreme Judicial Court, at Bristol, Rhode Island, A.D. 1842* (n.p. [March 1842]), copy in New York Public Library, was the major statement of the antirebel conservative ideology in 1842, considered by Dorrites a "furioso and bombastical" statement of "ultra-slavish doctrines." [7] Jacob Frieze composed two important anti-Dorr pamphlets in 1842, the first anonymously: *Facts For the People: Containing Comparison and Exposition of Votes on Occasions Relating to the Free Suffrage Movements in Rhode Island* (Providence: Knowles & Vose, 1842) and *Concise History of the Efforts to Obtain an Extension of Suffrage in Rhode Island From the Year 1811 to 1842* (Providence: B. Moore, 1842), copies of both in New York Public Library. *The Close of the Late Rebellion in Rhode-Island: An Extract from a Letter by A Massachusetts Man Resident in Providence* (Providence: B. Cranston & Co., 1842), copy in WLHU, written anonymously by Brown University librarian Charles C. Jewett after the arsenal fiasco, expressed conservative dismay. Samuel Kettell's anonymous *Daw's Doings, Or, the History of the Late War in the Plantations by Sampson Short-and-Fat* (Boston: White & Lewis, 1842), is a savage satire, especially when compared with Henry Bowen's fairly mild anti-Dorr lampoon *The Dorriad: Or, the Hero of Two Flights* (Boston: Justin Jones, 1842), published anonymously in verse. Copies of both are in WLHU. Judge John Pitman was an active, anonymous, conservative pamphleteer in 1842. His *To the Members of the General Assembly of Rhode Island* (Providence: Knowles & Vose, [January] 1842), copy in New York Public Library, and *A Reply to the Letter of the Hon. Marcus Morton, Late Governor of Massachusetts, On the Rhode-Island Question, by One of the Rhode-Island People* (Providence: Knowles & Vose, 1842), copy in WLHU, expressed the views of Rhode Island's governing elite. Elisha R. Potter, Jr., was a more moderate conservative. His *Considerations on the Question of a Constitution and Extension*

---

[7] Dorr to Duttee J. Pearce, March 18, 1842, Pearce Papers, Newport Historical Society.

of Suffrage in Rhode Island (Boston: Thomas H. Webb, 1842), interleaved author's copy in RIHSL, is a vigorous polemic. Dexter Randall, *Democracy Vindicated and Dorrism Unveiled* (Providence: H. H. Brown, 1846), copy in New York Public Library, deals extensively with the impact of the Rebellion on Rhode Island's party system. Brown University's president, Francis Wayland, delivered two important anti-Dorr sermons in 1842: *The Affairs of Rhode Island, a Discourse Delivered in the Meeting-House of the First Baptist Church, Providence, May 22, 1842* (Providence: Knowles & Vose, 1842) and *A Discourse Delivered in the First Baptist Church, Providence, R.I., on the Day of Public Thanksgiving, July 21, 1842* (Providence: Knowles & Vose, 1842), copies of both in RIHSL. The conservative polemic *Address of John Whipple to the People of Rhode-Island on the Approaching Election* (Providence: Knowles & Vose, [March] 1843), copy in WLHU, gave a foretaste of the bitter anti-Dorrite diatribe Whipple would launch five years later in his Supreme Court argument in *Luther v. Borden.* This argument, along with Daniel Webster's in the same case, is found in Webster and Whipple, *The Rhode-Island Question* (Providence: Charles Burnett, 1848), copy in RIHSL.

Reminiscences shedding light on the Dorr Rebellion include: Charles T[abor] Congdon, *Reminiscences of a Journalist* (Boston: James R. Congdon, 1880); Almon D. Hodges, Jr., ed., *Almon Danforth Hodges and his Neighbors: An Autobiographical Sketch of a Typical Old New Englander* (Boston: privately printed, 1909); Dan King's *Life and Times of Thomas Wilson Dorr, With Outlines of the Political History of Rhode Island* (Boston: published by the author, 1859), not a biography but mainly a reprinting of material from *Burke's Report* with a rudimentary connecting narrative; and Abraham Payne, *Reminiscences of the Rhode Island Bar* (Providence: Tibbitts & Preston, 1885), containing biographical data on some of the principal figures in the Dorr Rebellion.

B. Secondary Sources

The best account I have read of the Dorr Rebellion is Anne Mary Newton, "Rebellion in Rhode Island: The Story of the

Dorr War" (M.A. Thesis, Columbia University, 1947), the first full-scale study to use the Brown University manuscript collections. Her narrative is generally accurate and her interpretations insightful, with the major exception being her ascription of a Napoleonic complex to Dorr. (It is true that Dorr, in his photographs at least, amazingly resembles the young Napoleon. But the evidence is too slight to support any deeper connection.) Newton fails to explore adequately the intellectual roots of Dorrism and its eventual subsidence in the swirling currents of Rhode Island politics in the 1840s.

Another important unpublished study is George Marshel Dennison, "The Constitutional Issues of the Dorr War: A Study of the Evolution of American Constitutionalism, 1776–1849" (Ph.D. Thesis, University of Washington, 1967). Taking the *Luther v. Borden* litigation as his starting point, Dennison traces the authorities cited by Dorrite lawyers, who tried to delineate a legitimate right of "peaceful revolution." His interpretation is weakened by his treating the Rhode Island upheaval in strictly constitutional terms and confusing a supposedly genuine intellectual tradition of "peaceful revolution" with arguments and precedents seized haphazardly for the occasion of legal argument.[8] Dennison is most misleading in viewing thinkers like James Wilson as precursors of Dorrism.[9] Unable to discover an intellectual genealogy for Dorrism, Dennison merely summarizes the views of all the authorities the rebels cited, a huge bibliographical enterprise, but one of doubtful historical value. Nor is Dennison convincing in describing the Southern secession leaders of 1860 as the intellectual descendants of Dorr, especially as he cannot find a single Confederate spokesman citing the Dorrite example.

The major published work on the subject is Arthur May

---

[8] Similarly confused is Dennison's article drawn from his dissertation (but more deeply researched), "Thomas Wilson Dorr: Counsel of Record in *Luther v. Borden,*" *St. Louis University Law Journal,* XV (Spring 1971), 398–428.

[9] Cf. the brilliant interpretation of Wilson's political philosophy in Gordon S. Wood, *The Creation of the American Republic: 1776–1787* (Chapel Hill, N.C.: University of North Carolina Press, 1969), pp. 316, 330, 347–348, 353–354, 530–531, 535.

Mowry, *The Dorr War; Or, the Constitutional Struggle in Rhode Island* (Providence: Preston & Rounds, 1901), which was recently reissued in the "Cherry Pie" series on the history of violence in America.[10] Basic manuscript sources were not available to Mowry, who composed his careful, creditable but biased study mainly on the basis of pamphlets, newspapers and *Burke's Report*. Mowry essentially accepts the viewpoint of contemporary conservative ideologists that the rebel resort to arms was unjustified and unnecessary.[11] The Dorrite movement, he solemnly pronounced, "can have no upholders today," and the willingness of politically aroused groups in other states to support it must seem strange to "the quiet citizen of today." [12] Mowry's conservative biases not only lead him to outright falsification on occasion,[13] but to hostile judgments that preclude full understanding of what the Rhode Island rebels were contesting for so desperately.

Nor is Mowry the only twentieth-century writer on the Dorr Rebellion who allowed political biases to distort an interpretation of the upheaval. John Bell Rae's essay "The Issues of the Dorr War," *Rhode Island History,* I (April 1942), 33–44, echoes Mowry's judgment that the Rebellion was "regrettable and unnecessary" and that "it was just as well that Dorr lost" (p. 44). Despite his espousal of a militant liberalism, Arthur Schlesinger, Jr., in his *Age of Jackson* (Boston: Little, Brown & Co., 1945) reaches conclusions identical to those of conservative writers Mowry and Rae. Schlesinger concludes that Dorrism was an impermissible departure from legitimate political practices in America; if its principles were accepted, "it would be impossible to see how . . . disastrous consequences . . . could

---

[10] The allusion is to H. Rap Brown's observation that "violence is as American as cherry pie." The reissue, with a preface by Leon Friedman, was published by Chelsea House in 1970 and is available in a Vintage Books edition.

[11] *Dorr War,* pp. 298–299.

[12] *Ibid.,* pp. 299, 302. Cf. Mowry, "The Constitutional Controversy," pp. 369–370, his earlier essay.

[13] See above, pp. 34 (note 10), 50 (note 62), 56–57 (note 19), 112 (note 19), 157 (note 67), 173 (note 128), 200 (note 6), 242 (note 3).

be avoided." [14] Similarly, Willard Hurst sees in the Dorr Rebellion a "savage temptation to relieve discontent, frustration and fear" by an evil violence which always lurks "not far below the ordered surface of society." But Hurst perceives no savagery in the measures of the partisans of Law and Order. On the contrary, he maintains that the Charter Government in Rhode Island was bound to use its monopoly of "legitimate" violence against the rebels. "The use of the law's force might be costly," Hurst admits, "but the want of it would be costlier still to the values . . . to which this middle class society [in antebellum America] was so firmly committed." [15]

More balanced and objective accounts of the Dorr Rebellion may be found in Joseph Brennan, *Social Conditions in Industrial Rhode Island, 1820–1860* (Washington, D.C.: Catholic University of America, 1940); Peter J. Coleman, *The Transformation of Rhode Island, 1790–1860* (Providence: Brown University Press, 1963), pp. 254–294 (a path-breaking attempt at a social interpretation of the Dorr Rebellion which has deeply influenced my approach); and Chilton Williamson, *American Suffrage: From Property to Democracy, 1760–1860* (Princeton: Princeton University Press, 1960), Chap. 13 (a study based on a partial survey of the manuscript sources, which fruitfully views the Dorr Rebellion as a radical attempt to achieve reforms that elsewhere in America came with minimal struggle).

Students of legal history have produced some of the best scholarship on the Dorr Rebellion. Particularly useful have been Michael A. Conron, "Law, Politics and Chief Justice Taney: A Reconsideration of the *Luther v. Borden* Decision," *American Journal of Legal History,* XI (October 1967), 377–388, and C. Peter Magrath, "Optimistic Democrat: Thomas W. Dorr and the Case of *Luther vs. Borden*," *Rhode Island History,* XXIX (August–November 1970), 94–112, the latter study based on manuscript sources.

---

[14] *Age of Jackson,* p. 415.

[15] James Willard Hurst, *Law and Social Process in United States History: Five Lectures Delivered at the University of Michigan . . . 1959* (Ann Arbor, Mich.: University of Michigan Law School, 1960), pp. 258–261, 272–274, 278–281.

Finally, two studies that begin to uncover the role of Rhode Island blacks in the suffrage controversy are Julian Rammelkamp, "The Providence Negro Community, 1820–1842," *ibid.,* VII (January 1948), 20–33, and J. Stanley Lemmons and Michael A. McKenna, "Re-enfranchisement of Rhode Island Negroes," *ibid.,* XXX (February 1971), 2–13.

Index

251

About the Author

Born in New York in 1933, Marvin E. Gettleman was educated in the city's public schools. At first he studied art, spending a year at the Tyler School of Fine Arts, Temple University. Then he entered the City College of New York, where he majored in Philosophy and took his B.A. degree cum laude in 1957. Coming to The Johns Hopkins University on a National Woodrow Wilson Fellowship, he received M.A. and Ph.D. degrees there, studying with Pulitzer Prize-winning historian David Donald. Dr. Gettleman taught at his alma mater, CCNY, before taking a position at the Polytechnic Institute of Brooklyn, where he is now Associate Professor of History. He also teaches at the Hunter College School of Social Work. He has written articles in such journals as *The Nation, Science & Society, History of Education Quarterly, New Left Review, Studies on the Left* and *Social Research.* His books include *Vietnam: History, Documents and Opinions* (2nd ed., 1970); *Conflict in Indochina,* coedited with Susan Gettleman and Lawrence and Carol Kaplan (Vintage Books, 1970); and *The Failure of American Liberalism,* coedited with David Mermelstein (Vintage Books, 1971). Mr. Gettleman, his wife Susan and their four children divide their time between Manhattan and Fire Island.